# Reading Rochester

### EDITED BY
## EDWARD BURNS
Senior Lecturer in English
University of Liverpool

# LIVERPOOL UNIVERSITY PRESS

First published 1995 by
LIVERPOOL UNIVERSITY PRESS
PO Box 147, Liverpool, L69 3BX


Copyright © 1995 by
Liverpool University Press

**British Library Cataloguing-in-Publication
Data**
A British Library CIP Record is available for
this book
ISBN 0–85323–038–2 *cased*
0–85323–309–8 *paper*

Text set in Linotron 202 Baskerville by
Wilmaset Limited, Birkenhead, Wirral
Printed and bound in the European Union by
The Alden Press in the City of Oxford

# Contents

# Contributors

PAUL BAINES is a lecturer in the Department of English Language and Literature, University of Liverpool. He is a specialist on eighteenth-century literature and has published articles on Pope, Swift, Defoe, Johnson, Walpole and Chatterton. He has just completed a book on forgery in the eighteenth century.

TONY BARLEY is a member of the English Department at Liverpool University. His publications include articles on the poetry of Ben Jonson, Philip Larkin and Hamish Henderson, and he is the author of *Taking Sides: The Fiction of John le Carré* (1986).

BERNARD BEATTY is Senior Lecturer in the English Department at the University of Liverpool. He has published books on Byron's *Don Juan* and essays on Dryden, Bunyan, Gray, Keats, Shelley and Matthew Arnold. He is editor of the *Byron Journal* and chairman of *English Association North*.

EDWARD BURNS is Senior Lecturer in English at the University of Liverpool. His publications include *Restoration Comedy; Crises of Desire and Identity* (1987) and *Character: Acting and Being on the Pre-Modern Stage* (1990). He is currently editing *Henry VI Part One* for the Arden Shakespeare series.

STEPHEN CLARK teaches English at the University of Osaka, Japan. He has written extensively on eighteenth-century literature and ideas, and on modern literary theory. His books include *Paul Ricoeur* (1990) and *Sordid Images* (1995), in which another version of his chapter here appears.

NICK DAVIS, a member of the University of Liverpool English Department, works mainly on later Medieval and Renaissance literature. He has recently completed a book on projections of chaos in texts of the period, and is currently writing a study of *The Faerie Queene*.

## Contributors

SIMON DENTITH is Reader in English at Cheltenham and Gloucester College of Higher Education. He has written on George Eliot, rhetoric and on nineteenth- and twentieth-century topics; his most recent book is an introduction to Mikhail Bakhtin.

BREAN S. HAMMOND is Rendel Professor of English at the University of Wales, Aberystwyth. He is the author of several books and articles on seventeenth- and eighteenth-century literature, and is editor of the *British Journal for Eighteenth-Century Studies*. His current project is a study of the first era of professional writing in Britain.

JIM McGHEE is an Honorary Research Fellow at the Department of English Language, University of Glasgow. He is currently completing his novel, *The Syndrome*.

RAY SELDEN. Until his death in 1991, Professor Raman Selden had taught at Portsmouth Polytechnic, the Universities of Durham and Lancaster, and Sunderland Polytechnic. His published work includes many distinguished contributions to both modern literary theory and seventeenth-century scholarship, including the Clarendon edition (with Harold Brooks) of the poetry of John Oldham.

The essay printed here was commissioned for an earlier version of this anthology; the editor gave his permission for it to be printed in *The Seventeenth Century*, vol. vi, no. 1, Spring 1991.

HELEN WILCOX is Professor of English Literature and Head of the Department of English at the University of Groningen, The Netherlands. Her publications include *Her Own Life: Autobiographical Writings by Seventeenth-Century Englishwomen* (1989), *George Herbert, Sacred and Profane* (1995) and *Women and Literature in Britain 1500–1700* (1995).

# Acknowledgements

The editor would like to thank Christine Hughes and Louise Aylward: the first for checking the typescript, the second for her invaluable expertise and help in its first edit. Thanks are also due to Robin Bloxsidge and Julie Rainford at Liverpool University Press, for their patience and care in seeing the collection through its gestation.

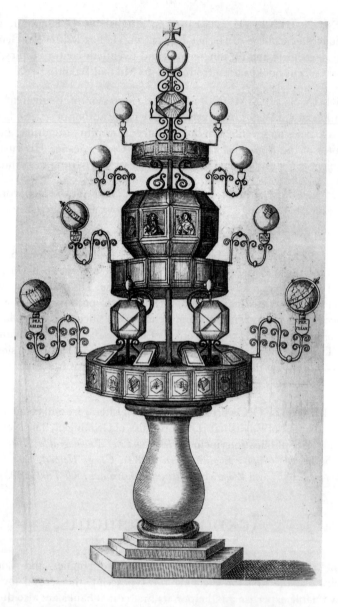

*Multiple sun-dial and time-reckoner, set up in Charles I's Privy Garden at Whitehall in 1669 and destroyed by Rochester and friends in 1675 (see further the essay by Nick Davis).* © *British Library*

# Introduction

Of all the major English poets, Rochester is the most irrepress-
ibly disruptive. The very idea of the anarchic libertine poet, as
created in the gossip of his contemporaries and in the notoriety
of unpublishably obscene texts, disrupts any attempt to
account for his writings from within the institutions and
procedures of the Academy. To submit Rochester to scholarship is to effect an even starker juxtaposition of a poet's
emotion and its eventual recollection into the tranquillity of
footnotes than that of Yeats's 'The Scholars':

> Bald heads forgetful of their sins
> Old, learned, respectable bald heads
> Edit and annotate their lines
> That young men, tossing on their beds,
> Rhymed out in love's despair
> To flatter beauty's ignorant ear . . .
> . . . Lord, what would they say
> Did Catullus walk that way?[1]

Yeats in mid-life is nervously defending a body of work that,
like the life inscribed on it, is already judged eminent, already
constructing an eternity for itself. Rochester did not live into a
premature and prolonged old age like Yeats's, nor did he
gather texts together to construct an *oeuvre*, with the result that
matters of authorship and ascription have dominated Rochester studies for most of this century. This, and the issue of
Rochester's obscenity, paradoxically delayed the appearance
of an authoritative text until the current era of critical fashion,
in which the author has been declared dead, and in which the
compilation is possible of 'Rochester' as a person-shaped
uncontestably authored text to replace the fragmented self–
obscuring 'Rochester' of historical gossip; the notoriety of
censorship no longer seems a natural or inevitable activity. In
any case, his writings themselves seem to be in flight from an

idea of individual identity; a stably identified 'Rochester' is the
last thing they want to establish. But we can scarcely read a
poem by Rochester without a consciousness of an individual
presence, whether or not we have the information and the
inclination to read that as the presence of the 'Rochester' of
literary anecdote. And the Rochester identity constructed in a
web of other texts—plays, letters, reminiscences all tending to
the condition of gossip—is, once we become aware of it,
strikingly difficult to shake off. Yet there are hardly any poems
by Rochester in which a 'Rochester' figure is centrally and
clearly placed. His avatars (to use Anne Righter's attractive
term[2]) crowd into the work of contemporary poets, playwrights
and gossips, but are seldom created in his own texts, for his
own contemplation. His writing is less a mirror to himself than
a withdrawal from variously painful situations into a position
of rancorous or rueful contemplation. In the satires, the satirist
has fled into a position free of external aggravation from which
he can speak, but in which he must admit himself impotent to
amend or counter the causes of such aggravation, and thus is
likely only to be wounded further, to wound and aggravate the
more. The lyrics too are written from a position that foregrounds withdrawal. 'Absent from thee . . .' else, why write?
In the 'mature' lyrics (if one can make that distinction in a
spectacularly accelerated career of writerly development)
death and absence are reflected on not simply as biographical
or sociological phenomena but as conditions of that writing. In
the love lyrics a conventional vocabulary allows 'death' to
figure as a euphemism for orgasm, as an hyperbole of extreme
feeling. But it is in the nature of Rochester's characteristic
discourse that euphemism and hyperbole are near-useless as
critical concepts—discrete registers don't stay long enough in
their place, the literal intrudes, perspectives shift, levels meld.
This is a condition of Rochester's language, and it is the source
of his ability to pull the gravely and challengingly simple for
self–reflexive baroque ironies, his ability to earth or perhaps to
short-circuit the high-flown in resonance-less colloquialism.
The post-Petrarchan wittily manipulable set of conceits that
Rochester inherits for the description of love are used by him in
a way that turns knowingness back on itself, that creates an
effect in which a favourite discourse of death, pain, despair can

come to operate as an impersonally well-worn code for feeling while at the same time throwing out, as a kind of shadow, the larger literal sense of those words.

Any defence of his work that Rochester makes is in the present, as a response to an immediate demand on the poet's patience that has him swerving off from and breaking the poem itself:

> You Wiser men despise me not;
>    Whose Love-sick Fancy raves,
> On Shades of Souls, and Heaven knows what;
>    Short Ages live in Graves.
>
> When e're those wounding Eyes, so full
>    Of Sweetness, you did see;
> Had you not been profoundly dull,
>    You had gone mad like me.
>          'The Mistress: A Song' (ll. 13– 20)[3]

The critic's challenge is of the moment; like that of Yeats's scholars it instates in the poem a sense of the passing of time, but a completely different sense, a sense that collapses futurity into an appeal to immediate experience—an insolent appeal, for 'we' his critics are necessarily outside his poem; its experience is insulated from us, we cannot be wounded by those eyes, whose-ever they are. At the same time this allows us a more congenial role than that of Yeats's ghosts of criticism future. The Rochester text does not seek to protect itself by simultaneously canonizing itself and aloofly inuring that canon from our scrutiny. Indeed, it hardly protects itself at all. A rawness of surface, a contact to the reader that is at the same time abrasive and abraded, is the condition of a collection of works that we call 'Rochester', haphazard in attribution and provenance, heterogeneous in form, aim and context, and, as individual texts, notoriously self-disrupting in their subversive and explosively obscene disregard for the discreteness of registers of language, of the proper categories of the literary, the written, the spoken and the unspeakable. Reading Rochester, teaching the texts and talking about them is always an unsettling experience, in that the work always contains the germ of some subversion of those normally safe situations.

Yeats's gibe seems hypocritical in that his poems are written
into an eternity of explication; the poem smugly pillories a
class of readers it has made necessary. Rochester leaves no-one
smug, least of all himself. The wounding eyes exist, unlike the
'ears' of Yeats's ignorant beauty, outside the transactional
possibilities of the poem, and so the woman of whom they are a
metonym cannot be arraigned, as Yeats's imagined loved one
is, as yet another insensitive reader. The poem makes us as
aware of the provisionality of its mode of statement as of its
doomed attempt to formulate a response in those eyes. Rochester is both an affront to his readers and their ally, in that his
anarchic assault on those structures of self-presentation and
required response that hold poems in their place succeeds in
destroying his own authority, and rendering the very idea of a
'canon', a 'corpus', an *oeuvre* unattainable; it is a strategy to
allow him to remain unfixed, and so can be taken by the reader
as an openness, the possibility of an equalizing engagement
with the texts.

   'Reading Rochester' is then the project of this volume, and if
a riposte emerges to the sublime *double entendre* of Leavis's
judgement that 'Rochester is not a great poet of any kind; yet
he certainly had uncommon natural endowments . . .',[4] then it
will be through an open engagement with the texts. Helen
Wilcox, in her essay on the 'Song of a Young Lady to her
Ancient Lover', raises immediately questions consequent on
reading Rochester in the often compromised arena in which he
is most frequently encountered: the Academy itself. Like
Stephen Clark, in his discussion of misogyny, and Jim McGhee
on the early censorship of Rochester's printed texts, Wilcox
reveals the complex and often unpredictable results of the
introduction of Rochester's discourse of sexuality into the
social situations of reading, writing, teaching. Clark's choice of
quotation for his title points to the 'something generous in mere
lust' which makes it impossible for the reader to feel simply
superior to Rochester's presentations of sexuality. Whether or
not one agrees with Germaine Greer's claim, made in a lecture
at the 'Voicing Women' conference at the University of
Liverpool,[5] that Rochester is 'the best woman poet of the
seventeenth century', it becomes clear that the construction of
Rochester as the purveyor of the forbidden pleasures of

misogyny is itself a sexist misappropriation. My own piece, tracking two occasional poems through their positioning of Rochester as sexual subject, ends a section entitled, safely enough, 'Text and Gender'.

Rochester, literally at his wit's end, thinks through trains of ideas that seem to break the bounds of language and of the formal demands of verse. Simon Dentith deals with Rochester's apparent aristocratic negativity of vision in terms of the kaleidoscopically dialogic diversity of language in the lyrics, while Tony Barley and Nick Davis explore the more explicitly philosophical poems in terms of their treatment of 'nothingness' and time and memory, respectively. Paul Baines's essay again looks at 'Nothing', but traces its genealogy and descendants, in a way that by leading us on to Pope, straddles the second and third sections, from 'Form and Intellect' to 'Rochester and Others'. Brean Hammond on Rochester and Shadwell presents, through the medium of the 'Allusion to Horace', a sense of the Restoration battle over the ownership and interpretation of the past, particularly in this case, the inheritance of Jonson. Raman Selden and Bernard Beatty both read Rochester against a strong contemporary, Oldham in the first case, Dryden in the second. It makes sense, I think, to end with Rochester perceived not as the challenging outsider, but as a figure central to his age, active in the articulation of a sceptical and committed language that offers us, as readers, a point of entry into late seventeenth-century culture as a whole.

## NOTES

1. W. B. Yeats, *The Scholars*, quoted from *The Collected Poems* (London, 1950), p. 58.

2. Ann Righter, 'John Wilmot Earl of Rochester', reprinted in *John Wilmot Earl of Rochester: Critical Essays*, ed. David M. Vieth (New York, 1988), p. 6.

3. *The Poems of John Wilmot, Earl of Rochester*, ed. Keith Walker (Oxford, 1984).

4. F. R. Leavis, *Revaluation: Tradition and Development in English Poetry* (London, 1936), p. 35.

5. April 1992.

# Gender and Artfulness in Rochester's 'Song of a Young Lady to Her Ancient Lover'

## HELEN WILCOX

> As to the Work itself, the very Name of *Rochester* is a sufficient Passport wherever English is spoken or understood: And we doubt not but it will give the highest Delight to all those who have Youth, Fire, Wit and Discernment.[1]

This essay arises primarily out of the experience of discussing Rochester's work with readers who possess plenty of 'Youth, Fire, Wit and Discernment', namely, fascinated but perplexed undergraduates. How does Rochester, they ask, achieve that astonishing rational directness, that surprisingly delicate lyric grace? Why does he so regularly challenge these, and his readers, with cynicism and obscenity? Is his wit sharpened in anger or love? Is it concerned or dispassionate? Is there a consistent perspective underlying and shaping the variety of poetic masks worn in and by the texts? More particularly, as a male author did he regard the human female with special distaste, or does the sometimes brutal attention given to her indicate attraction? How are human relations, Rochester-style, negotiated? And how are readers' relations and reactions to his texts to be understood and built upon?

This range of questions, adequate answers to which would fill a book, will be focused for the next few pages on just one lyric by Rochester, the one which has caused most impassioned disagreement and bewildered interest among my students—his 'Song of a Young Lady to her Ancient Lover'. The lyric raises issues of voice, gender, experience, wit, art and compassion; a close look at it may help to suggest ways of responding to Rochester's work and to late-twentieth-century readers' dilemmas concerning it.

1
Ancient Person, for whom I
All the flattering Youth defy;
Long be it e're thou grow Old,
Aking, shaking, Crazy, Cold;
  But still continue as thou art,
  Ancient Person of my Heart.

2
On thy withered Lips and dry,
Which like barren Furrows lye,
Brooding kisses I will pour,
Shall thy youthful Heat restore.
Such kind Show'rs in Autumn fall,
And a second Spring recall:
  Nor from thee will ever part,
  Antient Person of my Heart.

3
Thy Nobler part, which but to name
In our Sex wou'd be counted shame,
By Ages frozen grasp possest,
From his Ice shall be releast,
And, sooth'd by my reviving hand,
In former Warmth and Vigor stand.
All a Lover's wish can reach,
For thy Joy my Love shall teach:
And for thy Pleasure shall improve,
All that Art can add to Love.
  Yet still I love thee without Art,
  Antient Person of my Heart.²

As we might expect of Rochester, the immediate impact of
the poem is contradictory. It is clearly dramatic, with a
constructed female voice addressing her male lover intimately
and apparently, at times, with tenderness. Yet despite this
dramatized individuality, the lyric is strangely impersonal,
with unnamed participants not even honoured with pastoral
labels. What distinguishes them is simply their gender and
age—this is an anonymous young woman verbally caressing
an older man. It is important, though, to note that the title

defines the relative social roles and status of these stereotypical characterizations. The female speaker is not immediately identified as a whore,[3] nor even as a mistress; she is independent and as a 'lady' has some propriety. And in an already teasing inversion of conventional relationships and prevailing social conditions, the man is rendered secondary, dependent upon the 'lady' for his identity, as he is 'her lover'.

How significant, however, are the differences in age and gender between the speaker and her lover? Initially it could be assumed that in these respects the speaker is identified with a number of disadvantages, at least in terms of seventeenth-century society. She is youthful and thus inexperienced, naïve; she is female, and thus liable to be a possession of either her father or her husband—a legal nonentity, a nameless subordinate absorbed into patriarchy just as a 'rivulet' is incorporated into a larger river.[4] The anonymity of 'young lady' in the title is therefore perfectly apt: 'young' gives place to old, 'lady' to man. However, this is to reckon without Rochester's vision of the world, in which to be male is to be at the mercy of devouring females or unwilling physique, and to be old is to realize this all the more vividly. Timon, for example, is confronted with this assumption in the opening of Rochester's satire of that name:

What Timon does old Age begin t'approach
That thus thou droop'st under a Nights debauch?

(ll.1–2)

And in Rochester's portrait of 'rational' human nature in 'Satyr', the last stage of life is mercilessly characterized:

Then Old Age, and experience, hand in hand,
Lead him to death, and make him understand,
After a search so painful, and so long,
That all his Life he has been in the wrong;

(ll.25–28)

Perhaps, bearing in mind Rochester's undermining of the traditional wisdom and authority of old age, the youthful naïvety, pride and hope of the young lady are preferable to ancient disillusion.

Relationships between these two extremes, a young woman

and an old man, were common in seventeenth-century England, when so many women died in childbirth, leaving widowers who sought a new partnership and security of inheritance with a second, and sometimes even a third, young wife. Such relationships were often seen in mercenary terms, as in Dorothy Osborne's lighthearted account of

> An old rich Knight, that had promised mee this seven year's to marry mee whensoever his wife dyed, and now hee's dead before her, and has left her such a widdow it makes mee mad to think on it, 1200 a yeare Joynter and 20000 in mony and personall Estate, and all this I might have had, if Mr Death had bin pleased to have taken her instead of him. Well whoe can help these things . . .[5]

These partnerships, however, frequently ceased to satisfy either party, and Robert Burton listed difference of age as one cause of melancholy between men and women:

> A young Gentlewoman in *Basil*, was married . . . to an ancient man against her will, whom she could not affect; she was continually melancholy, and pined away for griefe.[6]

In Rochester's lyric, far from pining away, the autonomous young lady (who is not, it seems, married to her ancient beloved) puts all her energies into making the relationship physically and emotionally (and not necessarily financially) satisfying to them both. Yet again, Rochester is working against the grain of powerful social stereotypes.

Burton used the phrase 'ancient man' to refer simply to advancement in years, but it is worth pausing over the fact that Rochester distinguishes between 'ancient' and 'old'. The latter appears to refer to more extreme senility—'aking, shaking, Crazy Cold'—while 'ancient' implies the slightly less terminal, though not very flattering, 'Withered Lips and Dry'. The chief meaning of the word 'ancient', as used in the refrain, 'Ancient person of my heart', is probably time-worn but long established, suggesting continuing loyalty to what we would term (again without direct reference to age) an 'old friend' (*OED* 5). The young lady's 'heart' stresses the ancientness of their love, not his maturity. Despite the poem's sometimes insulting references to the actual signs of great age in the lover's body, there are at the same time hints that 'ancient' has the sense of 'venerable'(*OED* 7), a person deserving care and respect. Some versions of the text adopt the spelling 'antient', itself an old-fashioned variant reminding us of the rarity of precious or antique objects (Walker shifts between the two). Does the continuing stress on the lover's physical state suggest that he is, in fact, being treated as such an object? This is, once more, an intriguing reversal of the obsessive itemising attention to the female body found in so much Renaissance and seventeenth-century English love poetry. But is this materialist attentiveness destructive or emboldening?

The young lady's account of her ancient lover's body given in the second stanza is dominated by metaphors of the natural world, metaphors in which gender associations are disrupted and blurred:

> On thy withered lips and dry,
> Which like barren Furrows lye,
> Brooding kisses I will pour,
> Shall thy youthful Heat restore.
> Such kind Show'rs in Autumn fall,
> And a second Spring recall:
> (ll.7–12)

The male lover is the passive earth, the element so often regarded as the female principle; in Aristotle's binary world, the feminine is always associated with receptiveness and inactivity.[7] Here, it is the male lover's lips and (by association) wrinkled brow which are likened to the 'barren Furrows' of the ground, ploughed (in phallic manner) by life's hard experiences. This is in contrast to Rochester's more conventional gendering of nature in 'Upon his Leaving His Mistriss', in which the earth is a female 'seed-receiving' womb on whom 'no show'rs unwelcome fall' (ll.15–17, p. 37). The 'show'rs' which fall in the young lady's song are her own kisses; in her patently wishful account of the future, she herself is the active (masculine) life force whose loving rain ensures a springtime of renewed vigour in her autumnal partner. The gendered opposition, already thus inverted from traditional usage, is complicated. Although much of her activity appears to be associated with the masculine, the lady's language of concern and healing restoration has overtones of maternal care, introduced primarily by the adjective 'brooding' (1.9) and the action 'sooth'd' (1.19). And while she is thus credited with motherly reviving powers which restore her lover's 'Heat', in the third stanza, he is associated not with this giving of birth but with the ice of age[8] and the coldness of death, recalling the misery of a 'winter's day' in Rochester's 'The Mistress':

> Where Life and Light with envious hast,
> Are torn and snatch'd away.
> (ll.3–4)

If the young lady's metaphors and envisaged successes are ambiguously gendered, her modest voice in stanza 3 is a deliberately feminine construction:

> Thy Nobler part, which but to name
> In our Sex wou'd be counted shame,
> (ll.15–16)

The self-conscious reference to 'our Sex' is a reminder of the connection between the feminine and restraint, in language and action. Silence and chastity, not-naming and not-shaming, were closely interlinked in seventeenth-century expectations of womanhood, as the rhyme aptly underlines. Ironically of course, the ostentatious modesty of her carefully oblique reference to the lover's sexual organs ensures that the young lady's discussion is no longer oblique. It highlights her knowledge of male sexuality, as much as it demonstrates her awareness of what is expected of an innocent young lady's conversation. The personal and the social, though distinct, are shown to be inseparable here. The dangers of female obedience to the social code, when such coyness ran contrary to genuine female desire, were outlined bleakly by Rochester in the conclusion of 'Song':

> Then if to make your ruin more,
>     You'll peevishly be coy,
> Dye with the scandal of a Whore,
>     And never know the joy.
>     (ll.13–16)

However, the joyfully sensual language in the earlier stanza of the 'Song of a Young Lady' defies the subsequent prim deference to feminine verbal modesty. The context of the final stanza eventually clarifies what the 'Nobler part' refers to, though in the circumstances one wonders how ironic this reference is, bearing in mind the 'withered', 'barren' and 'frozen' state of her ancient lover. Elsewhere in Rochester's work, the physical has in fact shown itself to be 'the frailer part', while the 'nobler' is an adjective reserved for the 'tribute of a heart', the metaphysical aspect of love ('The Fall', ll.14–16). Contemporary understandings of love often identified the honourable realm of love with the feminine ideal—chaste, noble—and the physical realm with masculine initiative; as a real 'Young Lady' wrote in 1691, 'Female our Souls, all Masculine our Love'.[9] There may well, therefore, be several layers of irony in this reference to the 'Nobler part'. In its immediate application, the stark reality is that the lover's penis is feeble and in need of revival; by ironic transfer, nobility refers to the ideal of love rather than its inadequate physical reality; and in taking this transfer of meaning, the 'nobler part' ceases to be a reference to virile masculinity at all but becomes associated instead with the feminine soul. To 'name' the genuinely 'nobler part' would, then, lead to not 'shame' but to a transformation of values.

The 'Song' thus makes possible a number of metamorphoses within (and between) its lines: male to female, physical to spiritual, modesty to outspokenness, winter to spring. Perhaps most importantly, the progression of the poem marks a movement from the natural to the artful, as the strangely reversed cycle of seasonal growth is shown to have been brought about by 'all that art can add to love'. This is an artful lyric, as a look at its structure shows. The initial stanza is carefully framed in first and last lines by the 'ancient person' who is the focus and addressee of the poem. As the stanzas proceed they grow in length, mirroring the spring-like fertility recounted in the second stanza and the expansive revival of the third. Meanwhile, the underlying concept of constancy is expressed in the vocabulary and structure of the refrain, returning to the lover each time with terms implying continuation, notably the repeated 'still' of perpetuated loyalty. Even as the lyric speaks of improvements and additions—and the stanzas add their extra lines in mimicry—the unchanging refrain works in a contrary motion, defying the very notion of change which the young lady promises. That change, too, is knowingly artful, a conscious reversal of the conventional romance narrative in which the love of a young man transforms an old hag into a beautiful maiden; in this newly engendered tale, the loyalty of a young lady transforms an ancient person into a vigorous lover.

The word 'art' occurs three times during the lyric, and its developing meanings epitomize the progress of the poem. Its first appearance is not as a noun at all, but incidentally, as part of the verb to be: 'But still continue as thou art' (1.5). This provides both an aural anticipation of the artistry referred to later and an indication of the status quo at the beginning of the poem, a kind of naturalness, the state of being. The second and third uses of 'art' come in adjacent lines towards the end of the poem:

> All a Lover's wish can reach,
> For thy Joy my Love shall teach:
> And for thy Pleasure shall improve,
> All that Art can add to Love.
>> Yet still I love thee without Art,
>> Antient Person of my Heart.
>> (ll.21–26)

What is it that 'art' can add to love? Clearly this is a use of art as skill (*OED* 1), a reference to a lover's techniques learned, perhaps, from Ovid's *Ars Amatoria* and undoubtedly echoing its title. There is an implication that pleasure in love may be learned (and taught); that the young lady is 'mistress' of these arts is implied in the steady growth of the stanzas and their ever more hopeful sense of improvement. Similarly in Rochester's poem 'Verses Put Into a Lady's Prayer-Book', the speaker urges that, with the aid of love, he and his lady:

> . . . By easie steps may rise
> Through all the Joys on Earth, to those Above.
> (ll.16–17)

In both poems the lovers' experience of joy is progressively upgraded, the 'easie steps' here echoing the idea of the lover as a pupil in the young lady's school of love. But in contrast to this practical sense of art as learned skills, the final use of the word in 'Song of a Young Lady' introduces overtones of undesirable unnaturalness (*OED* 2), deceit and trickery, as she assures her lover that her affection for him is 'without Art'—in other words, unaffected and without guile. But if such meanings are prominent in this final usage, may they not also lurk in the earlier references to art? Can any interference of art in nature ever be trusted?

This question, one which underlay many Renaissance and seventeenth-century debates about love, is particularly pointed when we recall the artfulness of the poem itself, not just in its self-conscious lyric structuring but also as an artifact, a 'counterfeit' as Sidney would have it.[10] If this is potentially true of most poems, it is especially true here when the character of the speaker is so obviously artificial: a female voice constructed by a poet known to be male. There are, moreover, significant implications in the idea of artistry when applied to a female writing verse, suggesting extra layers of deceit and danger. As Rochester famously wrote in 'A Letter From Artemiza in the Towne to Chloe in the Countrey' (p. 83), a woman speaking in poetry was hardly to be trusted:

> Whore is scarce a more reprochable name,
> Than Poetess:
>
>                        (ll.26–27)

Nor was Rochester alone in implying this. Margaret Cavendish, who wrote prolifically at this time, knew that to be a 'writing lady' was seen as an aberration and a threat; her texts encroached upon male rights, for men

> hold books as their crown, and the sword as their sceptre, by which they rule and govern.[11]

Literary artistry and the arts of social control were not far apart in the later seventeenth-century. Even the outspoken Cavendish distinguished between her writing and that of her husband: while he 'wrote' with 'wit', she 'scribbled' with mere 'words'.[12] And as the anonymous female author of 'The Emulation' wrote in 1683, men

> let us learn to work, to dance, to sing,
> Or any such like trivial thing,
> Which to their profit may Increase or Pleasure bring.
> But they refuse to let us know
> What sacred Sciences doth impart
> Or the mysteriousness of Art.

Yet, despite being denied access to the sanctuary of high art, this female poet concluded that women can produce poetry in their own way:

> To Nature only, and our softer Muses, we
> Will owe our Charms of Wit, of Parts, and Poetry.[13]

This recalls the statement of the 'young lady' at the end of her song, that she loves 'without Art' both in her honest passion and her simple lyricism. A plain style without the counterfeits of complex rhetoric was also favoured by Dorothy Osborne, who commented that, in contrast to the frank artistry of a female writer, it was

> an admirable thing to see how some People will labour to find out term's that may obscure a plain sence, like a gentleman I knew, whoe would never say the weather grew cold, but that Winter began to salute us.[14]

So, while the artful 'young lady' risks her reputation as a woman by making so bold as to write in verse at all, her conclusion in its denial of art typifies the peculiar entanglement of the female writer, who uses art to hide it in order to retain some vestige of acceptable and apparently honest femininity.

However, within her 'Song' the young lady makes reference to other arts than poetry. The art which 'teaches' love is a particularly brazen subject for a female speaker, and introduces ideas not only of sensual prowess but also of the art so often associated with the feminine: making the female body itself into a work of art, to attract a lover. In contrast to this female social artistry, Rochester depicts the equivalent art of the masculine in military terms, using the vocabulary of

conquest in the 'Imperfect Enjoyment': the male approaching
with 'stiffly resolv'd' penis like a 'dart of love' which violently
'pierc'd' its object (ll.41–43). Female 'arts' are rarely seen by
Rochester as so direct or aggressive; even the less accomplished women in 'Upon His Leaving His Mistriss' attempt 'by
their Arts' to make '*one* happy Man' (ll.10–11). And if they are
deceptive or underhand, female arts are generally shown to be
manipulative rather than destructive. As another of Rochester's female voices comments in 'Artemiza to Chloe':

> They little guesse, who att Our Arts are griev'd,
> The perfect Joy of being well deceaved.
>                                       (ll.114–15)

How well, then, are we readers deceived by the arts of 'Song
of a Young Lady'? Initially we tend to connive contentedly in
the fiction of a crafted female persona, a double counterfeit
because of the known gender of the author. But beyond this,
what are the possible deceptions operating? The young lady
asserts at the beginning that she defies 'all the flattering Youth'
in order to remain true to her ancient lover; but how far is her
song itself an instance of superficial flattery rather than tender
concern? And if such flattery has a hollow ring to it, how far
can 'age' turn the tables on youth and defy its deceiving
flattery? But when we pause to consider the possible reactions
of the ancient person(a), we realize that, for all the female
artfulness, the focus of the poem, in addition to being the
current inadequacies of his physical being, is in fact his own
joy, his 'pleasure'; the song holds out tempting mirages of new
life and restored virility for him. Equally, there is a strong sense
of the lady's delight in her powers of restoration and her
proffered arts, recalling the lines in 'To a Lady in a Letter':

> For did you love your pleasure lesse,
> You were noe Match for mee.
>                                       (ll.27–28)

The lady and her lover, despite imbalances of weakness and
power, experience and innocence, seem to be on equal terms
when it comes to agreeing to the pursuit of pleasure. Or is this

another of the song's riddling deceptions, making us forget temporarily the inevitable inequalities also explored in the poem?

With all its layers of irony, the 'Song' has to be read as a wryly amusing poem; it certainly contains the ingredients of a comic scenario in its complex juxtapositions of youth and age, art and nature, loving and insulting language. But is the laughter affectionate or mocking, and does the lady laugh, or just her reader? There is undoubtedly some irony at the expense of her ancient lover, particularly focused on his 'Nobler part' and all that is signified by that phrase and its careful contextualising in the song. But it is difficult to discern how knowing the young lady is, especially with regard to her own self-ridicule. The mock-modesty of the beginning of the third stanza seems to me to be well under her control; she has assumed too many powers in stanza 2 to remain unaware of the falseness of her coy tones in the subsequent lines. But the denial of 'art' at the end of a precisely-constructed work of art in which the 'arts' of love have been so ostentatiously displayed, is a layer of irony which appears to be the poet's own rather than that of his persona. There is an implication that the male poet will not permit his 'young lady' to get away with controlling the ambivalences in a woman's role as simultaneously experienced and naive lover, as artful but required by social and literary convention to be artless. The lady, then, is mocked by her creator for thinking that she can really love 'without Art' when the very statement is an acknowledgement of her social arts. Her loyalty, too, which might be seen as her genuinely 'Nobler part', is perhaps itself the subject of mockery; why should a young lady turn down all the attentive youth to devote her time to this 'withered' ancient? It is possible, however, that this devotion is not a cause of amusement but of hope, offering reassurance to the male author (and male readers) that a powerful woman (despite all kinds of powerlessness) can be a source of restoration rather than intimidation. The poem is in some ways an answer to the obsessive male fear of dependency and impotence, expressed most forcefully by Rochester in the mock-heroic lines of the 'Imperfect Enjoyment':

> Eager desires, confound my first intent,
> Succeeding shame, does more success prevent,
> And Rage, at last, confirms me impotent.
> Ev'n her fair Hand, which might bid heat return,
> To frozen *Age*, and make cold *Hermits* burn,
> Apply'd to my dead *Cinder*, warms no more,
> Than Fire to *Ashes*, cou'd past Flames restore.
>                                        (ll.28–34)

The 'Song', echoing the metaphors of passionate heat and 'frozen age' employed here, is the antidote to this fear, the assertion that a fair female 'hand' as both caresser and written art can indeed kindle new fires, even in the most ancient of men.

But no poem, especially by Rochester, is likely to be quite as simple as that in its optimism. The 'Song' appears to be simultaneously a railing of the male ventriloquist-poet against his own sex's vulnerability to the frailness of the physical (and to the attentions of women), and a searching for an image of the youthful life force—which mingles male and female as the lady's metaphors reveal—to ensure rejuvenation. It is a reassuring assertion of the potential of loyalty and affection against the odds; yet it is also a disconcerting exploration of the power of art (particularly female arts) to conceal and trick as well as to heal. William Hazlitt said of Rochester that 'his verses cut and sparkle like diamonds',[15] and like diamonds they also have innumerable surfaces, the source of their teasingly unfathomable wit. The 'Song' sparkles with a multiplicity of implications about women and men, about art and truth. As readers we have to learn, like Artemiza, to be 'Pleas'd with the Contradiction' (l.30) and to perceive within that the beginnings of a vision. In the case of the 'Song', this entails an understanding of the social and personal constraints on women and the implications of 'art' in their hands, but further, hints at the possibility of a destabilising of fixed gender roles in language and in relationships. What is perhaps most startling about the poem is the almost impudent control taken by the young lady, despite her comments on the possible 'shame' of her attitude. In Rochester's poem 'Womans Honor' (p. 22) he establishes gendered meanings of honour, conventionally

regarded in the seventeenth-century as chastity in women and
public integrity in men:[16]

> Consider reall Honour then,
>   You'll find hers cannot be the same,
> 'Tis Noble confidence in Men,
>   In Women, mean mistrustful shame.
>
> (ll.21–24)

These terms are triumphantly inverted in 'Song of a Young
Lady'; her tone and approach ring with 'Noble confidence', the
serenely perceived vision of a lover restored through her art
and her love. 'Shame' is absent from her dealings (even
ironically, banished from her language) and is transferred
instead to the unspoken shame of male sexual failure. What
makes it, finally and surprisingly, into a love song, is the fact
that the bitterness of the often discomforting contradictions is
subsumed into a refrain of overriding affection. 'Art' and 'heart'
remind us of the constraining opposition of the constructed and
the natural, in poetry and in gender, but these binaries are
allowed, for the duration of the poem at least, the harmony of a
rhyme:

> Yet still I love thee without Art,
> Antient Person of my Heart.
>
> (ll.25–26)

## NOTES

1. From the preface to *The Poetical Works of Rochester* (1761 p. v, in
*Rochester: The Critical Heritage,* ed. David Farley-Hills (London, 1972), p. 202.
2. The text is taken from *The Poems of John Wilmot, Earl of Rochester,* ed.
Keith Walker (Oxford, 1984), pp. 32–33. All subsequent references to
Rochester's works are from this edition; page numbers are given in the main
text.
3. See Rochester's 'A Letter from Artemiza in the Town to Chloe in the
Countrey' (pp. 83–85) on pp. 129–34 and further discussion below.
4. See T. E., *The Lawes Resolutions of Womens Rights* (1632), pp. 124–25.
5. Dorothy Osborne, *Letters to Sir William Temple,* ed. Kenneth Parker
(Harmondsworth, 1987), p. 87.
6. Robert Burton, *The Anatomy of Melancholy,* ed. Thomas C. Faulkner,

Nicolas K. Kiessling and Rhonda L. Blair (Oxford, 1989), part 1. Sect.2 Memb.4. Subs. 7, Vol.I. p. 366.

7.  See discussion of this and other fundamental ideas of women 'coming second' in Patricia Parker, *Literary Fat Ladies: Rhetoric, Gender, Property* (London, 1987), pp. 178–233.

8.  Because of the uncertainty of seventeenth-century punctuation, some modern texts print 'ages" instead of 'age's' in line 17, following it with 'From their ice' instead of 'From his ice' (Veith's emendation). Rochester may well have intended the initial ambiguity, implying ancientness across the ages as well as in one man's age. Walker's text respects this by printing 'Ages', though he adopts the emendation to 'his'.

9.  A Young Lady, 'Maria to Henric' (1691) in *Kissing the Rod: An Anthology of Seventeenth-Century Women's Verse*, ed. Germaine Greer, Jeslyn Medoff, Melinda Sansone and Susan Hastings (London, 1988), p. 371.

10.  Sir Philip Sidney, *An Apology for Poetry*, ed. Geoffrey Shepherd (Manchester, 1973), p. 101.

11.  Margaret Cavendish, preface 'To All Writing Ladies', *Poems and Fancies* (1653), no pagination.

12.  Cavendish, 'A True Relation of my Birth, Breeding and Life' (1656) in *Her Own Life: Autobiographical Writings by a Seventeenth-Century Englishwoman*, ed. Elspeth Graham, Hilary Hinds, Elaine Hobby and Helen Wilcox (London, 1989), p. 93.

13.  'Triumphs of Female Wit, in some Pindarick Odes. Or the Emulation' (1683), in *Kissing the Rod*, pp. 310–12.

14.  Osborne, *Letters*, p. 131.

15.  William Hazlitt, *Lectures on the English Poets* (1818), in *Rochester: The Critical Heritage*, p. 214.

16.  For a contemporary reference to this difference of meaning according to gender, see 'The Memoirs of Ann, Lady Fanshawe' in *The Memoirs of Anne, Lady Halkett and Ann, Lady Fanshawe*, ed. John Loftis (Oxford, 1979), p. 116.

# 'Something Genrous in Meer Lust'?: Rochester and Misogyny

## STEPHEN CLARK

Given Rochester's undisputed status as 'one of the dirtiest poets in the canon',[1] one might think that any sustained consideration of his work would at some point involve detailed attention to the issue of misogyny. This has not, however, proved to be the case. It is not that feminist criticism has neglected his writing: in the last 20 years Fabricant, Wilcoxon, Wintle and Nussbaum have all provided illuminating commentaries.[2] Yet considering the attention devoted to niceties of satiric form or problems of textual attribution, this aspect of his work has suffered at least comparative neglect, the issues involved apparently being regarded as simultaneously too self-evident and too problematic. The general impression given is that Rochester has been too readily indulged by his proponents and too easily dismissed by his detractors, and that both parties have tended to rest their respective cases upon the more restricted question of obscenity.

In degree of physical specificity, lines such as 'whether the *Boy* fuck'd you, or I the Boy' (The Disabled Debauchee', (1.40) look positively anodyne in comparison with Dorset's 'strange incestuous stories / Of Harvey and her long clitoris', or claims that Mulgrave 'rears a little when his feeble tarse' is presented with 'a straight well-sphincter'd arse'.[3] As Dustin Griffin observes, 'his obscenity and misogyny are mild when compared to Oldham or Robert Gould or a number of anonymous Restoration satirists'.[4] Barbara Everett finds these terms evidence of 'betrayal of human sense and meaning to mere grunting phatic gesture'.[5] Perhaps, but they may equally well be seen as part of the Royal Society ideal of purifying the dialect of the tribe.[6] Lines such as 'Her Hand, her Foot, her very look's a *Cunt*' ('The Imperfect Enjoyment', 1.18) content themselves with the naming of parts as a talismanic invocation.

Rochester may not be quite as briskly common-sensical as
Suckling ('As for her Belly, 'tis no matter, so / There be a Belly,
and a Cunt, below'),[7] but there is still little sense of uneasy
lingering on threatening physicality. As Farley-Hills points
out,[8] a line such as 'A thing whose bliss depends upon thy will'
('The Discovery', l.23) seems almost to disdain innuendo, the
impulse to 'cry cunt' in order to 'friske his frollique fancy' ('An
Allusion to Horace', l.74). Instead there is a kind of tactile
empiricism concerned to define the qualities of the object at
hand. Rochester's 'And a Cunt has no sence of conscience or
law' ('Against Marriage', l.8) makes the same play as Shakespeare's 'Love is too young to know what conscience is'
(Sonnet 151, l.5); but without an equivalent erotic charge of
phonetic decomposition: 'con-science', 'con-sense', 'cunt-
sense'.[9] Rochester is equally disinclined to extend the trope in
the manner of Oldham's 'Her conscience stretch'd, and open as
the Stews' ('A Satyr upon a woman', l.85).[10] Elusiveness within
a formulaic diction is far more characteristic than lurid or
surreal metaphoric extrapolation.

   I take it for granted that sexual explicitness is not a regrettable
occasional blemish in Rochester's poetry, but one of its chief
attractions. Attempts to segregate the salacious, or if one
prefers, pornographic, elements from the aesthetic are misguided and inappropriate, if not downright hypocritical. The
phenomenon is, however, by no means a simple one. The
powerful misogynistic elements would lead one to expect a
reinforcement of authority, covert or explicit strategies of
dominance: 'And therefore what they fear, at heart they hate'
('A Satyr against Reason', l.45). Yet this is not supported by the
history of reception. The '*Lady*' in 'Timon' famously 'Complain'd our love was course, our *Poetry*, / Unfit for modest Eares'
(ll.102–03); the 'Prologue' to *Sodom* declares, 'I do presume there
are no women here / 'tis too debauch'd for their fair sex I fear';
and Robert Wolsley insisted in 1785, 'neither did my *Lord
Rochester* design those Songs the *Essayer* is so offended with . . .
for the Cabinets of Ladies'.[11] Nevertheless, of an admittedly
sparse documentary record, female readers from Aphra Behn to
Barbara Everett have proved singularly undeterred by this
aspect of his work and willingly heeded the opening address of
'Signior Dildo': 'You Ladyes all of Merry England' (l.1).

For this response to be possible, Rochester's poetry must offer 'something Genrous in meer Lust' ('A Ramble', l.98). In order to locate and define this quality, I will assess the degree of 'progressiveness' in his libertinism, in the context of recent models of homosocial bonding. I shall then analyse his distinctive plaintiveness and vulnerability, and explore some of the paradoxes of the truth of the failure of the body in his verse.

## II

The perennial problem of Rochester criticism has been to link his satirical and lyric modes, and Hobbesian individualism has regularly been invoked to perform this generic unification. The only truth is that provided by the none too reliable senses: the only legitimate ethics must be founded on their possibilities and limitations. In Lockean epistemology, awareness of the 'flying Houres . . . Whose Images are kept in store / By Memory alone' ('Love and Life', ll.4–5) produces an imperative to conserve, hoard and protect a finite and dwindling 'stock of ideas': in fairly simplistic terms, a bourgeois philosophy of accumulation. The libertine recuperation of Hobbes, in contrast, provokes a spendthrift pursuit of immediate and intense sensation: 'The Pleasures of a Body, Lam'd with lewdness, / A meer perpetual motion makes you happy'.[12]

It has frequently been argued that the libertine ideal of mutually reciprocated desire ('For did you love your pleasure lesse, / You were not fit for me' ('Song', ll.19–20) has implications for the social and political domain: as Sarah Wintle puts it, 'pleasure through sexual variety' may 'lead to an attitude which grants rights or equal pleasure and promiscuity to women'.[13] This potentially emancipatory aspect is, however, embedded in and impeded by a matrix of reactionary attitudes. Rochester's poetry 'oscillates' between the two, providing an empirical confirmation of their continued incompatibility.

Several immediate objections may be lodged against such an approach. It divests Rochester's poetry of cognitive status by treating it as a secondary manifestation of intellectual debates that precede it, and so reduces it to a merely symptomatic status. Secondly, the ameliorative nature of an atomistic individualism may be questioned. Even celebration of female sexual desire defines the gender in terms of an innate eroticism rather than an autonomous subjectivity. It requires immediate reconstitution in terms of contract, which Hobbes simply underwrites an authoritarian status quo. It is simple enough to regard the variety of relations women have with men—sexual, familial, economic—as entered into a formal if unspecified point. Hobbes may point out that 'If there be no contract, the Dominion is in the Mother',[14] but this is surely one reason why one always seems to exist. Thirdly, the relative equality of 'In Love 'tis equal measure' ('Song', 1.14) relies on a fictitious balance, disregarding the actual economic and political status underlying the 'nice allowances of Love' ('A Ramble', 1.110), such as those made by, for example, Rochester to his mistress, Elizabeth Barry. 'For none did e're soe dull, and stupid, / But felt a God, and blest his pow'r in Love' ('Artemiza', 1.48–49); but that 'power' manifests itself in a variety of cultural forms unavailable to a woman.

Mastery is not so much absent in Rochester as reversible: to be enslaved is quite as appealing an option as to enslave, though the question of who ultimately stages the scenario remains. In 'Fair Cloris', the swain, although 'Lustfull' remains a 'Slave' (1.26). The language of decorous sado-masochism abounds in the early lyrics: 'To see my Tyrant at my Feet; / Whil'st taught by her, unmov'd I sit / A Tyrant in my Turn' ('Pastoral Dialogue' ll.53–55). 'Kindness' itself 'guilds the Lovers Servile Chaine and makes the Slave grow pleas'd and vaine' ('Song', ll.15–16). In 'Insulting *Beauty*', it is boasted, 'I triumph in my Chain', (1.14); and the speaker of 'The Discovery' goes so far as to regret 'dying' only because 'I must be no more your slave' (1.44). In this context it is even possible to put a positive gloss on the power of the testicles to 'make a Man a Slave / To such a Bitch as *Willis*' ('On Mistress Willis', ll.3–4).

Mutuality, equality, in Rochester, tends to be achieved in terms of stand-offs, explicit negotiation, rather than persuasion, consummation. This needs to be reduced, as Wintle does, to a 'bleak notion of contract: I use you, you use me'.[15] There is an unusual (if not unprecedented) sense of considering one's mistress worth talking to even after sleeping with her. There is no influx of power through casual disparagement, none of the animus in excess so deplored by Ricks in Donne.[16] Whatever hostility there is seems primarily self-directed, a point to which I wish to return.

Adult equals are by no means the automatic paradigms for sexual encounters. Rochester's erotic landscape is inhabited by a broad and varied cast, including Signior Dildo, the oceanic Duchess of Cleveland and a herd of grunting pigs. It is mistaken to presume condemnation of or repulsion from grotesquerie. There remains something uniquely calm, unflustered, practical, about the attitude of the 'Young Lady' towards her 'Ancient Lover', whatever the relative proportions of nature and 'Art' in the 'reviving hand' (ll.25, 19).[17]

The 'something Genrous in meer lust' permits an unmisgivingness about a wide variety of sexual scenarios that extends far beyond the point of simple amoralism: 'Things must go on in their lewd natural way' ('Fragment'). Where Keats's proclamation 'even now, clammy dew is beading on my brow' implies solitude and self-absorption,[18] in Rochester, the 'clammy joys' ('The Imperfect Enjoyment', l.20) seem to involve actual and specific modes of conduct. The attention of the poetic voice is concentrated on the niceties of its etiquette: Everett rightly stresses 'its power of latency, its character of reserve'.[19]

Restoration anti-feminist satire habitually denounces women for both harbouring animal lust and then pretending to restrain it: 'Poor helplesse Woman, is not favour'd more. She's a sly Hypocrite, or Publique Whore' ('An Epistolary Essay', ll.95–96). In Rochester, the *grande dame* becomes a figure of urgent self-gratification: in 'Mistress Knights Advice to the Dutchess of Cleavland in Distress for a Prick', despite the demurral, 'Though Cunt be not Coy, reputation is Nice', the Duchess states a forthright preference for being 'Fuct by Porters and Carmen / Than thus be abus'd by Churchill and German', (ll.4, 11–12), a contest between female desire and male hypocrisy that recurs throughout Rochester.

The ethic of 'generosity' is espoused in numerous contexts: in addition to the title of this essay, 'Be generous, and wise and take our part'. ('Second Prologue', l.38); be not 'Generous and grateful never' ('Dialogue', l.26); seek 'true gen'rous *Love*'

('Woman's Honor', l.11); praise those 'whose Principles most gen'rous are, and just' ('A Satyr against Reason', l.125); 'In a generous Wench theres nothing of Trouble' ('Against Marriage', l.10); and 'Love, the most gen'rous passion of the mynde' ('A Letter from Artemiza', l.40).

From here it would seem a short step to celebration of a universal principle of fecundity: the Lucretian Venus. This, it seems, is provided in 'Upon his leaving his Mistress':

> Whilst mov'd by an impartial Sense,
> Favours like *Nature* you dispense,
> With Universal influence.
>
> See the kind Seed-receiving Earth,
> To Ev'ry Grain affords a *Birth*;
> On her no Show'rs unwelcome fall,
> Her willing *Womb*, regains 'em all,
> And shall my *Celia* be confin'd?
> No, live up to thy mighty *Mind*,
> And be the Mistress of *Mankind*.
>
> (ll.12–21)

'Confin'd' expands beyond possession by an individual male ('To damn you only to be mine', l.4) to a vision of unlimited universal access. However, the problem with such a celebration of impassive abundance is that the iconography cannot be kept on a solely mythological level: it must necessarily become involved in narratives of contract and estrangement. In 'Song', 'She's my delight, all Mankinds wonder; But my Jelous heart would break, should we live one day asunder' (ll.14–16), the speaker fears being asunder from 'Mankind' as much as from his mistress. To be included is always to be included alongside, amongst: the most forceful assertion of female autonomy is simultaneously the strongest confirmation of the social bond between men. Thus the 'Mistress of *Mankind*' (typically endowed with a 'mighty *Mind*') fuses personal with cultural libido: 'By merit, and by inclination, the joy at least of one whole *Nation*' (ll.6–7). Or, more crudely, 'Each Man had as much room, as *Porter*, *Blunt*, or *Harris*, had, in *Cullens*, *Bushel Cunt*' ('Timon', ll.93–94).[20]

This communalizing function is evident in the middle

section of 'A Ramble in St James's Park', a conjunction of
satiric commentary on sexual mores, specific, empirical, concrete, with the apostrophic mode, more usually delivered from
an unspecified vantage to an unidentified mistress:

> Gods! that a thing admir'd by mee
> Shou'd fall to so much Infamy.
> Had she pickt out to rub her Arse on
> Some stiff prickt Clown or well-hung Parson
> Each jobb of whose spermatique sluce
> Had fill'd her Cunt with wholesome Juice
> I the proceeding shou'd have prais'd
> In hope she had quence'd a fire I'd raised.
> Such naturall freedomes are but Just
> There's something Genrous in meer lust . . .
>                                   (ll.89–98)

Corinna retains initiative, choice, the power of 'picking out':
the speaker bewails his exclusion from the her 'Divine Abode',
(l.39). (The initial 'Consecrate to Prick and Cunt', (l.10) and
final 'dares prophane the Cunt I swive' (l.166) gives a religious
framing to the whole poem.) Everett describes the poem as a
'savage, dangerous, yet obscurely innocent fantasy—innocent
from the sensed rectitude which its upside down fury violates,
the contained and quashed romantic idealism'; and her
instinct is sound, I believe, to see the poem as 'an actual if
finalizing perpetuation (for all its grossness) of earlier Renaissance modes of idealization'.[21] The sexual 'thing' is initially
'admir'd', and the note of limpid self-pity retains a sense of
etiquette, humility, deference ('praised'). The 'Infamy' to
which it is opposed remains indeterminate. The capacity of the
narrator to make such a judgement is uncertain after his initial
departure from the 'grave discourse'. Hence the oddness of the
subsequent accusation, 'To bring a blott on Infamy', (l.104):
not so much to exceed the bounds of shame as bring the
category itself into disrepute. 'Thing' can also be read as penis
(with a play on 'fall'): and it is tempting to make the
psychoanalytic extrapolation, of Corinna representing the
virility that the speaker lacks.

There is a querulous comic note in the feminine rhymes; and
also an absence of hierarchy recalling the social as well as

sexual dimensions of the 'all-sin-sheltering Grove': 'And here promiscuously they swive', (1.25, 32). The 'spermatique sluce' of 'stiff-prickt Clowns' and 'well-hung Parson' provides not corruption or disease but a 'wholesome Juice'. 'To rub her arse on' continues the 'proud bitch' image: but as with the later 'longing Arse' (1.41) has a potential homo-erotic dimension. 'Quence'd the fire' is a typical literalization of a precieux diction, dousing the 'flame' with other men's semen.[22] 'I'd raised' suggests the arousal of the 'knight errant Paramours' by the speaker himself. The 'natural freedomes' represent not liberation from but facilitation of exchange between men: 'meer lust' is not an underlying impulse, basic motivation, but an unattainable, longed-for, standard.

The relation of 'I' to 'all Mankind' initially seems antitheti-cal, but in the course of the passage undergoes a physical assimilation. There is a typically determinist note in the severity of 'Fate'. 'Priviledge above' and 'nice allowances' attribute a certain authority to the speaker, but this is immediately compromised by the infantile dependence of 'humble fond believing me'. The 'meanest part' could be genitals of either sex or a role in 'loves Theatre the Bed' ('Leave this gawdy guilded Stage', 1.5). 'Ungratefull' most immediately refers to the flouting of contract by Corinna, but can be extended to the speaker's own behaviour or the reader, pre-emptively rebuked for simultaneously witnessing and violating the erotic intimacy. There remains a sense of decorum, almost gentility, in the 'digestive surfiet water' served up; and an infinite poignancy in 'content', whose obvious sexual play cannot detract from the peculiar resonance of 'Grace'.

'Pleasure for excuse' seems to ascribe a libertine autonomy, 'naturall freedomes': 'abuse' refers to his own 'dram of sperm' as much as Corinna's behaviour. 'Meer lust' cannot be taken as simply an anti-inflationist view of 'pleasure': a secular pastime. (Though there is no compunction about describing Corinna as 'joyfull and pleas'd' (1.80) at her liaison.) The poem would be much simpler and more manageable if this were a clearly available standard. Yet the 'pleasure' of the speaker lies more in his relation with Corinna's other lovers than in any momentary spasm of ejaculation. Indeed, orgasm as an entity in itself is immediately redefined in term of two overlaid relations: an apostrophic address to Corinna, and an indirect communion with 'halfe the Town'. 'Spewing home' seems more appropriate to the behaviour of the narrator himself; and if one pursues this somewhat lurid transference, he receives as well as adds to the 'seed' within. The voracity of the 'devouring Cunt' seems part of its attraction rather than a cause of repulsion. 'Full gorges' would seem attached to 'Cunt', but transfers itself to the speaker in both active and passive senses: he is himself swallowed up[23] but also bloated by receiving the 'vast meal'. The 'nasty slime' is displaced from the juices of female arousal onto the male ejaculate; but the point is that the two are inseparable, and satisfaction is received from contact with both.

One might go so far as to say that the affair is only fully consummated in the moment of infidelity. The term 'betray' comes to represent both revelation and exposure. The expression that gives public significance is brought into existence by a movement inseparable from fickleness and duplicity.[24] As Everett says, the narrator of a Rochester poem is always hoping 'that he will betray love enough'.[25] Logically, Corinna cannot reveal 'secrets' until they have been confided in her, but the implication seems to be that she already has been 'faithless'. This, of course, conforms to the argument for mutable desire espoused in some of the lyrics. Nevertheless, the implication is that she is attractive precisely because of, not in spite of, her 'Treachery'. 'When leaneing' refers both backwards to the 'Paramours' engaged in love-making and forward to the narrator seeking comfort: the two are telescoped into being simultaneously present. 'And Reason lay dissolv'd in Love' is not the prelude to disaster, Samson in Delilah's lap, but the desired outcome, the culmination of the preceding accelerated pattern of inversions.

The primary tension of the passage lies in its conflation of third-person satire with second-person apostrophe: 'But mark what Creatures women are How infinitly vile when fair', (ll.41–42). The definition is not the result of taxonomy, categorization, but of the movement between vileness and fairness: the apparent stability containing progressively more estranged extremes. There is a summoning and making-present of physical residue, an inverted and arguably perverse idealization of a gluttonous absorption of the male body. The hostility towards the male rivals is merely an inversion of the attraction towards physical contact via the 'devouring Cunt'. I now wish to discuss the relation of this mutual accentuation to the presence of communal judgement in Rochester's verse.

## III

One by-product of the foregrounding of the instance of utterance in Rochester's lyrics is the reduction of the masculine community to 'The false Judgement of an Audience / Of Clapping-Fooles' ('An Allusion to Horace', (ll.13–14). In Rochester there is never any sense of transmission of a received and proven wisdom. 'The Mistress', for example, offers a series of outward addresses: 'You Wiser men despise me not'; 'Had you not been profoundly dull, You had gone mad like me'; 'Nor Censure us You who perceive My best belov'd and me' (ll.13, 19–20, 21). These are not apologies or appeals for social endorsement so much as a kind of pre-emptive debunking. Yet there is no corresponding idealization of the lovers: where Donne's 'The Good Morrow' celebrates the power which 'makes one little roome an every where',[26] the lines, 'To make the old *World*, a new withdrawing Room, Whereof another *World* she's brought to *Bed*!' provoke nothing but mockery in 'Timon' (ll.148–49).

The testimony of the isolated speaker is displaced onto an almost phenomenological emphasis on the personal body; it articulates not the authority of collective experience but an estrangement from and within it. There is no protective persona of a public self, but equally no post-romantic subjectivity conflating the two spheres. Not only Rochester, but also Sedley, Dorset and the rest seem almost devoid of political and social identities in their verse. It has often been noted how little Rochester deals with the public sphere: attempts such as Paulson's to read the obscene as 'the private half of a basic analogy between public and private life',[27] have little purchase compared to the reverse movement that transforms Charles II into an alter-ego and displaced father-figure, and his mistresses into demonic maternal presences.

It can, of course, be argued that Rochester's verse at all

times presupposes a homosocial bonding. There would seem ample support for this in comments such as Pope's 'Mob of Gentlemen who wrote with Ease', Marvell's 'merry gang', and Dryden's 'men of pleasant conversation . . .' ambitious to distinguish themselves from the herd of gentlemen, by their party![28]

> Scorne all Applause the Vile Rout can bestow,
> And be content to please those few, who know . . .
> I loathe the Rabble, 'tis enough for me,
> If Sidley, Shadwell, Shepherd, Witcherley,
> Godolphin, Buttler, Buckhurst, Buckingham,
> And some few more, whom I omit to name,
> Approve my Sense, I count their Censure Fame.
> ('An Allusion to Horace', ll.102–03, 120–25)

There is a predictable hauteur in the roll-call perhaps, but the 'few, who know' have scarcely any significant presence in Rochester's verse. There is a peculiar solipsism, a sense of self-directedness, with little or no sense of a Rochester poem being for anyone, whether wife or mistress, specific male confidante or broader circle.

'Love a *Woman*! y'are an *Ass*' advises staying at home with a 'lewd well-natur'd *Friend*, Drinking, to engender *Wit*' (ll.11–2). Yet there is no equivalent to the cheerfully louche exchanges between Buckhurst and Etherege. Where their verse-letters celebrate a benign itinerary of collective indulgence ('Then the next morning we all hunt / To find whose fingers smell of cunt'),[29] Rochester's 'Regime d'viver' offers an irascible filofax of cyclic, solitary debauchery, whose culminating animus— 'Then crop-sick, all Morning, I rail at my *Men*, And in Bed I lye Yawning, till Eleven again' (ll.13–14)—expands out from an immediate circle of servants onto a whole gender: '*Men*' in general.

Even in Sade, as has often been noted, there is an ethic of friendship[30] and a certain clubbability has accompanied most outbursts of ethical antinomianism and romantic diabolism. In contrast, Rochester's ultimate slight in 'On Poet Ninny', 'The worst that I cou'd write, wou'd be noe more, Than what thy very Friends have said before' (ll.27–28), reflects much more on the companions than the supposed target. No distinction is drawn between Artemiza's 'To heare, what Loves have past, In this Lewd Towne' (ll.32–33), and the 'grave discourse, Of who Fucks who and who does worse' ('A Ramble', ll.1–2). The monkey that she addresses as a 'curious Minature of Man' is a 'dirty chatt'ring Monster' ('Artemiza', ll.143, 141) and while 'dirty' may do no more than reflect contemporary standards of hygiene, 'chatt'ring', voluble, gossipy, empty-headed, reverses the stereotype of feminine volubility.

The 'dull dining *Sot*' pursues Timon, 'but as a *Whore*, With modesty enslaves her *Spark*, the more' (ll.9–10), a comparison that both refuses to differentiate between male honour and female modesty, and gives an explicitly sexualized dimension to male social intercourse. After attributing a libel to Timon (which may or may not be the poem itself, yet to be written), 'to his dear mistake, Which he, by this, had spread o're the whole Town, And me, with an officious Lye, undone' (ll.28–30). This vulnerability to public opinion again feminized ('undone'), is powerfully prefigured in Strephon's early dialogue with Alexis:

> As Trees are by their Barks Embrac'd,
> Love to my Soul doth cling;
> When torn by th' Herd's greedy taste,
> The injur'd Plants feel they're defac't,
> They wither in the Spring.
> ('Pastoral Dialogue', ll.61–65)

The arboreal 'Soul' is divided into 'Tree', 'Bark' and the 'Herd's greedy taste': 'Love' serves the function of a protective surface, but is itself 'defac't', 'torn', and 'injur'd'. In 'Timon', the congregation of 'all brave *Fellows*', the rompish camaraderie of the 'tough *Youth*', provokes a fastidious shudder (ll.37, 86):

> Their rage once over, they begin to treat,
> And six fresh *Bottles*, must the peace compleat.
> I ran down Stairs, with a Vow never more
> To drink Bear Glass, and hear the *Hectors* roar.
> (ll.174–77)

The persona never dominates, seldom interjects, but rather witnesses with varying degrees of tacit fascination and contempt. There is no single *adversarius*, but rather a whole social group, and Timon hates himself for being unable to differentiate himself from them: 'No means, nor hopes, appear of a retreat' (l.42). The speaker of 'Tunbridge Wells' responds similarly to the 'crowd':

> Endeavouring this irksome sight to Balke,
> And a more irksome noyse, their silly talke,
> I silently slunke down to th' lower walke:
> ('Tunbridge Wells', ll.35–37)

He repeatedly attempts to absent himself from his own poem: 'th' hearing what they said, I did myself the kindness to evade' (ll.34–35), and 'Tir'd with this dismall Stuffe, away I ran' (ll.26). Even the narrator of 'Upon His Drinking Bowl' defines himself in terms, not of belonging to, but of separation from: 'I'm none of those that took *Mastrich*, Nor *Yarmouth Leaguer* knew': 'For I am no Sir Sydrophell, Nor none of his *Relations*' (ll.11–12, 15–16).

Given a masculine community as brutish and rapacious in its pleasures as one could wish (or perhaps envy), an explanation is needed of how Rochester speaks (or appears to be speaking) from a point outside this collectivity.

One tradition of feminist reading would stress the residual equality of desires: 'When neither overcomes Loves triumph greater is' ('Leave this gawdy guilded Stage', l.10). There is undoubtedly a willingness to allow independent female voices into the poems. Satiric modes are directed as (if not more) frequently against men than women; and the conventions of cavalier lyric themselves become feminized, transposable, in poems such as 'Against Constancy', 'The Platonick Lady', and 'The Song of a Young Lady to her Ancient Lover'. There is a complex empathy with the host's wife in 'Timon' (ll.49–56).

The '*Lady*' has scarcely worn worse than Timon himself; and the passage reflects the same ambivalence towards its object as the reader feels towards its narrator. '*Age*' is the 'incurable disease of others beside '*Beauty*'; and the gap between 'desire' and 'pow'r to please' is famously commented upon by Rochester himself: 'soe great a disproportion twixt our desires and what has been ordained to content them'.[31] 'Fit to give love' is almost the finest compliment that can be paid; 'prevent

despair' is a gently unrecriminative term for sexual availability. '*Cocks*' gives a momentary masculinity, force, not
wholly retracted by 'old bleer *Eyes*', no less to be respected than
the disabled debauchee; 'smite' has overtones of both heroic
endeavour and social flirtation. There is a note of admirable
defiance, 'in despight of time'; 'affection' also acquires a certain
dignity as a conscious role-playing. She shares her preoccupation with love with Rochester himself; and the resulting
dialogue is closer to Eliot's 'Portrait of a Lady' than to the
witches' sabbath of Pope's 'Ghosts of Beauty' ('To a Lady',
l.241). Her tone is gently reproachful, unflustered, graceful,
with a note of disdain towards the 'Hair-brain'd *Youth*', deemed
'Too rotten to consummate the Intrigue' (ll.104, 106). In
perhaps the morally finest line in Rochester, and certainly the
most understated epithet, she is allowed to depart undispar-
aged, undiminished: 'And decently my *Lady*, quits the Room'
(l.110).

Wintle dismisses this persistent tactic of gender-reversal as
simply offering a 'parody of a woman',[32] but this is to
underestimate the slitheriness of role-playing in Rochester.
The demand for 'mutual Love' ('The Advice', l.16) precludes
full appreciation of the instability, the solipsism, and the
impassioned lyricism of sexual failure.

Sex is ethical, even conceptual, before it is erotic; and the key
instances to be debated are not those of ecstasy and fulfilment
but disappointment and inadequacy. There is a truth of the
body to be found through its very humiliation, in the pursuit of
a pleasure known to be insufficient beforehand.

In 'The Women about Town', 'a Fate which noe man can
oppose; The losse of his heart and the fall of his Nose'
('Lampoone', ll.9–10) does not merely refer to possible
infection, but extends to a whole betrayal by the body. It is not
'just' but nevertheless inevitable that 'our Tarses be burnt by
our hearts taking fire' (ll.15–16). There is no specific guilt or
punishment for indulgence beyond the acceleration of an
inevitable decline. There is little or nothing of the *poète maudit* in
Rochester, seeking transgression as an end in itself. Despite
ultimate conversion, there is similarly little sense of blasphemy
as an inverted mode of belief. Physical corruption is not the
correlative of sin; and, as previously noted, there is no sense of

the disgusting in itself arousing. Instead there is a certain stoic dignity in conscious acceptance, even pursuit, of this corporeal transformation.

The disabled debauchee boasts of the 'Honourable scars, Which my too forward valour did procure'; and in 'To the Post Boy' even the more graphic 'Sear cloaths and ulcers from the top to toe' remain 'Heroick scars' (ll.8–9). The couplet, 'So charming Oyntments, made an Old *Witch* flie, And bear a Crippled Carcass through the Skie' ('A Satyr against Reason', ll.86–87) also has something of this last-standness. There is a stark pathos to 'Old', an unsparing naturalism but no disgusted recoil in 'Carcass', and an immense respect for the refusal of the '*Witch*' to capitulate to the state of 'Crippled'. The 'Oyntments' are 'charming' because they are casting a spell, but also felicitous, because they are successful in doing so when there is no alternative but to inculcate an illusion.

> Trembling, confus'd, despairing, limber dry,
> A wishing, weak, unmoving lump I ly.
> This *Dart* of Love, whose piercing point oft try'd,
> With *Virgin blood*, *Ten thousand Maids* has dy'd;
> Which *Nature* still directed with such *Art*,
> That through it ev'ry *Cunt*, reacht ev'ry Heart.
> Stiffly resolv'd, twou'd carelessly invade,
> *Woman* or *Man*, nor ought its fury staid,
> Where e're it pierc'd, a *Cunt* it found or made.
> Now languid lies, in this unhappy hour,
> Shrunk up, and Sapless, like a wither'd *Flow'r*.
> Thou treacherous, base, deserter of my flame,
> False to my passion, fatal to my *Fame*;
> Through what mistaken *Magick* dost thou prove,
> So true to lewdness, so untrue to Love?
> (ll.35–49)

The 'Satire on Charles II' is concerned with the obvious political dimension to virility in terms of the royal succession, but what is striking is his more universal masculine ungainliness: 'Yett his dull graceless Ballocks hang an arse' (l.27). There is no political respect, but a biological empathy. A displaced self-loathing and curious solicitation are directed towards the bodily imperatives of the ageing debauchee:

clapped out in every sense. This extends to Mistress Willis, who, like Charles, represents a persona to be occupied. She 'Rails and Scolds when she sits down, And Curses when she Spends' (ll.15–16), terms with both a generic and psychological appositeness to Rochester and Restoration satire in general, with its close conjunction of arousal and abuse. Further points of connection are the odd poignancy of 'And yet with no man Friends'; in what might be seen as a highly apposite summation of Rochester's own style, 'Bawdy in Thoughts, precise in Words'; and even perhaps an oblique glance at the poet's constipation, the 'Belly' which is 'a Bagg of Turds' (ll.13–14, 17, 19–20).

In the rivalry between Count Cazzo and Signior Dildo, there is only one winner: the substitute clearly surpasses the original, a situation which 'Flesh and Blood cou'd not bear' (l.80). Witnessing the subsequent ambush and pursuit by 'A Rabble of Pricks' (l.83):

> The good Lady Sandys, burst into a Laughter
> To see how their Ballocks came wobbling after,
> And had not their weight retarded the Fo
> Indeed't had gone hard with Signior Dildo.
>                     (ll.89–92)

'Retarded' is delayed, but also rendered imbecilic; and 'gone hard' merely reinforces the superiority of the intruder, and the dispensability of the original. Harold Weber astutely notes how the poem demonstrates that 'from the female point of view the male body provides an essentially comic spectacle'. 'Reducing men to their pricks' makes them 'objects of derision', and there is unsparing indictment of the 'anatomical insufficiency of the male body', in particular, the ballocks as 'the male body's betrayal of itself'.[33] As Weber points out, the inadequacy of feminist models built around the unitary phallus becomes immediately apparent when confronted with the testicles, in all their queasy dangling vulnerability. But he fails to follow through this insight, instead reverting to ascribing to Rochester a 'conventional misogynous understanding of hierarchical relations between the sexes' (1992; p. 115).[34]

The poems represent, Weber claims, 'an attempt to transform the penis into the phallus, to recapture an endemic wholeness which would banish death'. It is 'their inability to effect this transformation' which 'generates the rate and anxiety that so often disfigure the verse, marking the moment when the male will discovers the limits of its own power and authority' (1992; p. 110).[35] Like Robinson, Weber is reluctant to acknowledge that 'rage and anxiety' might be what we read for. That which 'disfigures the verse' might be what produces it in the first place.

In Rochester, however, there is not a failed attempt to 'transform the penis into the phallus', but often a strikingly literal dramatization of the reverse process: what is sought is not power, but powerlessness. If, as Timon insists, he 'never Rhym'd, but for my *Pintles* sake', this may imply not self-aggrandizement but self-deprecation. 'The Imperfect Enjoyment' offers the most complex display of what Claude Rawson called Rochester's 'machismo of sexual debility' (1985; p. 335).[36] Weber argues that 'the failure to control desire, to overcome the gap between the mind and the body, transforms a genuinely erotic moment into a bitter litany of foul complaints' (1992; p. 103).[37] A more productive way of looking at the poem is that it exposes this 'gap'. The genuinely erotic' cannot be simply opposed to the 'bitter litany': the one is implicit within and generated out of the other. The speaker's inability to respond to his mistress's desires with 'wisht Obedience', what 'The Advice' dubs 'the Freedom to Obey' (I.12), prompts the final outburst of '*Rage*' (1.25).

The speaker appears not merely to address but actually to become his penis. The vain-glorious boast of previous exploits is delivered from the point of minimum performance, leading to the suspicion that they are purely verbal and compensatory. Yet it should be stressed that erotic failure is the condition rather than the cessation of this indiscriminate assault, which, as in 'Mock Song', subjects an infinitely penetrable body to a random incision that verges on the sadistic and grotesque. It is noteworthy that the previous description of ejaculation might easily be transposed into female orgasm: 'In liquid *Raptures*, I dissolve all o're, Melt into Sperme, and spend at ev'ry Pore' (ll.15–16). 'Stiffly resolv'd' reverses the relation of conscious purpose to sexual arousal from one of prohibition and restraint. The '*All-dissolving Thunderbolt*' (1.10) becomes a display of authority, the antithesis of the yielding assimilation of the 'wishing, weak, unmoving lump'. Yet this state is broadly continuous with the ideal of protective enclosure prevalent elsewhere. An obvious parallel may be found in the masturbatory passivity of Bloom's 'languid floating flower',[38] suggesting that the 'wither'd *Flow'r* that 'languid lies' might be truer 'to love' than the rampaging virility with which it is contrasted.

> Worst part of me, and henceforth hated most,
> Through all the *Town*, a common *Fucking Post*:
> On whom each *Whore*, relieves her tingling *Cunt*,
> As *Hogs*, on *Gates*, do rub themselves and grunt.
> May'st thou to rav'nous *Shankers*, be a *Prey*,
> Or in consuming *Weepings* waste away.
> May *Strangury*, and *Stone*, thy *Days* attend,
> May'st thou ne're Piss, who didst refuse to spend,
> When all my joys, did on false thee depend.
> And may *Ten thousand* abler *Pricks* agree,
> To do the wrong'd *Corinna* right for thee.
>
> (ll.62–72)

Abuse of the penis seems a more than adequate substitute for utilization of it. A dismemberment of his own body is performed through a series of violently repudiatory apostrophes; a making present of that which, as it were, had been gouged out of himself.

Rancour is drained away from all other possible targets: the unqualified intimacy of the opening lines paradoxically presupposes this eventual outlet. There is, as Treglown points out (1982; p. 85),[39] a disconcerting urbanity to the pun on 'depend' and on the previous 'confirm me impotent' (l.28), ushering in a final compliment to the 'wrong'd *Corinna*'. The 'Worst part' is not so much expelled as expanded to fill the narrative present of the poem. It is then denounced for precisely what it is manifestly failing to do: provide 'a common *Fucking Post*'. The ferocity of invective is thus displaced from the state of powerlessness onto the state of potency, apparently only invoked as a negative contrast. The punishment becomes a jubilant kind of release: not from the 'drudgery' of heterosexual intercourse, but from the necessity to 'agree' with, conform to, the hallucinatory array of 'abler *Pricks*'. Belief, opinion, scandal, are all set aside in favour of a reiteration of common physical limitation, whose buoyant explicitness refuses the grotesque or macabre. The 'Consuming *Weepings*' of venereal sores might be seen as Rochester's version of 'lacrimae rerum'; and, in their more restricted fashion, as partaking of some of the grandeur of the Virgilian pathos.

Rochester may be seen as the great articulator of the malfunctioning body, a typology superimposed upon its most flagrant and ostentatious debaucheries. In the context of my original concern, misogyny, it is possible to offer a provisional conclusion. The generic continuities with anti-feminist satire, and inventive, occasionally horrifying, results of generic inversion of lyric, are of little consequence compared to the foregrounding and evocation of masculinity as a cultural bond. The continual recourse to a negative testimony of the body represents a kind of obdurate refusal of a culturally endorsed mastery, and it is in this precarious movement, I believe, that we may discover and applaud the generosity of Rochester's poetry.

## NOTES

1. The Professional Amateur', in *Spirit of Wit: Reconsiderations of Rochester's Wit*, ed. Jeremy Treglown (Oxford, 1982), pp. 58–74.

2. Carole Fabricant, 'Rochester's World of Imperfect Enjoyment', *Journal of English and German Philology*, (1974), pp. 338–50. Reba Wilcoxon 'Rochester's Sexual Politics', *Studies in Eighteenth-Century Culture* (1979), pp. 137–49 reprinted in *John Wilmot: Earl of Rochester: Critical Essays*, ed. David M. Vieth (New York, 1988), pp. 113–26; Sarah Wintle 'Libertinism and Sexual Politics', in Treglown, pp. 133–65; and Felicity A. Nussbaum, *The Brink of All We Hate: English Satires Upon Women, 1660–1750*, (Lexington, 1984), pp. 57–60.

3. All quotations from *The Poems of John Wilmot, Earl of Rochester*, ed. Keith Walker (Oxford, 1984). The Dorset quotations are taken from 'Colon', ll.44–45 and 'A Faithful Catalogue of our most Eminent Ninnies', ll.112–13, in *The Poems of Charles Sackville Sixth Earl of Dorset*, ed. Brice Harris (New York and London, 1979), pp. 125–26, 140.

4. 'Rochester and the "Holiday Writers" ', in *Rochester and Court Poetry*, ed. Alan Roper (Los Angeles, 1988), pp. 33–66.

5. 'The Sense of Nothing', in Treglown, ll.1–41.

6. 'As they conceiv'd lewdly, so they wrote in plain *English*, and took no care to cover up the worst of their thoughts in clean Linnen', Daniel Defoe, in

*The Works of Sir Charles Sedley* (1722 for 1721), i ll.8–9; cited in *Rochester: The Critical Heritage*, ed. David Farley-Hills (London, 1972), p. 192.

7. 'The Deformed Mistress', in *The Works of Sir John Suckling: The Non-Dramatic Works*, ed. Thomas Clayton (Oxford, 1971), p. 34, ll.27–28.

8. Farley-Hills, *Rochester's Poetry*, (London, 1978), p. 45.

9. 'See the exhaustive commentary by Stephen Booth in *Shakespeare's Sonnets* (New Haven, 1977), pp. 525–26.

10. 'A Satyr upon a woman, who by her falshood and scorn was the death of his friend', *The Poems of John Oldham*, ed. Harold F. Brooks and Raman Selden (Oxford, 1987), p. 82. Compare also Robert Gould, 'Nor are their consciences (which can betray / Where e're they're sworn to love) less large than they', in *Love Given O're: Or, a Satyr against the Pride, Lust and Inconstancy etc. of Women* (London, 1682). Reprinted in *Satires on Women* (Augustan Reprint Society no. 180, intro. Felicity A. Nussbaum (Los Angeles, 1977).

11. *Rochester's Sodom*, ed. L. S. A. M. von Romer (H. Welter: Paris and Amsterdam, 1904, 1905). For discussion of the problem of attribution, see J. W. Johnson, 'Did Lord Rochester write *Sodom*?' *Papers of the Bibliographical Society of America* (1987), pp. 119–53. Wolsey's comment comes in 'Preface to *Valentinian*' (1685), in *Rochester: the critical heritage* ed. D. Farley-Hills, p. 155.

12. '*Valentinian: a tragedy: as 'tis altered by the late Earl of Rochester* (London, 1685), 5ii, 61.

13. Sarah Wintle, 'Libertinism and Sexual Politics', in Treglown, p. 155.

14. *Leviathan*, ed. C. B. Macpherson (Harmondsworth, 1968), p. 253.

15. Sarah Wintle, 'Libertinism and Sexual Politics', in Treglown, p. 134.

16. 'Donne after Love', *Literature and the Body*, ed. Elaine Scary (Baltimore, 1988), pp. 33–69.

17. 'The Imperfect Enjoyment' also stresses the 'busie hand' and the 'fair hand, which might bid heat return / To frozen *Age*' (p. 13, ll.31–32).

18. *Endymion* III, pp. 567–68, in the *Poetical Works of John Keats*, ed. H. W. Garrod (Oxford, 1970), p. 119.

19. Everett, 'The Sense of Nothing', in Treglown, p. 17.

20. The most graphic illustration comes in Sedley's 'In the Fields of Lincoln Inn', published in *Poems on Several Occasions* (London, 1680), p. 57. Phillis, faced with two gallants, acts decisively: '*Coridon's* Aspiring Tarse, she fitted / To her less frequented *Arse*' while Strephon 'into her *Cunt* she thrust: Now for Civil Wars prepare, / Rais'd by fierce intestine Bustle. / When these Heroes meeting Justle / In the Bowels of the Fair'. 'Nature had 'twixt *Cunt* and *Arse* / Wisely plac'd firm separation, / God knows else what desolation / Had insu'd from warring *Tarse*'. Compare Gloria, in *The Devil in Miss Jones*, similarly circumstanced: 'can you feel his cock against yours, can you feel it'. Cited in Anne McClintock, 'Gonad and the Barbarian and the Venus Flytrap: Portraying the female and the male orgasm', *Sex Exposed: sexuality in the pornography debate* (London, 1992), pp. 111–31.

21. Everett, 'The Sense of Nothing', in Treglown, pp. 25, 27.

22. Compare 'Dialogue' (ll.33–40): 'the Show'rs that fall / Quench the fire, and quiet all;' and 'The Advice' (ll.23–24): 'for even streams have desires, / Cool as they are, they feel Love's powerful fires'.

23. Compare *Sodom*, where Flux comments: 'Men's Pricks are eaten of the secret parts / Of Women' (l.51).

24. From a host of examples: 'To betray, and engage, and inflame my Desire' ('The Submission', l.6); 'employ that Art / Which first betray'd, to ease my heart' ('Dialogue', ll.6–7); 'my unfaithfull eyes / Betray a kinder story' ('Song', ll.7–8); and 'But Virgins Eyes their hearts betray, / And give their Tongues the lie' ('Song', ll.19–20). In 'A Satyr against Reason', 'But Savage *Man* alone, does Man Betray' (l.130), allows, by the logic of its own argument, that the primitive impulses are superior because they are closer to the spontaneous behaviour of the animal kingdom.

25. Everett, 'The Sense of Nothing', in Treglown, p. 19.

26. 'The Good Morrow', *The Elegies and the Songs and Sonnets*, ed. Helen Gardner (Oxford, 1965), p. 70.

27. 'Rochester: the Body Political and the Body Private', in *The Author in his Work: Essays on a problem in criticism*, ed. Louis L. Martz and Aubrey Williams (New Haven and London, 1978), pp. 103–21; reprinted in Vieth, 1988, pp. 45–67. See also Robert Holton 'Sexuality and Social Hierarchy in Sidney and Rochester', *Mosaic*, 24:1 (1991), pp. 47–65.

28. *The Twickenham Edition of The Poems of Alexander Pope*, ed. John Butt *et al.* (New Haven and London, 1939–1969), vol. 4, *Imitations of Horace*, ed. John Butt, III 108, 203; to Sir Edmund Harley, 1677; *The Poems and Letters of Andrew Marvell*, ed. H. M. Margoliouth, vol. 2 (Oxford, 1972; 2nd edition, 1981), p. 329; Dryden, 'Preface to "All for Love" ' (1678), cited in *Rochester: The Critical Heritage*, ed. Farley-Hills, p. 32.

29. 'Mr Etherege's Answer' (to 'Another Letter by the Lord Buckhurst to Mr Etherege'), in *Poems of Dorset* (ll.34–35), p. 115.

30. Simone de Beauvoir, 'Must we burn Sade?' Introduction to Marquis de Sade, 'One Hundred and Twenty Days of Sodom' (London: Arrow, 1989), pp. 3–64; Angela Carter, *The Sadean Woman: an exercise in cultural history* (London, 1979), p. 90.

31. *The Letters of John Wilmot, Earl of Rochester*, ed. Jeremy Treglown (Oxford, 1980), pp. 241–42. Compare Dorset's 'The Antiquated Coquette': 'Desire's asleep and cannot wake / When women such advances make: / Both time and charms thus Philis Wastes, / Since each must surfeit ere he tastes. / Nothing escapes her wand'ring eyes, / No one she thinks too mean a prize' (pp. 39–45).

32. Sarah Wintle, 'Libertinism and Sexual Politics', in Treglown, p. 151.

33. Harold Weber, 'Drudging in fair Aurelia's Womb: Constructing Homosexual Economies in Rochester's Poetry', *The Eighteenth Century*, 33:2 (1992), pp. 99–117, 110, 108.

34. *Ibid.*, p. 115.

35. *Ibid.*, p. 110.

36. Claude Rawson, 'Systems of Excess', *Times Literary Supplement*, 29 March (1985), pp. 335–36.

37. 'Drudging In Fair Aurelia's Womb: Constructing Homosexual Economics in Rochester's Poetry', *op. cit.*, p. 103.

38. *Ulysses*, 3 vols, ed. Hans W. Gabler (New York, 1984), 1:175.

39. Treglown, p. 85.

# Obscene Libel and the Language of 'The Imperfect Enjoyment'

## JIM McGHEE

In his bestselling sermon for Rochester's funeral, Robert
Parsons, chaplain to the Earl's mother, claimed that Rochester
had made a last request that 'those persons, in whose custody
his Papers were', would 'burn all his profane and lewd
Writings, as being only fit to promote Vice and Immorality'.[1]
Parsons' image of Rochester's shameful and blasphemous texts
ablaze with the flames of Holy Religion is particularly apt in
the light of their subsequent publication history. Part of the
ritual of press control still current at this time was the public
burning by the hangman of a symbolic copy of the banned
book. In the gesture of Rochester's 'last request' this ritual
erasure of difference and subversion intersects with those
promiscuously-employed seventeenth-century metaphors, the
flames of desire and the fires of venereal disease.

But as a practical request it was a futile gesture. Handwritten copies of Rochester's poems had been circulating round the
town throughout the past decade. Several individual poems
had been printed as pamphlets over the previous couple of
years, and some handwritten copies had also fallen into the
hands of opportunistic publishers of poetical anthologies.
Moreover, even as the dying Rochester was (supposedly)
consigning his writing to the flames, some enterprising London
printers were busy preparing for an eager public the first
collection of the Earl's poems.

Evidently, a manuscript collection of about 60 poems
connected with Rochester and his court circle had fallen into
the hands of these printers. These poems appeared in print as
*Poems on Several Occasions By the Right Honourable, the E. of R---*
within a month or two of Rochester's death in July 1680.[2] Even
by seventeenth-century standards of printing the book is
shoddy workmanship. It is a grubby octavo of 152 pages, with

the text scrunched up as closely as possible to save on paper costs. All the signs of a rush job are there. The text is littered with typographical errors and presented without such time-consuming details as running titles or prefatory matter; the punctuation is mindless rather than careless; and its printing was anonymous—no names on the title page, no printer, publisher or bookseller—the product of a fly-by-night operation which preferred not to be identified. As an extra detail to throw troublesome enquirers off the scent, a false imprint on the title-page claims the book was 'Printed at Antwerp'.

But this edition of August/September 1680 is only one of a group of 11 *almost* identical editions of *Poems on Several Occasions* that were produced before the end of the seventeenth-century. For convenience I shall refer to the 11 editions as the '1680' group, with 1680 in heavily inverted commas because some of them may have been printed as late as 1698.[3] All 11 editions print the same poems in the same order.[4] No effort was made to improve the quality of the text or the product with each new setting of type. Successive editions introduce as many new errors as they correct in a sort of stasis of sloppiness, and a uniformly low standard of printing—blotchy inking, broken type, type shortages, squinty typesetting—runs through the whole '1680' group.

The printers of the '1680' group went out of their way to preserve their anonymity, which survives intact to the present day. What did they have to fear? What reprisals could they have expected from the machinery of press control?

The principal legal engine of press control in the late seventeenth-century was the licensing system, whereby the printer or publisher of a book was obliged to submit a manuscript copy of the text to a state-appointed licenser *before* setting it in type. In addition, the title-page of each book had to carry certain information that identified responsibility for its publication: the names of the author, the printer, the publisher and the licenser who approved the book.[5] But in January 1679, amidst the chaos of the Popish Plot, Parliament was hastily prorogued without having passed the legislation necessary to renew the 1662 Printing Act which was shortly due to expire. Accordingly, the legal apparatus of pre-publication licensing lapsed on 13 March 1679 and remained inoperative for the next six years.[6]

When the first few editions of the '1680' group were printed, therefore, the machinery of press-control was in temporary abeyance. The '1680' group was thus able to ignore the licensing system's fundamental requirement of explicit accountability by naming no printer, no publisher or bookseller as responsible for the book's production.

As far as prosecution for obscenity was concerned, these anonymous printers seem to have had little to fear from the law. Legal action on such grounds had been sporadic and arbitrary in the 20 years prior to 1680. In 1661 John Garfield had been imprisoned in Newgate for writing the pamphlet-series *The Wandring Whore*,' but the only other comparable case before 1680 seems to have been in 1677 when George Wells, a bookseller, had his shop closed by the licenser, Sir Roger L'Estrange, for stocking *L'Escole des Filles* and *Satyra Sotadica*.[8] In 1680 John Coxe was prosecuted at the Middlesex County Sessions for publishing a translation of *L'Escole des Filles*, *The School of Venus* 'with the intention of debauching and corrupting young men and others of the said King's lieges and subjects', but the result of the prosecution has not survived.[9] In the first half of the 1680s only two of the many prosecutions of the press seem to have been for what was shortly to become obscenity. An adaptation of an Italian satire called *The Whore's Rhetorick* landed its printer and publisher John Wickins in the Guildhall Sessions in 1683.[10] He was fined 40 shillings. The result of the case against William Cademan (or Cadman) in 1684 is not on record: he was accused of 'exposing, selling, uttering and publishing the pernicious, wicked, scandalous, vicious and illicit' translation of *Satyra Sotadica*.[11]

In 1685 there were two important developments in this story: the appearance of the first edition of *Poems on Several Occasions* to bear its publisher's name on the title-page,[12] and Parliament's enactment of the bill to revive the Licensing Act.

The name on the title-page of the 1685 edition of Rochester's *Poems* was that of Andrew Thorncome. Thorncome (or 'Thorncomb') does not seem to have been a prolific publisher. Only two other books bearing his name have survived, both published in 1684: a 'comicall dialogue' and a manual of animal husbandry.[13] Thorncome seems to have migrated to Boston, Massachusetts the year after the publication of his Rochester edition. In his autobiography *Life and Errors*, the bookseller John Dunton mentions meeting him there in 1686 and provides the only description we have of Thorncome:

> His company was coveted by the best Gentlemen in Boston. Nor is he less acceptable to the Fair Sex; for he has something in him so extremely charming, as he makes them very fond of his company. However, he is a virtuous person, and deserves all the respect they shewed him.[14]

No further trace of him in England is to be found: he doesn't seem to have returned.[15]

Thorncome's edition has very strong similarities to the editions of the '1680' group in overall content, generally grubby appearance and low standard of workmanship. But where the '1680' group consistently declared the book to be poems 'by the E. of R---', Thorncome uses the cautious formula 'Written by a late Person of Honour'. Thorncome also abandons the phoney 'Antwerp' imprint and gives prominence to the London location by printing it in large italic capitals. These changes are the consequence of naming, of declaring accountability for the printed product; the words 'Printed for *A. Thorncome* and are to be sold by most Booksellers' appear on the title page. This declaration of accountability was in turn a result of the revival of licensing legislation[16] which meant that, once again every book was required to declare on its title-page those responsible for its contents—those who got into trouble if the book proved dangerous—author, printer, publisher, bookseller or licenser. In the 1685 edition of Rochester's poems this naming set in motion a series of changes in the texts of the poems.

The poem 'Naked she lay, claspt in my longing Arms' belongs to a seventeenth-century genre of 'Imperfect Enjoyment' poems concerned with premature ejaculation.[17] The English 'Imperfect Enjoyment' poem ranges from close translations of the French sources, through clever paraphrases such as Aphra Behn's 'One Day the Am'rous *Lisander*' (which appears in all the '1680' group editions and is printed by Thorncome[18]) to Rochester's poem, which only occasionally borrows from the earlier French versions. Rochester's poem climaxes much earlier than the other poems in the genre (at l.15), and introduces a long curse (ll.46–72) addressed to his prick.

That Thorncome insisted on the removal of those parts of the poem which did 'so much offend' is evident from the most cursory comparison of the 1685 text with that of any '1680' group edition.[19] The first problem in such a project was the poem's rhyming-couplet structure: so many of the words to be removed were at the end of the line. The simplest way of dealing with this problem was one-word substitution—for example, 'drive' replaces 'Swive' (to rhyme with 'strive' in the previous line at 1.27). Only rarely, however, can this substitution be achieved without disturbance of the surrounding text. At line 64 'Tingling want' (to rhyme with 'grunt') clearly seemed almost as unsatisfactory as the 'tingling *Cunt*' of the '1680' group readings, for the adjective too is replaced by 'lustful'. Entire phrases are re-written to remove the offending rhyme. 'Her very look's a *Cunt*' (1.18) becomes 'her very looks had charms upon't' and 'who didst refuse to spend' (1.69) is translated into 'who didst so much offend'.

'Swive', 'cunt', 'spend': there seems to have been a short-list of words triggering alteration of the text, a lexis to which Thorncome was not prepared to put his name. 'Sperm', 'fuck' and 'prick' could be added to the list. The removal of this vocabulary didn't stop at mere excision, but involved smoothing the surface of the poem to prevent the realization that it had ever been anything different: maintaining the rhyme, changing an iambic pentameter to an alexandrine (1.18), re-writing an entire line. To remove 'sperm' and 'spend' line 16 is drastically altered from:

> 'Melt into Sperme, and *f*pend at ev'ry Pore':

to

> 'Meling in Love, *f*uch joys ne'r felt before'.

But in the course of this translation the smooth continuity of the new line is disrupted by a typographical slippage, the 't' dropped from the word 'melting'.

Sperm becomes love, spending turns into joy. A process of abstraction is at work in these anxious moments that provoke transformation of the text. The 'literal' words are translated into metaphors that encode what is no longer there. 'Cunt' is variously abstracted into 'Port' (l.40) and 'entrance' (l.43); the prick as 'the common *Fucking Poſt*' (l.63) becomes 'the common rubbing poſt'. But it is precisely at those junctures in the 1680 text, where these words perform metaphorical functions, that the transformation into abstract metaphor takes place in the 1685 text. Identity is 'dissolved' into ejaculate in the moment of an orgasm which transforms the entire body into a pulsing prick (ll.15–16). The rake's prick has the power to change any orifice of either gender into a cunt (l.43), but later it is reduced to an inanimate phallus, a dildo, a '*Fucking Poſt*' (l.63). The moments of anxiety in the production of the 1685 text coincide with those moments in the 1680 text when metaphor enacts acute crises of subjectivity. Thorncome's evaporation of parts and functions of the body into metaphor provides a further twist to the poem's complex plot of problematized male identity.

The most radical instance of this operation occurs in the final couplet, where '*Pricks*' are transformed into 'Men' (ll.71 and 72):

A-1680    And may *Ten Thouſand* abler *Pricks* agree,
A-1685    And may ten thouſand abler Men agree,
A-1680    To do the wrong'd *Corinna*, right for thee.
A-1685    To do the wrong'd *Corinna* right for thee.

Now, the fundamental joke, the mainspring of the poem, is the commonplace that 'the prick has a mind and life of its own'. This not only informs the initial situation of premature ejaculation and subsequent impotence, it enables the subject of the poem to detach his wayward member from his self and address to it the long curse that begins (l.46) 'Thou treacherous, base, deserter of my flame' and reaches its climax in the final couplet. In this curse the prick is endowed with a life independent of the rest of the body: it is a 'Rude-roaring *Hector*' (l.54), a subject rebelling against its '*Prince*' (l.61). The body is dismantled into limbs, members and orifices in a state of anarchy, each pursuing its own ends.[20] The simple substitution of '*Pricks*' with 'Men' attempts nothing less than the reintegration of the fragmented body into a single unified subject.

In Thorncome's 1685 edition there was, then, what Foucault might have described as a policing of the statements of the '1680' group.[21] But this policing of statements went further than the expurgation of the unauthorized vocabulary of the '1680' group. The policing of the text entailed the excision of the offensive image and the insertion of new material to conceal the vacancy. This new material papers over the gap, obviating the possibility that there was ever anything else there. The couplet: 'Smiling, *f*he chids in a kind murm'ring Noi*f*e, / And *f*ighs to feel the to too ha*f*ty joys'; (ll.19–20) seems an elegant and funny description of the mistress's reaction to her lover's premature ejaculation. There is hardly any reason to believe that the second line is 'infill' that takes the place of the image removed: 'And from her *Body* wipes the clammy joys;'. Thorncome's vocabulary of anxiety is absent from this line—sperm is expressed metaphorically in the '1680' version—yet the image of the woman's body spattered with 'the clammy joys' has to be removed. Even the word 'body' has been distilled into breath, a sigh.

But *who* was policing these statements? Who was the 'author' of this new material? Someone with the metrical skill to turn an iambic pentameter into an alexandrine, with a facility for rhyme, and a familiarity with contemporary literary metaphor. Not the compositor: it seems likely that the compositor was working from a '1680' group edition which had been marked up with the required changes.[22] That is, an editor was involved in the production of this text. But Thorncome's editor attempts to conceal his own presence, to disguise the work he has carried out. Working to establish what Foucault calls 'areas . . . of tact and discretion',[23] he is himself tactful and discreet to the point of near invisibility.

The wisdom of Thorncome's judicious cuts and imaginative alterations became apparent three years later, in 1688, when a consistent policy towards 'obscene and lascivious bookes' began to emerge, together with a co-ordinated move against them that involved all the agencies of press control. For printers and distributors of racy fiction and poetry, the heat was on.

Over three days in March 1688 a Messenger of the Press went on a shopping trip round various London bookshops (the

Messengers of the Press were the bloodhounds and retrievers of the agencies of press control, combining the roles of spy, informer and policeman of the printing-trade[24]). Among other books and prints, Henry Hills junior bought four copies of Rochester's *Poems* at bookshops in Tower Hill, Westminster Hall and Pall Mall, paying one shilling and sixpence for three of the copies, a shilling for the fourth. These purchases were not for his own private enjoyment. A few days before this shopping expedition three men had appeared before the Guildhall Sessions charged with trading in 'obscene and lascivious bookes'. Hills was out shopping for evidence.[25]

The three books concerned in the case were Rochester's *Poems*, *The School of Venus* and *A Dialogue between a Marridd Lady & a Maide*, a translation of *L'Academie des Dames* which was in its turn derived from the mid-seventeenth-century Latin text by Nicholas Chorier, *Satyra Sotadica*.[26] (This, as detailed above, was one of the two books known to have been the subject of prosecutions during the previous decade, the other being *L'Escole des Filles*. Rochester's poems were now joining their select company.) When the case came to court a few months later, Benjamin Crayle was fined 20 shillings and Joseph Streater was fined 40 shillings for the publication of *The School of Venus*—fairly low amounts compared with fines for political seditious printing which, in the 1680s, seem to have ranged from £10 to £20. The case against Francis Leach for Rochester's *Poems* appears to have been dropped: his bond was discharged in April, and there the record of his involvement ends. The repercussions for Crayle and Streater, however, were to rumble on for the next two years. At the end of 1689 they were again back in court, this time for publishing and printing *Sodom: or the Quintessence of Debauchery*.[27] This time it was the infamous Robert Stephens (nicknamed 'Robin Hog') who was the Messenger of the Press involved in the case.[28] Streater got off comparatively lightly with a fine of 20 shillings, half the cost of his fine for *The School of Venus* the year before, but Crayle fared far worse. He was given a fine of £20 and imprisoned for being unable to pay it.

Crayle's sentence represents a real escalation in the state's moves against 'obscene and lascivious' books. For the first time obscenity is elevated to the same degree of seriousness as political sedition. The trick of imposing a fine beyond the means of the defendant was a common method of ruining a printer of seditious books—isolate a tradesman from the means of production and you neutralize his opposition by bankrupting him. Obscenity in England had come of age and was being taken as seriously as those more traditional problems of press control, sedition, libel and blasphemy.

For Crayle, imprisonment was contingent on an unpaid fine; when Rochester's *Poems* re-entered the story in 1693, imprisonment was an intrinsic part of the publisher's sentence. In May of that year Elizabeth Latham was given bail of £40 after being charged with publishing the book. Again the tireless Robert Stephens, Messenger of the Press, was involved in the case. When she was tried at the Guildhall Sessions the following month, Elizabeth Latham was given a lighter fine than Crayle's, a fine of five marks (about £3). But she was sentenced to imprisonment, cut off from her livelihood, and there is no record of when she was released.[29] Three years after Elizabeth Latham's imprisonment the relentless Robert Stephens publicly burned 'a Cart load of obscence [sic] Books and Cards, tending to promote Debauchery', the stock of an Italian bookseller called Bernardi.[30] But the intensification of pressure on the producers and distributors of obscene books is most clearly seen in the promotion of these trials from local lower courts such as the London Guildhall and the Middlesex Guildhall to the Court of the King's Bench. A major shift in the state's perception of the crime, of the nature and seriousness of the threat presented by these books, is evident in this change of venue.

In 1698 someone called 'Hill' was indicted by the King's Bench for 'printing fome obfcene poems of my lord *Rochefter's* tending to the corruption of youth'.[31] Whether this is Henry Hills junior, who as a Messenger of the Press had bought four copies of Rochester's *Poems* back in 1688, and later pirated Tonson's edition of Rochester in 1710, is impossible to tell from the brief mention of the case given in Strange's *Reports* of 1755.[32] The case did not come to court: Hill 'went abroad, and was outlawed'. As the defendant in a precedent-setting King's Bench prosecution, Hill could expect only to be bankrupted through imprisonment either by direct sentencing or by being unable to pay an exorbitant fine. Though Hill's flight left the case inconclusive, the seriousness of the case against him can be deduced from his rapid departure. Such a conclusion was certainly reached 30 years later in a trial that used the Hill case as a precedent: 'he went abroad, and was outlawed; which he would not have done if his counsel had thought it no libel.'[33]

The inconclusive Hill case of 1698 was only the first attempt to obtain a successful prosecution for obscenity from the Court of the King's Bench. Nine years later, in 1707, two such prosecutions took place. The prosecution of John Marshall involved the two books for which Streater and Crayle had been fined in the lower courts, *Sodom* and *Tullia & Octava*.[34] Angell Carter and James Read were charged with publishing a small pamphlet of mildly bawdy poems entitled *The Fifteen Plagues of a Maidenhead*.[35] All three men were found guilty of publishing the books. But then the campaign against 'diabolical and cupidinous' books seems to have gone wrong.

The lawyers of James Read questioned the power of the court to deal with obscenity in the first place, and moved for an arrest of judgement. When the case was put before Justice Holt the following year Holt, surprisingly, agreed, arguing that 'matters of bawdry' could only be tried by the ecclesiastical courts. 'There are ecclesiastical courts: why may not this be punished there?'[36] There is no evidence that such cases ever were tried by what remnants of the 'bawdy courts' were still operating in 1707.[37] Holt readily admitted the obscenity of *The Fifteen Plagues of a Maidenhead*, but believed there was no precedent for trying such a case in the temporal courts: 'If we have no precedent we cannot punish. Shew me any precedent'. The lower court precedents of Streater, Crayle and Latham from the previous century were not produced; Hill's King's Bench indictment seems to have been forgotten. Read's case was adjourned *'sine die'*. This had the immediate effect of causing the prosecutions against Angell Carter and John Marshall to collapse. The agencies of press control had failed spectacularly in their attempts to obtain a precedent of obscene libel in the Queen's Bench.

In 1707, the same year as Read, Carter and Marshall were tried unsuccessfully before the Queen's Bench, a new collection of Rochester's poems appeared. This was the first issue in the

'C-series',[38] the version that was to become the dominant collection of Rochester's poetry for the duration of the eighteenth century.

The name on the title-page of this edition was that of Benjamin Bragge, a distinctly shady character who operated a publishing outfit that specialized in sensational crime-reporting, sizzling atrocities and titillating confessions straight from the lips of those waiting to be hanged in Newgate.[39] Bragge also operated as a 'trade publisher', lending his name to books produced by other publishers but considered too hot for them to handle: for a cut, Bragge would take the risk.[40] It may well be in such a capacity as front-man for invisible others that Bragge's name appears on the title-page of the Rochester edition.

The book is very different from the previous Rochester collections: more of a poetical miscellany than the collection of one poet, both in the way the title-page presents the contents and in the way the material is laid out. Bragge's title-page describes the book as 'The Miscellaneous Works of the Right Honourable the Late Earls of Rochester and Roscommon . . . To which is added, a curious Collection of Original Poems and Translations by . . .', and there follows a list which includes the names of Dorset, Otway, Prior, Rowe and, interestingly, the former licenser Sir Roger L'Estrange. The book is divided into two parts, basically 'Rochester' and 'others'. The 'others' section is further divided into a section of 'Poetical Works' of the Earl of Roscommon, and an anthology section that includes three poems assigned to Rochester. Bragge's book also boasts the first published portrait of Rochester, an engraved frontispiece that was to recur, in increasingly cruder reworkings, in the rest of the C-series editions throughout the eighteenth-century.

But Bragge's association with Rochester's poetry was brief. Before the year was out Bragge (or his backer?) seems to have sold the loose sheets of the book and the plate for the frontispiece to Edmund Curll, who was at that time just beginning his career as the most flamboyant and controversial character in eighteenth-century publishing.[41] Curll replaced the title-page to delude the book-buying public into thinking it was getting a second edition, shoved in an extra sheet,[42] and passed the book off as one of his own devising.

Curll reprinted the edition at the end of March 1709.[43] Within months a group of envious publishers had pirated the book. Their piracy makes the editions of the '1680' group seem like coffee-table books by comparison: the same text that occupied the first part of Curll's edition is compressed into less than a third of the space in a jumble of different typefaces.[44] It was just at that moment that the interest of the Queen's Bench prosecutors in Rochester's poems suddenly revived. Three of the pirates, Thomas Harrison, Anne Croom and Anne Smith, found themselves summoned before the Queen's Bench charged with publishing 'a profane, lascivious and pernicious lampoon called "The Works of the Right Honourable the Earle of Rochester and Roscommon with some Memoirs of the Earle of Rochester's Life by Monsieur St. Evremont" '.[45]

In the same year the Queen's Bench prosecutors initiated the first trial of a medical book for obscenity. A barber-surgeon called John Martin had been publishing a series of treatises on venereal disease over the previous five years, drumming up business for his practice as a pox-doctor. None of these books had attracted the attention of the prosecutors.[46] But in 1709 Martin produced a sequel to his popular series, a book that was more a sex manual than a guide to cures for clap. Although no fewer than seven publishers' names were listed on the title-page, it was John Martin who was hauled before the Queen's Bench as the author of the 'diabolical and cupidinous' *Gonosologium Novum*.[47]

The obscenity of both books prosecuted in 1709 was unquestioned; that Harrison, Croom, Smith and Martin were held responsible for their production was expressed in the verdicts of guilty on the fact of publication. But the Queen's Bench prosecutors still had to contend with Justice Holt's decision in the Read case of 1707, that obscenity was not punishable in the temporal courts. The prosecution in both cases failed to overturn this decision, and both cases were adjourned '*sine die*'; the category of obscenity remained unrecognized as a punishable offence at the Queen's Bench.

The failure of the 1709 prosecution of Rochester's *Works* had an enormous effect on the development of the C-series. Edmund Curll clearly believed it gave him *carte blanche* to publish whatever Rochester poems he chose, without fear of prosecution. His 1714 edition of the *Works* was considerably expanded from the 1709 text.[48] To accommodate the additional material, Curll split the book into two volumes following the two-part division of the previous editions, 'Rochester' and 'Roscommon and others', and added a new section to the end of the book entitled 'The Cabinet of Love'—a selection of particularly 'obscene and lascivious' poems. One of the new poems in the Rochester section was 'The Imperfect Enjoyment'.[49]

Although Curll's 1714 'Imperfect Enjoyment' was, like Thorncome's version, derived from one of the '1680' group editions, the textual tactics involved in its production were very different. Rather than re-write the text, Curll replaced certain words with lacunae, dashes typically between three and five letters long: a kind of printing under erasure. But the cleverness of Curll's deletions is in their transparency: the rhyme reveals what isn't actually printed. 'Her very Look's a ----', and it rhymes with 'don't' (l.18); the 'tingling ----' (l.64) rhymes with 'grunt'. Sometimes, for those readers devoid of any aptitude for rhyme, Curll helpfully provides a clue by supplying the first letter of the word. Thus '*f*--' (l.69) rhymes with 'attend' and 'depend', and Curll's reader is dissuaded from rhyming 'drive' with '*f*trive', like Thorncome, by the provision of the initial '*f*' of the absent 'swive' at (l.27). Note that the same sign ('*f*--') signifies two different words (spend or swive) depending on context: the technique relies heavily on rhyme-prompted reader response. That is, the *reader*, not the printer or the publisher, completes the rhyme. The word doesn't hide behind the dash, it simply isn't there. It exists only in the mind of the reader, who then becomes responsible— accountable—for the meaning produced: it is the reader's voice that violates tact and discretion in the enunciation of these words. If it is a crime to utter these words, then it is the reader, not the publisher or the printer, who is the criminal.

With deleted words that are internal to the line, Curll is careful to reinforce contextual clues with supplied letters. The first and last letters of the word 'sperm' are supplied, with a five-letter-long dash between the 's' and the 'm' (l.16). This contextual prompt is supplemented by the provision of the initial letter in the next deletion two words later, '*f*----' for 'spend':

'Melt into S----m, and *f*---- at ev'ry Pore.'

The first of three occurrences—or rather absences—of the word 'Cunt' is a rhyme at the end of l.18; the rhyme-prompted reading of the word then substantiates local contextual clues and the supplied initial letter when the sign '*C*---' appears internally at ll.40 and 43. The dash-deletions suggest a shortlist of possible readings. Using clues like rhyme and supplied letters, a vocabulary is delineated: the cryptic sign of the dash *can only refer* to one of a limited subset of words, a restricted range of meanings.

Through such tactics of textual production we can see a vocabulary of the unprintable in the process of formation; not a repertoire of unprintable texts—Curll interpreted the 1707 and 1709 verdicts as dispensations that allowed him to publish poems omitted from previous C-series editions—but a lexicon of specific unprintable words. Yes, Curll's dashes do point towards these words in a clear obvious way, proclaiming their absence rather than erasing the evidence of textual difference as Thorncome's 1685 re-writes had done. But the words themselves are not there on the page. In the moment that these words in this poem are 'read' in print for the first time in nearly 20 years, in that moment those words construct a lexicon of impropriety, participating in what Foucault describes as an 'expurgation—and a very rigorous one—of the authorized vocabulary'.[50]

The 50 years after the first publication of Rochester's *Poems* saw a significant consolidation of state censorship of 'obscene' books. Variations in the texts of poems such as 'The Imperfect Enjoyment' inscribe the traces of this intensification of legal pressure on the book trades; but the poems also played a key part in the formation of the law of obscene libel by being one of a select group of texts targeted in precedent-setting prosecutions. When, in 1728, this process of consolidation reached its climax in the first successful King's Bench prosecution for obscenity, the defendant was none other than Edmund Curll. Rochester's poems were not involved in the case—Curll was fined 50 marks (about £32) for publishing a translation of a French dialogue called *Venus in the Cloister, or the Nun in her Smock* and Meibomius's *Treatise of the Use of Flogging in Venereal*

*Affairs.*[51] But by a strange twist of both coincidence and logic, one of the precedents used to overturn Justice Holt's 1707 ruling and inaugurate modern obscenity law was the case of Rochester's friend Sedley hurling abuse and worse on a crowd during a drunken binge at Covent Garden:

> Sir Charles Sedley was indicted at common law for several misdemeanours against the king's peace, and which were to the great scandal of Christianity; and the cause was, for that he showed his naked body in a balcony in Covent Garden to a great multitude of people, and there did such things, and spoke such words, &c. . . as throwing down bottles (pissed in) *vi et armis* among the people.[52]

Such are the precedents that lie behind the prosecutions of Byron, Lawrence, Burroughs . . . The list is a long one; it continues to lengthen.

## NOTES

1. *A Sermon Preached At the Funeral of the Rt. Honourable John Earl of Rochester.* . . (Oxford, 1680), pp. 28–29; quoted in James Thorpe *Rochester's Poems on Several Occasions* (Princeton, 1961), p. ix.

2. Samuel Pepys owned a copy by 2nd. of November 1680: letter to William Hewer in R. G. Howarth, *Letters and The Second Diary of Samuel Pepys* (London, 1933), pp. 104–05. Pepys' copy is one of only two surviving copies.

3. See below.

4. Thorpe, *ibid.*, p. xiii.

5. For the changing conditions of licensing legislation, see Raymond Astbury, 'The Renewal of the Licensing Act in 1693 and its Lapse in 1695', in *The Library*, 5th. series, vol. XXXIII, pp. 296–322; Cyprian Blagden, *The Stationers' Company* (London, 1690); Laurence Hanson, *Government and the Press* (Oxford, 1936); Harry Ransom, *The First Copyright Statute* (Austin, Texas, 1956); Lyman Ray Patterson, *Copyright in Historical Perspective* (Nashville, 1968); and F. S. Siebert, *Freedom of the Press in England* (Urbana, Illinois, 1952).

6. Astbury, *ibid.*, p. 9.

7. David Foxon, *Libertine Literature in England 1660–1745* (New York, 1965), pp. 8–9; Roger Thompson, *Unfit for Modest Ears* (London, 1979), pp. 65–66.

8. Foxon, *ibid.*, p. 9.

9. Roger Thompson, 'Two Early Editions of Restoration Erotica', in *The Library*, 5th. series, vol. XXXII, p. 45.

10. Foxon, *ibid.*, p. 9.

11. Thompson, 'Two Early Editions of Restoration Erotica', pp. 47–48.

12. Prinz numbers the edition XII in his bibliography of early editions of Rochester (Johannes Prinz, *John Wilmot Earl of Rochester: his life and writings* [Leipzig, 1927: Palaestra 1541]). David Vieth assigns to it the identifier 'A-1685' (David Vieth, *Attribution in Restoration Poetry: A study of Rochester's Poems of 1680* [Yale, 1963], pp. 9–10, 500).

13. *Registers of the Stationers' Company 1640–1708* (London, 1914), vol. II, pp. 219, 229. From his examination of type and variants in the '1680' group, James Thorpe believed that Thorncome 'may possibly' have published the edition identified as the 'Harvard' edition (Thorpe, *ibid.*, p. xxiv).

14. John Dunton, *The Life and Errors of John Dunton, Citizen of London* (London, 1703), pp. 97–98.

15. The 1701 reprint of Thorncome's edition (Prinz XV; Vieth 'A-1701') claims on the title-page to have been 'Printed for A. T.'. If this does indeed refer to Andrew Thorncome it is the only evidence I have come across of his presence in England after 1686. See Vieth, *ibid.*, p. 10.

16. See Astbury, *ibid.*, p. 296.

17. Richard E. Quaintance, 'French Sources of the 'Imperfect Enjoyment' Poem', in *Philological Quarterly*, vol. XLII, pp. 190–99; see also John H. O'Neill, 'An Unpublished 'Imperfect Enjoyment' Poem', in *Papers on Language and Literature*, 13 (Spring, 1977), pp. 197–202.

18. 'A-1680' (Huntington edition), F6–G1; 'A1685', F1–F4.

19. See *Appendix*, below.

20. An even more extreme disassembling of the body takes place at the end of *Signior Dildo*, where the animated dildo is chased by a 'Rabble of Pricks' and escapes only because the pursuers are slowed down by the weight of the 'Ballocks' that 'came wobbling after'. Keith Walker, *The Poems of John Wilmot Earl of Rochester* (London, 1984), p. 78.

21. Michel Foucault, *The History of Sexuality Volume One: An Introduction* (London, 1981), pp. 17–18.

22. These changes are the only departures from a '1680' group text slavishly followed on punctuation, spelling and error. Only one correction is introduced in A-1685, 'May'st thou Piss' (l.69) to 'May'st thou not Piss'. See Thorpe, *ibid.*, pp. xxiii, 162; and also David Vieth, 'The Text of Rochester and the Editions of 1680', in *Papers of the Bibliographical Association of America*, vol.50, pp. 243–63.

23. Foucault, *ibid.*, p. 18.

24. Foxon, *ibid.*, pp. 10–11. For the Messengers of the Press, see Foxon, *ibid.*, pp. 7–8, and Seibert, *ibid.*, pp. 252–54.

25. The expense-account of Henry Hills junior for the cost of the books has survived in the archives of the Stationers' Company. This document is reproduced in Foxon, *ibid.*, plate I.

26. Foxon, *ibid.*, pp. 11, 39–41; see also Donald Thomas, Prosecutions of *Sodom: or, the Quintessence of Debauchery*, and *Poems on Several Occasions by the E of R*, 1689–1696 and 1693, in *The Library*, 5th series, vol. XXIV, pp. 51–53.

27. *Sodom*, a charmingly filthy play, has been closely connected to Rochester since the 1670s.

28. For Robert Stephens, see Leonie Rostenberg, *Publishing, Printing and Bookselling in England 1551–1700* (New York, 1965), volume two, pp. 343–67. For a variant reading of this case, see J. McGhee, *The Publication of the Poetry of John Wilmot, Earl of Rochester, from 1680 to 1728*, unpublished Ph.D. thesis, 2 vols (University of Glasgow, 1991).

29. Thomas, *ibid.*, p. 54.

30. Foxon, *ibid.*, pp. 11–12.

31. Sir John Strange, *Reports of Adjudged Cases in the Courts of Chancery, King's Bench, Common Pleas, and Exchequer* (London, 1755), vol. ii p. 790; see also Thomas, *ibid.*, p. 52.

32. James Thorpe considered Henry Hills junior as a possible printer of some of the '1680' group editions 'in that he was a notorious pirate, he regularly produced poor work on cheap paper, and he was apparently at loose ends in London in 1680 having recently returned from his unsuccessful venture in India' (Thorpe, *ibid.*, p. xxvi).

33. Strange, *ibid.*, p. 790. The Hill case was used as a precedent in the prosecution of Edmund Curll (see p. 55). It is probable that the editions of Rochester's poetry prosecuted in the cases of Leach, Latham and Hill belonged to the '1680' group. The indictment in the Latham case quotes the title of a poem absent from both the Thorncome and the Tonson editions ('Say Heav'n-born Muse, for only thou canst tell'): see Thomas *ibid.*, p. 54.

34. Foxon *ibid.*, p. 13; Donald Thomas, *A Long Time Burning* (London, 1969), p. 77.

35. Foxon, *ibid.*, pp. 12–13; Thomas, *A Long Time Burning*, pp. 77–78, 337.

36. William Cobbett, *A Complete Collection of State Trials and proceedings for high treason and other crimes* (London, 1813), column 157.

37. For the ecclesiastical courts, see Edward J. Bristow, *Vice and Vigilance: purity movements in Britain since 1700* (Dublin, 1977), pp. 11–12, and Christopher Hill, *Society and Puritanism in Pre-Revolutionary England* (London, 1969), pp. 291–93, 331–32.

38. Prinz, XVIII; Vieth, 'C-1707-a'. Vieth classifies the early editions of Rochester's poetry into 'series', 'A', 'B' 'C' and 'D' (Vieth, *ibid.*, pp. 9–15). The A-series includes the '1680' group editions and Thorncome's 1685 edition, and also those editions reprinted from Thorncome's; the B-series consists of those editions reprinted or pirated from Tonson's edition of 1691.

39. See Michael Harris, 'Trials and Criminal Biographies', in *The Sale and Distribution of Books from 1700*, Robin Myers and Michael Harris eds. (Oxford, 1982), p. 5.

40. Michael Treadwell, 'London Trade Publishers 1675–1750', in *The Library*, 6th. series, vol. IV, pp. 99–134, and 'On False and Misleading Imprints in the London Book Trade, 1660–1750', in *Fakes and Frauds: varieties of deception in print and manuscript*, Robin Myers and Michael Harris eds. (Winchester, 1989).

41. See Ralph Straus, *The Unspeakable Curll* (London, 1927), which includes a useful handlist of books connected with Curll.

42. Vieth 'C-1707-b'. The extra sheet contains the *Satyr againft Man*: for some reason the previous issue contained only *An Addition to the Satyr againft Man*, Thorpe, *ibid.*, p. xxxiii, note 34.

43. Prinz, XIX; Vieth, 'C-1709'. Curll advertised the new edition in *The Post Boy*, 24–26 March 1709.

44. Prinz, XX; Vieth, 'C-1709-P'. Material that took up fourteen octavo gatherings of Curll's 1709 edition has been squeezed into four octavo gatherings; three different typefaces have been used, the type changing alarmingly in mid-page, mid-poem.

45. Thomas, *A Long Time Burning*, p. 78. Records of this trial are to be found in the Public Record Office, K.B. 28/32/9.

46. Straus, *ibid.*, pp. 26–32.

47. Foxon, *ibid.*, p. 13 and Plate IV; Thomas, *A Long Time Burning*, p. 78; P.R.O. K.B. 28/31/20.

48. Prinz, XXV; Vieth, 'C-1714-1' and 'C-1714-2'. Curll's new edition includes a series of five new engravings illustrating the poems and a portrait of Roscommon as frontispiece to the second volume.

49. In Curll's edition 'Naked she lay, clasp'd in my longing Arms' is entitled 'The Disappointment'; 'The Imperfect Enjoyment' is used as the title for another poem in the Rochester section, 'Fruition was the question in Debate'. A three-way interchange of titles has taken place: Aphra Behn's poem 'One Day the Am'rous *Lifander*', had been entitled *The Disappointment* when it appeared in the '1680' group editions, but now becomes *The Insensible* in Curll's 1714 edition, where it is printed in the Rochester section.

50. Foucault, *ibid.*, p. 17.

51. Cobbett, *ibid.*, cols 153–60; Straus, *ibid.*, 101–11; Thomas, *A Long Time Burning* pp. 77–79. Curll had increased the government's determination to ruin him by publishing *The Memoirs of John Ker of Kersland*, the *Spycatcher* of the 1720s; for this he was fined 20 marks and sentenced to an hour in the pillory (Straus *ibid.*, 111–21; Foxon *ibid.*, pp. 14–15).

52. Cobbett, *ibid.*, col. 155. Judge Reynolds opined that Curll's crime was 'surely worse than sir Charles Sedley's case, who only exposed himself to the people then present, [naked,] who might chuse whether they look upon him or not; whereas this book goes all over the kingdom' (Cobbett *ibid.*, cols. 159–140).

# APPENDIX

A comparison of the following three printed texts of 'Naked she lay, claspt in my longing Arms':

A-1680 = *POEMS ON SEVERAL OCCASIONS By the Right Honourable, the E. of R---* ('Antwerp', 1680, Huntington edition)

A-1685 = *POEMS ON SEVERAL OCCASIONS Written by a late Perfon of Honour* (London, 1685)

C-1714 = *The Works of the Earls of Rochester, Roscommon, Dorset, &c.* (London, 1714)

| | |
|---|---|
| A-1680 | *The Imperfect Enjoyment.* |
| A-1685 | *The Imperfect Enjoyment.* |
| C-1714 | *The Disappointment.* |

1   A-1680   NAked ʃhe lay, claʃpt in my longing Arms,
    A-1685   NAked ʃhe lay, claʃpt in my longing Arms,
    C-1714   NAked ʃhe lay, claʃp'd in my longing Arms,

2   A-1680   I fill'd with Love, and ʃhe all over charms,
    A-1685   I fill'd with Love, and ʃhe all over Charms,
    C-1714   I fill'd with Love, and ʃhe all over Charms,

3   A-1680   Both equally inʃpir'd with eager fire,
    A-1685   Both equally inʃpir'd, with eager fire,
    C-1714   Both equally inʃpir'd with eager Fire,

4   A-1680   Melting through kindneʃs, flaming in deʃire;
    A-1685   Melting through kindneʃs, flaming in desire;
    C-1714   Melting through Kindneʃs, flaming in Desire;

5   A-1680   With *Arms, Legs, Lips*, cloʃe clinging to embrace,
    A-1685   With *Arms, Legs, Lips*, cloʃe clinging to embrace,
    C-1714   With Arms, Legs, Lips, cloʃe clinging to embrace,

6   A-1680   She clips me to her *Breaʃt*, and ʃucks me to her | *Face.*
    A-1685   She clips me to her *Breaʃt*, and ʃucks me to her | *Face.*
    C-1714   She clips me to her *Breaʃt*, and ʃucks me to her *Face.*

7   A-1680   The nimble *Tongue* (*Love's* leʃʃer Lightning) plaid
    A-1685   The nimble *Tongue* (Love's leʃʃer Lightning) plaid
    C-1714   The nimble *Tongue* (Love's leʃʃer Lightning) plaid

8   A-1680   Within my *Mouth*, and to my thoughts convey'd.
    A-1685   Within my *Mouth*, and to my thoughts convey'd.
    C-1714   Within my Mouth, and to my Thoughts convey'd

9   A-1680   Swift Orders, that I ʃhou'd prepare to throw,
    A-1685   Swift Orders, that I ʃhou'd prepare to throw,
    C-1714   Swift Orders, that I ʃhou'd prepare to throw

10  A-1680   The *All-diʃolving Thunderbolt* below.
    A-1685   The All-diʃʃolving *Thunderbolt* below.
    C-1714   The All-diʃʃolving Thunderbolt below.

11  A-1680   My flutt'ring *Soul*, ʃprung with the pointed kiʃs,
    A-1685   My flutt'ring *Soul*, ʃprung with the pointed Kiʃs,
    C-1714   My flutt'ring Soul, ʃprung with the pointed *Kiʃs*,

12  A-1680   Hangs hov'ring o're her *Balmy Limbs* of Bliʃs.
    A-1685   Hangs hov'ring o're her balmy Limbs of bliʃs.
    C-1714   Hangs hov'ring o're her balmy *Lips* of *Bliʃs*:

13  A-1680   But whilʃt her buʃie hand, wou'd guide that part,
    A-1685   But whilʃt her buʃie hand wou'd guide that part,
    C-1714   But whilʃt her buʃy *Hand* wou'd guide that *Part*,

14  A-1680  Which ʃhou'd convey my *Soul* up to her *Heart.*
    A-1685  Which ʃhou'd convey my *Soul* up to her *Heart.*
    C-1714  Which ʃshou'd convey my Soul up to her *Heart.*

15  A-1680  In liquid *Raptures*, I difʃolve all o're,
    A-1685  In liquid Raptures I difʃolve all o're,
    C-1714  In liquid Raptures I difʃolve all o're,

16  A-1680  Melt into Sperme, and ʃpend at ev'ry Pore:
    A-1685  Meling in Love, ʃuch joys ne'r felt before.
    C-1714  Melt into S-----m, and ʃ---- at ev'ry Pore:

17  A-1680  A touch from any part of her had don't,
    A-1685  A touch from any part of her had don't,
    C-1714  A Touch from any Part of her had don't;

18  A-1680  Her Hand, her Foot, her very look's a *Cunt.*
    A-1685  Her *Hand*, her *Foot*, her very looks had charms | upon't.
    C-1714  Her *Hand*, her *Foot*, her very Look's a ----.

19  A-1680  Smiling, ʃhe chides in a kind murm'ring *Noiʃe,*
    A-1685  Smiling, ʃhe chids in a kind murm'ring Noiʃe,
    C-1714  Smiling, ʃhe chides in a kind murm'ring Noiʃe,

20  A-1680  And from her *Body* wipes the clammy joys;
    A-1685  And ʃighs to feel the to too haʃty joys;
    C-1714  And from her *Body* wipes the clammy Joys;

21  A-1680  When with a Thouʃand Kiʃʃes, wand'ring o're,
    A-1685  When with a Thouʃand Kiʃʃes, wand'ring or'e
    C-1714  When with a thouʃand Kiʃʃes, wand'ring o'er

22  A-1680  My panting *Breaʃt*, and is there then no more?
    A-1685  My panting *Breaʃt*, and is there then no more?
    C-1714  My panting *Breaʃt*, And is there then no more?

23  A-1680  She cries. All this to Love, and *Rapture's* due,
    A-1685  She cries. All this to Love, and *Raptures* due,
    C-1714  She cries. All this to Love and Rapture's due,

24  A-1680  Muʃt we not pay a debt to pleaʃure too?
    A-1685  Muʃt we not pay a debt to pleaʃure too?
    C-1714  Muʃt we not pay a Debt to Pleaʃure too?

25  A-1680  But I the moʃt forlorn, loʃt *Man* alive,
    A-1685  But I the moʃt forlorne, loʃt Man alive,
    C-1714  But I, the moʃt forlorn, loʃt Man alive,

26  A-1680  To ʃhew my wiʃht Obedience vainly ʃtrive,
    A-1685  To ʃhew my wiʃht Obedience vainly ʃtrive,
    C-1714  To ʃhew my wiʃh'd Obedience, vainly ʃtrive,

27   A-1680   I ſigh alas! and Kiſs, but cannot Swive.
        A-1685   I ſigh alas! and Kiſs, but cannot drive.
        C-1714   I ſigh, alas! and kiſs, but cannot ſ----.

28   A-1680   Eager deſires, confound my firſt intent,
        A-1685   Eager deſires, confound my firſt intent,
        C-1714   Eager Deſires confound my firſt Intent,

29   A-1680   Succeeding ſhame, does more ſuccceſs prevent,
        A-1685   Succeeding ſhame, does more ſucceſs prevent,
        C-1714   Succeeding Shame does more Succeſs prevent,

30   A-1680   And *Rage*, at laſt, confirms me impotent.
        A-1685   And Rage, at laſt, confirms me impotent.
        C-1714   And *Rage* at laſt confirms me impotent.

31   A-1680   Ev'n her fair Hand, which might bid heat return
        A-1685   Ev'n her fair Hand, which might bid heat return
        C-1714   Even her fair Hand, which might bid heat return

32   A-1680   To frozen *Age*, and make cold *Hermits* burn,
        A-1675   To frozen Age, and make cold *Hermits* burn,
        C-1714   To frozen *Age*, and make cold *Hermits* burn,

33   A-1680   Apply'd to my dead *Cinder*, warms no more,
        A-1685   Apply'd to my dead Cinder, warms no more,
        C-1714   Apply'd to my dead *Cinder*, warms no more

34   A-1680   Than Fire to *Aſhes*, cou'd paſt Flames reſtore.
        A-1685   Than Fire to *Aſhes*, cou'd paſt Flames reſtore.
        C-1714   Than Fire to *Aſhes* cou'd paſt Flames reſtore:

35   A-1680   Trembling, confus'd, deſpairing, limber, dry,
        A-1685   Trembling, confuſ'd, deſpairing, limber, dry,
        C-1714   Trembling, confuſ'd, deſpairing, limber, dry,

36   A-1680   A wiſhing, weak, unmoving lump I ly.
        A-1685   A wiſhing, weak, unmoving lump I ly,
        C-1714   A wiſhing, weak, unmoving lump I lie:

37   A-1680   This *Dart* of love, whoſe piercing point oft try'd,
        A-1685   This Dart of Love, whoſe piercing point oft try'd
        C-1714   This *Dart* of love, whoſe piercing point oft try'd

38   A-1680   With *Virgin blood, Ten thouſand Maids* has dy'd.
        A-1685   With Virgin Blood, a hundred Maids has dy'd.
        C-1714   With *Virgin blood, Ten thouſand Maids* has dy'd;

39   A-1680   Which *Nature* ſtill directed with ſuch Art,
        A-1685   Which Nature ſtill directed with ſuch Art,
        C-1714   Which *Nature* ſtill directed with ſuch Art,

| 40 | A-1680 | That it through ev'ry *C---t*, reacht ev'ry Heart. |
|    | A-1685 | That it through ev'ry Port, reacht ev'ry Heart. |
|    | C-1714 | That it through ev'ry *C---* reacht ev'ry Heart; |

| 41 | A-1680 | Stiffly refolv'd, twou'd carelefly invade, |
|    | A-1685 | Stiffly refolv'd, twou'd carelefly invade, |
|    | C-1714 | Stiffly refolv'd, 'twou'd carelefly invade |

| 42 | A-1680 | *Woman* or *Boy*, nor ought its fury ftaid, |
|    | A-1685 | Where it effay'd, nor ought its fury ftaid, |
|    | C-1714 | *Woman* or *Boy*, nor ought its Fury ftaid, |

| 43 | A-1680 | Where e're it pierc'd, a *Cunt* it found or made. |
|    | A-1685 | Where e're it pierc'd, entrance it found or \| made. |
|    | C-1714 | Where e'er it pierc'd, a *C ---* it found or made: |

| 44 | A-1680 | Now languid lies, in this unhappy hour, |
|    | A-1685 | Now languid lies, in this unhappy hour, |
|    | C-1714 | Now languid lies in this unhappy hour, |

| 45 | A-1680 | Shrunk up, and Saplefs, like a wither'd *Flow'r.* |
|    | A-1685 | Shrunk up, and Saplefs, like a wither'd Flow'r. |
|    | C-1714 | Shrunk up and faplefs, like a wither'd *Flow'r.* |

| 46 | A-1680 | Thou treacherous, bafe, deferter of my flame, |
|    | A-1685 | Thou treacherous, bafe, deferter of my flame, |
|    | C-1714 | Thou treacherous, bafe Deferter of my flame, |

| 47 | A-1680 | Falfe to my paffion, fatal to my *Fame*; |
|    | A-1685 | Falfe to my paffion, fatal to my Fame; |
|    | C-1714 | Falfe to my Paffion, fatal to my *Fame*; |

| 48 | A-1680 | By what miftaken *Magick* doft thou prove, |
|    | A-1685 | By what miftaken Magick doft thou prove, |
|    | C-1714 | By what miftaken *Magick* doft thou prove |

| 49 | A-1680 | So true to lewdnefs, fo untrue to Love? |
|    | A-1685 | So true to lewdnefs, fo untrue to Love? |
|    | C-1714 | So true to Lewdnefs, so untrue to Love? |

| 50 | A-1680 | What *Oyfter, Cinder, Beggar,* common *Whore*, |
|    | A-1685 | What Oyfter, Cinder, Beggar, common Whore, |
|    | C-1714 | What *Oyfter, Cinder, Beggar,* common *Whore*, |

| 51 | A-1680 | Didft thou e're fail in all thy Life before? |
|    | A-1685 | Didft thou e're fail in all thy Life before? |
|    | C-1714 | Did'ft thou e'er fail in all thy Life before? |

| 52 | A-1680 | When *Vice, Difeafe* and *Scandal* lead the way, |
|    | A-1685 | When Vice, Difeafe and Scandal lead the way, |
|    | C-1714 | When *Vice, Difeafe,* and *Scandal* lead the Way, |

53   A-1680   With what officious haſt doſt thou obey?
     A-1685   With what officious haſt didſt thou obey?
     C-1714   With what officious Haſte doſt thou obey?

54   A-1680   Like a Rude roaring *Hector*, in the *Streets*,
     A-1685   Like a Rude-roaring *Hector*, in the Streets,
     C-1714   Like a rude roaring *Hector* in the *Streets*,

55   A-1680   That Scuffles, Cuffs, and Ruffles all he meets;
     A-1685   That Scuffles, Cuffs, and Ruffles all he meets;
     C-1714   That scuffles, cuffs, and ruffles all he meets;

56   A-1680   But if his *King*, or *Country*, claim his Aid,
     A-1685   But if his King or Country, claim his Aid,
     C-1714   But if his *King* or *Country* claim his Aid,

57   A-1680   The *Raſcal Villain*, ſhrinks, and hides his head;
     A-1685   The Raſcal Villain ſhrinks, and hides his Head:
     C-1714   The *Raſcal Villain* ſhrinks, and hides his Head:

58   A-1680   Ev'n ſo thy *Brutal Valor*, is diſplaid,
     A-1685   Ev'n ſo thy Brutal Valor, is diſplaid,
     C-1714   Ev'n ſo thy *brutal Valor*, is display'd,

59   A-1680   Breaks ev'ry *Stews*, does each ſmall *Whore invade*,
     A-1685   Breaks ev'ry Stews, does each ſmall Crack invade,
     C-1714   Breaks ev'ry *Stews*, does each ſmall *Whore invade*;

60   A-1680   But if great *Love*, the onſet does command,
     A-1685   But if great Love, the onſet does command,
     C-1714   But if great *Love* the Onſet does command,

61   A-1680   Baſe Recreant, to thy *Prince*, thou darſt not ſtand.
     A-1685   Baſe Recreant, to thy Prince, thou darſt not ſtand.
     C-1714   Baſe Recreant, to thy Prince thou dares not ſtand.

62   A-1680   Worſt part of me, and henceforth hated moſt,
     A-1685   Worſt part of me, and henceforth hated moſt,
     C-1714   Worſt Part of me, and henceforth hated moſt,

63   A-1680   Through all the *Town*, the common *Fucking Poſt*;
     A-1685   Through all the Town, the common rubbing Poſt;
     C-1714   Through all the Town the common ----- Poſt,

64   A-1680   On whom each *Whore*, relieves her tingling *Cunt*,
     A-1685   On whom each wretch, relieves her luſtful want,
     C-1714   On whom each Whore relieves her tingling ----,

65   A-1680   As *Hogs*, on *Goats*, do rub themſelves and grunt.
     A-1685   As *Hogs*, on *Goats*, do rub themſelves and grunt,
     C-1714   As Hogs on Gates do rub themſelves and grunt.

66   A-1680   May'ſt thou to rav'nous *Shankers*, be a *Prey*,
     A-1685   May'ſt thou to rav'nous Shankers be a Prey,
     C-1714   May'ſt thou to rav'nous Shankers be a Prey,

67   A-1680   Or in consuming *Weepings* waſte away.
     A-1685   Or in conſuming Weepings waſt away.
     C-1714   Or in conſuming Weepings waſte away.

68   A-1680   May *Stranguries*, and *Stone*, thy *Days* attend,
     A-1685   May Stranguries, and Stone, thy Dayes attend.
     C-1714   May Strangury and Stone thy Days attend;

69   A-1680   May'ſt thou Piſs, who didſt refuſe to ſpend,
     A-1685   May'ſt thou not Piſs, who didſt ſo much offend,
     C-1714   May'ſt thou ne'er piſs, who did'ſt refuſe to ſ---,

70   A-1680   When all my joys, did on falſe thee depend.
     A-1685   When all my joyes, did on falſe thee depend.
     C-1714   When all my Joys did on falſe thee depend.

71   A-1680   And may *Ten thouſand* abler *Pricks* agree,
     A-1685   And may ten thouſand abler Men agree,
     C-1714   And may ten thouſand abler *P---* agree

72   A-1680   To do the wrong'd *Corinna*, right for thee.
     A-1685   To do the wrong'd *Corinna* right for thee.
     C-1714   To do the wrong'd *Corinna* Right for thee.

# Rochester, Lady Betty and the Post-Boy

## EDWARD BURNS

An early pastoral finds Rochester in transition between fluency in a received language and an abrupt acknowledgement of his more personal concerns. The conventional language of love seems at first to spin itself out without any focused emotional reference.

### I

> *Alex*. There sighs not on the Plain
>     So lost a swain as I;
> Scorcht'd up with Love, frozen with Disdain,
> Of killing sweetness I complain
>     *Streph*. If 'tis Corinna, die.
>         (A Pastoral Dialogue Between Alexis and Strephon,
>         ll.1–5)

But when Strephon says that 'Like ruin'd Birds, rob'd of their Young, / Lamenting, frighted, and alone, / I fly from place to place' (ll.8–10), we receive an albeit miniaturized image of a vulnerability to a sense of death as felt loss, and of an aimless and evasive movement consequent on this, which seems typical of later, more ambitious poems. The loose improvisatory feel of even the most carefully worked of these—their abruptness of beginning and end, the provisionality of statement in poems that rethink themselves as they go—suggests that if despair or pain must be acknowledged, writing's business is to keep in flight. 'Absent from thee I languish still . . .' but a return to 'thee' can only be projected and deferred when that return is also to an 'everlasting rest'.[1] Such poems move away from even the possibility of dialogue, shifting from the often confrontational stance—mocking, flirtatious or accusing—of earlier lyrics, to a writing that describes absence and is poised at a point of withdrawal. I shall focus on a group of occasional, even atypical poems, in order to try to track the Rochesterian absence, the flight from centre-stage, in terms of its opposites; in terms of the insistently self-defining subject, the attempt to extort acquiescence or belief through rhetorical closure, which annoys him so much in the work of his contemporaries.

'To the Post-Boy' catches Rochester centre-stage, but in the service of an extreme self-dislocation, of a kind of prescience of death. The atypicality of the poem has been commented on by Anne Righter who places it in contrast to the shape-changing histrionic Rochester, hard to catch in his 'own' role.[2] There is no holograph, and the manuscripts in which the poem is ascribed to Rochester also ascribe to him a number of poems which seem uncharacteristically crude. John Harold Wilson, in the first argued ascription of the poem, can link it to its historical situation, but must also remark on the apparent unlikeliness, the shockingness even, of a poet writing this way about himself.[3] This seems to have been the factor which struck a seventeenth-century copyist, who combined part of the poem with some self-exculpatory lines from 'The Imperfect Enjoyment'.[4] At the same time, out of this uncharacteristic/ unlikely text, a voice sounds that one finds hard to disown as 'Rochester' . . . whatever *that* means. The poem imports a *frisson* into the business of attribution. The textual situation alone effaces whatever might be behind the mask (no authenticating mark survives), but the 'performance' is so complete, the mask so compelling, that on that basis alone we allow the poem to 'be' 'Rochester'. 'Rochester' becomes a theatrical persona split off from the assumed writer, insistent on establishing his identity by reference to events in the life of the historical Rochester. The effect is rather as if the writer had created a kind of puppet of himself who then tries to present credentials entitling him to his creator's identity, an effect Vieth's edition compounds, by adding '*Rochester*' as a speech-heading at the start of the poem.[5]

> Son of A whore God dam you can you tell
> A Peerless Peer the Readyest way to Hell?
> Ive outswilld Baccus sworn of my own make

> Oaths wod fright furies and make Pluto quake.
> Ive swived more whores more ways than Sodoms walls
> Ere knew or the College of Romes Cardinalls.
> Witness Heroick scars, look here nere go
> 　　　　　　　　　(ll.1–7)

A sense of the eerie is dramatized in the addressee's implied attempt to move away, to withdraw and to leave the Rochester figure centre-stage. 'Rochester' attempts to fix the boy by making him look, and thus fixes himself as the object of an unwilled gaze, whose intentions or responses we can only supply from our own. Again, the writer has effected a kind of alienation—between reader and writer, between the figure who stands uneasily in for the writer and the writer himself. The poem continues:

> Sear cloaths and ulcers from the top to toe.
> Frighted at my own mischiefes I have fled
> And bravely left my lifes defender dead.
> 　　　　　　　　　(ll.8–10)

Invited to 'witness Heroick scars', the boy has been placed in the position of a Doubting Thomas, the apostle to whom Christ appeared after his Resurrection and whom he invited to test the reality of his risen body by examining and touching his wounds. The analogue is not explicitly invoked, but it is consistent with Rochester's interests and methods elsewhere. The Rochester of the poem is a Christ on his way to, rather than from, a Harrowing of Hell, in search of a Thomas to give him belief in himself, to give substance to a tissue of anecdote and self-mythologizing. That the undeniable tokens of this reality are 'scars . . . and ulcers' should not surprise us, offered as they are by the man who wrote that 'pain can ne're deceive'.[6] As a recurrent subject in seventeenth-century religious painting, the story focuses a Baroque concern with the relation of the visual arts to belief—the materiality, the fleshiness of oil and canvas offer the promise of a realization of Christ's presence, while the framing, the self-conscious theatricality of the medium with holds that from us, and instates Thomas as our representative. Just as touch is the medium of belief in an anecdote represented visually by painting (or religious theatre), so sight is the medium of belief in a verbally enacted encounter. The theatrical form of the poem shapes the encounter as a present moment, as a picture offers us the illusion of our presence, our witnessing, at the event. Neither enables us to use the senses—tactile in the picture, seeing in the poem—on which belief depends for the depicted characters. Our belief is thus withheld.

The incident to which the poem refers is recounted in a letter of Charles Hatton's, dated 29 June 1676:

> Mr Downs is dead. The Lord Rochester doth abscond, and so doth Etheridge and Capt. Bridges who occasioned the riot Sunday sennight. They were tossing some fiddlers in a blanket for refusing to play, and a barber, upon the noise, going to see what the matter, they seized upon him, and, to free himself from them, he offered to carry them to the handsomest woman in Epsom and directed them to the constable's house, who demanding what they came for, (they) told him a whore, and, he refusing to let them in, they broke open his doors and broke his head and beat him very severely. At last he made his escape, called his watch, and Etheridge made a submissive oration to them and so far appeased them that the constable dismissed his watch. But presently after the Lord Rochester drew upon the constable. Mr Downs, to prevent his pass, seized on him, the constable cried out murther and, the watch returning, one came behind Mr Downs and with a sprittle staff cleft his skull. The Lord Rochester and the rest run away and Downs, having no sword, snatched up a stick and striking at them, they run him into the side with a half pike and so bruised his arm that he was never able to stir it after . . .[7]

The 'Rochester' of the poem is in flight from himself; 'Frighted at my own mischiefes I have fled'. The incident is schematized as an allusion to a self-splitting, to the panic-induced creation of a *doppelgänger*. In leaving his 'life's defender dead' Rochester's 'past life' is his 'noe more'[8]—but it is insistently present, and becomes the property of this challenging persona, this puppet-like other self. Downs has defended a life that can be Roches-

ter's no more, in that the very act of pusillanimity has erased
the dashing Rochester who instigated the incident, and left—
what? It is up to the post-boy to decide. Rochester ends by
confessing, or boasting, that he:

> Broke houses to break chastity and died
> That floor with murder which my lust denied.
> Pox on it why do I speak of these poor things?
> I have blasphemed my god and libelld Kings;
> The readyest way to Hell come quick—.
>
> (ll.11–15)

House and woman are identified with each other—both are
'broken', but the woman is imaginary, so that invaded enclosure becomes something other—this is a rush into emptiness, in
to the house of death. The pun on 'dyed/died' informs us of this.
Rochester *has* thus died—the word hangs on the end of the line,
the break giving one sense which is then recouped for a literal
sense, of having marked, or coloured, left some sign of himself,
but a sign (like the other signs that attest to his reality, the
'scars . . . / Sear cloaths and ulcers . . .') that comes of
wounding, of vulnerability. He has in some sense rushed into
the house of death, *has* harrowed Hell. The syntax of 'witness
Heroick scars' is ambiguous; do the scars witness, or is he
commanding the boy/to witness them? In which case we can't,
and the boy doesn't let on whether he will or not. Downs' blood
is the token of Rochester's wound, the wound to the life that is
Rochester's no more. The spilling on 'that floor' of body fluid
other than that which Rochester had meant to enter the non-
existent woman signals a double failure, a double death—had
he 'died' on entering *her*, the familiar seventeenth-century
euphemism would have made the poem into a celebratory
trophy of '*la petite morte*'. But to have 'dyed' thus . . . that stain is
ineradicable, and another kind of death. The boy at the end of
the poem gives his answer:

> The readyest way my Lord's by Rochester
>
> (l.17)

So where 'Rochester' tried to fix the boy still by transfixing him
with the spectacle of his wounds, the boy here fixes him—
'Ne'er stir'—by naming him. The name has to be introduced

surreptitiously as a pun on a place name, an evasive strategy necessary to 'charm' the revenant in order to escape it. I have referred intermittently to the second speaker as the boy, but strictly speaking, it is only here that he is directly identified; the opening of the poem allows only a blurred distinction between a figure to be realized in an anecdotal narrative, and the reader, thus addressed/constructed in a moment of unease. But as 'boy', the post-boy belongs with a series of other figures in Rochester's self-dramatizingly libertine poems. Like the 'well-look'd Link-Boy' in 'The Disabled Debauchee', or the 'sweet soft Page' in 'Love a Woman . . .', he is a marginal figure in the simplest sense of being at the edges of the poem—only just in view.[9] The literal occupation of the boys is to light and/or guide the way of the central figure, the libertine whose portrait the poem is. They thus 'illuminate' or 'position' that figure for us, as they might reveal or deictically emphasize the presence of their master in a painted portrait. In the other poems the link-boy and the page are peremptorily summoned centre stage to demonstrate the speaker's libertine credentials by having sex with him—the move from margin to centre is a formal joke to sharpen the erotic shock—but the post-boy's distance from even this ambiguous complicity again points up the impotence of the 'Rochester' figure. The post-boy charms the apparition into stillness by giving it back its name, a notorious name in which it must thus confront both its reputation and its own consciousness of failure. The encounter has not revealed it as risen and real, but as fled/dead/died/denied. The boy is no validating 'witness'.

To define oneself in verse, to engage in the egotistical sublime of placing oneself, as subject, centre-stage, is reserved in Rochester for the butts of his satires—the insistent 'I' in these ventriloquial exercises betrays emptiness. In the manuscript fragment of a comedy, one Mr Dainty complains of the necessity to sleep '. . . naturally I hate to be so long absent from myself, as one is in a manner those seven dull hours he snores away . . .'.[10] To Rochester, to fear rather than to desire absence from oneself is self-evidently arrogant and foolish. Rochester's lyrics of self-definition, of self-portraiture (where the speaker of the poem is identified with the writer only in so far as they share some familiar traits of libertinism—this makes classification of the poems into persona-based or own-voiced more difficult than Righter allows) present figures in withdrawal: the disabled debauchee, the lover leaving his mistress to her own devices ('Whilst I my pleasure to pursue / Whole nights am taking in / The Lusty Juice of Grapes, take you / The Juice of Lusty Men'),[11] the libertine foreswearing woman for his 'lewd well-natur'd *Friend*' and 'the sweet soft Page'.[12] This seems to be, for Rochester, the proper position from which to write, when writing is a partial self-negation, an impotent, even despairing, kind of engagement with others that at the same time is inevitable, and in some sense desired. 'A Very Heroicall Epistle in Answer to Ephelia' mocks the Earl of Mulgrave, nick-named 'Bajazet' by Rochester, for the opposite tendency:

> How is it then, that I inconstant am?
> He changes not, who always is the same.
> In my deare self, I centre ev'ry thing,
> My Servants, Friends, my Mistresse and my king,
> Nay Heav'n, and Earth, to that one poynt I bring:
> (ll.5–9)

In another attack by Rochester on a personal and literary enemy, the insistent, unchanging, undislodgeable subject of Carr Scroope's lyric 'I cannot change as others do'—an opening line that is immediately and irredeemably un-Rochesterian—is presumably what motivates a raucous parody entitled 'The Mock Song'—'I swive as well as others do; / I'm young, not yet deform'd' (ll.1–2)—a parody that opens the original out to a kind of defensive boasting, a nervous comparison of self to self-image anathema to Rochester in his own habitual stance. Then Rochester's poem gives us Scroope's mistress, Cary Frazier, answering him, and it becomes a statement of her insatiability:

> Were all my Body larded o're,
> With Darts of Love, so thick,
> That you might find in ev'ry *Pore*,
> A well stuck standing *Prick*,
> Whilst yet my *Eyes* alone were free,
> *My Heart*, wou'd never doubt,

In Am'rous Rage and Extasie,
To wish those *Eyes*, to wish those *Eyes* fuckt out
(ll.9–16)[13]

A martyr to lust, like the 'Rochester' of 'To the Post-boy', Cary is conversely without 'doubt', as securely centre-stage as Bernini's St Theresa, in an 'ecstasy' that allows her to transcend the need for the 'I's/'eyes' that Mulgrave/Bajazet in an unconscious and 'Rochester'/Rochester in a conscious insecurity rely on to look at the post-boy or Ephelia within the frame, to look out at/address us from inside it. The obscenity of the parody relies of course on her 'centre-stage', positioning; the obscene is on-scene, a grosser version of the movement into frame of the eroticized servant boys. However, like all Rochester's burlesquely pornographic monsters, she exists in happy confidence—the pose of martyrdom is always grotesque in Rochester's work, but he can take grotesquerie to a heroic extreme which is perhaps for him martyrdom's only validation. He celebrates self-containment and self-confidence in women in every bit as extreme a way as he conveys his revulsion from it in men.

The poems I have mentioned so far belong to a series of personal attacks on court figures which seem to increase in volume and ferocity towards the end of Rochester's output. More generally, they overlap with two interlinked literary phenomena of the late 1670s and 1680s, the revival of interest in Ovid's *Heroides*, as represented by Dryden's collection, *Ovid's Epistles, Translated by Several Hands* (1680) and a sequence of poems published under the pseudonym 'Ephelia'. The volume *Female Poems* (1679)[14] is the main collection of verses ascribed to 'Ephelia', but the name is also used by Rochester and his circle for the female complaint in *Heroides* style verses designed to embarrass Mulgrave.

Mulgrave's social and marital ambitions focused on the Princess Anne, later Queen Anne, daughter of the Duke of York. The use of the *Heroides* as a form for the Ephelia/Bajazet poems fits the circumstance of the mistress abandoned by the egotistical 'hero'. The politics of love in Ovid, its implication in a court world ('all his Poems bear the Character of a Court' according to Dryden),[15] and especially the play of class difference between lovers, provide apt material for Restoration Ovidians. Behn's *Oenone to Paris*[16] can be paired with a poem less securely but very probably attributable to her, where she gives the form another twist; in the epistle written by 'Ovid' to 'Julia', the daughter of Augustus in whose disgrace and exile the historical Ovid was implicated. He is presented here as an ambitious wooer, in a poem which also appears in *Poems on Affairs of State* (1696) with the names changed to Bajazet and Gloriana.[17] But leaving personalities aside, the form itself is an irritant to Rochester's imagination; the self-importance of the court-circle matches the egotistical drive of the self-justifying dramatic monologue, its insistent centring of the speaking subject, its push to validate its rhetoric in an appeal to the evidence of psychic wounds and the threat of their physical realization. If 'To the Post-boy' acquires its force from its atypicality, from the awkwardness and alienating effect of Rochester's pushing 'himself' centre stage (so that by virtue of this uncharacteristic manoeuvre he is then not himself), the distasteful insistence of the *Heroides*, like the crass mock-modesty of the parodied Scroope lyric, focuses the challenging and enraging self-importance of others into a formal affront to Rochester's own sense of the subject in writing.

A very late, short, perhaps extempore, piece by Rochester puts the *Heroides* in the context of his own lived life, at least as anecdotally described in the editor's title in the 1693 *A Collection of Poems by Several Hands*, its earliest known text:

'*The Earl of* ROCHESTER'S *Answer, to a Paper of* Verses, *sent him by* L. B. Felton *and taken out of the Translation of* Ovid's *Epistles*, 1680.

> What strange Surprise to meet such Words as these?
> Such Terms of Horrour were ne'er chose to please:
> To meet, midst Pleasures of a Jovial Night,
> Words that can only give amaze and fright,
> No gentle thought that does to Love invite.
> Were it not better for your Arms t'employ,
> Grasping a Lover in pursuit of Joy,
> Than handling Sword, and Pen, Weapons unfit;
> (ll.1–8)

The reference to sword and pen seems to suggest that the verses Lady Betty sent were from the opening of 'Canacee to Macareus', in Dryden's translation from the 1680 *Ovid's Epistles, Translated by Several Hands*.

> If streaming blood my fatal Letter stain,
> Imagine, er'e you read, the Writer slain:
> One hand the Sword, and one the pen employs,
> And in my lap the ready paper lyes.
> Think in this posture thou behold'st me Write:
> In this my cruel Father wou'd delight.
>
> (ll. 1–6)[18]

The narrative situation of the poem is as follows. Canacee and Macareus are brother and sister, children of the wind-god, Aeolus. She has borne Macareus's child, after an unsuccessful abortion attempt, and Aeolus has had the child exposed on a mountainside 'and, withal, sent a sword to *Canacee*, with this Message, That her Crimes would instruct her how to use it. With this Sword she slew herself: but before she died, she writ the following Letter to her Brother . . .'.[19] The 'situation' that might exist between Lady Betty and Rochester can only be a matter of speculation—we only have the 1693 editor's word for this anecdotal identification of the poem. But the title amplifies the text whatever the 'real' situation was. In this kind of playfully gossip-orientated writing, contexts and, more frustratingly, authorial identification, must be seen to dissolve into a game of masking and innuendo. But the poem itself provides enough of a context in its relation to the idea of the *Heroides*, and in its set of tropes—sword, pen, blood, letter—for the female writer, especially as amplified by the passage from 'Canacee'.

It is, of course, of the essence of *The Heroides* that they are male impersonations of the female. If Aphra Behn *is* the author of 'Ovid to Julia' she thus performs a doubly witty reversal, as a woman impersonating the male impersonator, himself trapped, as an injured man pleading with the absent and more powerful woman, in a reversal of the kind of situation about which he himself wrote. This seems to be typical of the kind of attention to *The Heroides* by this circle of writers, an attention to the rhetorical cross-dressing made possible by that foregrounding of the cultural signals of gender equally typical of Ovid and of Restoration writing. Just as the 'several hands' engaged in Dryden's volumes include writers of both sexes (one of them, in the 1712 volume, the eighth edition of this popular collection, being Rochester's niece, Anne Wharton,[20] so the *Female Poems* and related 'Ephelia' texts engage in a discourse of gender that by using explicit and distinct 'male' or 'female' voices as a matter of writerly convention, makes those voices equally available as writing strategies to both men and women. Etherege's hand in 'Ephelia to Bajazet' seems clearly documented. Germaine Greer guesses at Cary Frazier as the 'Ephelia', who wrote *Female Poems* but this only takes us into the game of identification that one suspects the anonymous authors intended to start by their playful masking and doubling of gender which the Ovidian genre amplifies and formalizes.

The opening of 'Canacee' presents us with an explicit and symmetrical image of the woman writer, or perhaps a caricature of a male view of a woman writing—pen in one hand, the equally phallic sword in the other, and the paper in her lap, the last focusing still further the worrying idea that *ecriture feminine* in this case is written out of wounds, or from the gash of the womb. The image is made more claustrophobic by a kind of *mise en abime*—'Think in this posture thou behold'st me Write' (1.5)—Canacee writes a description of herself writing a description of herself writing . . . and so on. Dryden confuses the issue further by introducing 'er'e'—'Imagine, er'e you read, the Writer slain' (1.2)—but how are we to imagine what the writing creates for us, how can we obey this injunction, *before* we read it? Formal games of this kind seem to inform the *Heroides*, and seem very much a piece with that quizzical foregrounding of gender that tends both to extort admiration for the writer's 'wit' while undermining empathetic responses to the heroines, or our belief that the writer translator and imitator are themselves responding somehow empathetically. Dryden's preface, like his comments elsewhere on Shakespeare and Chaucer, pushes a Cartesian terminology of 'the passions' to an appeal to universal common sense in order to make his claim for the poem's quality:

> If the Imitation of Nature be the business of a Poet, I
> know no Authour who can justly be compar'd with ours,
> especially in the Description of the Passions. And to prove
> this, I shall need no other Judges than the generality of his
> readers: for all Passions being inborn with us, we are
> almost equally Judges when we are concern'd in the
> representation of them.[21]

But at the same time, the rhetorical contortions that the form
imposes on its constructed speakers—the self-conscious
manipulation of narrative and image, the urge to consolidate
or prove while simultaneously affirming helplessness—mili-
tate against commonsensical empathy. That aspect of the
rhetorical self-consciousness of the *Heroides* which Restoration
versions tend to minimize—a focus on the materiality of the
text as a letter, as an object with an imperilled life of its own is
exactly the premise on which the Rochester verses are based.
Aphra Behn, for example, omits the harassed and waspish first
lines of the *Oenone*—'Will you read my letter through? or does
your new wife forbid? Read . . . [22] There is perhaps a
contradiction here between the sense of the *Heroides* as passionate outpouring, to be empathetically received, and the
medium, the letter, which is also a kind of barrier, a delay of
communication in which self-consciousness on the writer's
part and suspicion on the reader's can crystallize.

Lady Betty has taken on and given a personal meaning to, in
that sense acted or impersonated, a text in which a man
imitates a woman, that text translated by another man and
then appropriated and 'performed' by her. As Lady Betty
Howard, she had spoken lines written for her by Rochester as
'The Second Prologue at Court to *The Empress of Morocco* spoken
by The Lady Elizabeth Howard'.

> Wit's bus'ness is to please, and to fright
> 'Tis no Wit to be always in the right:
> You'l find it none, who dare be so to night.
>                    (ll.12–4)

In forsaking these precepts for Ovidian 'terms of horror . . .
ne'er chose to please' ('Answer . . .' l.2), Lady Betty has moved
from the Rochesterian evasion of self-assertion, to its loathed

opposite, the self-justifying egotism of *The Heroides*. In both
instances she is speaking the words of a man, but in the second
she seems to have forgotten this, perhaps to have lost the
rhetorical awareness Rochester credits her with in the prologue.

> Few so ill bred will venture to a Play,
> To spy out Faults in what we Women say.
> For us no matter what we speak, but how:
> How kindly can we say—I hate you now.
> (ll.15–18)

The rhetoric that depends on interaction, on the just sense of a
situation—of the kind that Rochester in the later poem accuses
Lady Betty of lacking—is the 'how' rather than the 'what' of a
discourse that allows women to negotiate these situations. The
self absorption which is here (and usually in Rochester) a male
characteristic allows women (like the audience addressed by
Lady Betty) freedom at the expense of being unheard:

> And for the men, if you'l laugh at e'm do;
> They mind themselves so much, they'l ne're mind you.
> (ll.19–20)

When Lady Betty addresses the King in her prologue, she
focuses attention on herself—literally 'centre stage'—while
using the power of that position to shift attention into the
audience, to indicate the King.

> But why do I descend to lose a Prayer
> On those small Saints in Wit, the God sits there.
> To you (Great Sir) my Message hither tends,
> From Youth and Beauty, your Allies and Friends.
> See my Credentials written in my Face,
> They challenge your Protection in this place:
> And hither come with such a Force of Charms,
> As may give check even to your prosp'rous Armes:
> (ll.21–28)

This sets up a kind of triangular displacement of authority.
Lady Betty angles and redirects potentially offensive words of
Rochester's, reflecting on the King's 'soft captivity' to women.

> . . . 'tis well known for your own part (Great Prince)
> 'Gainst us you still have made a weak Defence.
>
> (ll.36–37)

The ambiguous relation of male writer to female speaker is
resolved here, and Rochester's safety assured, by the 'Credentials written' in Lady Betty's face, credentials to her identity (of
the kind 'Rochester' could not convince the post-boy he
possessed) which override the ambiguities of literary cross-
dressing. Betty and Charles validate each other, she as beauty,
he as captivated king—Rochester as writer occupies a more
slyly occluded position, using the prologue as a kind of Trojan
horse for the disruption of Charles's authority, an authority
displaced in any case by the shifting spotlight that prevents
any of the three occupying a central originating or authoritative position.

One could argue that Rochester had himself 'written' those
'credentials', in constructing the idea of Lady Betty's beauty,
or at least of presenting that beauty in the terms his prologue
requires. But the obvious contrast with the 'Answer to . . .
L. B. Felton' and its assumed point of reference in 'Canacee',
is between opposed modes of writing on the body. When
Rochester refers to her 'handling sword and pen, weapons
unfit' it is not clear whether the sword is an offensive or a self-
directed weapon—but come to think of it, that isn't clear of
the pen either, and so we are brought to another essential
aspect of the *Heroides*, that the pen and sword (or whatever
other means of self-destruction is employed) are identified as
what 'writes' the text, and that that writing is both a suicidal
undoing of the writer and a 'weapon' wielded at the recipient.
Fictional recipient and reader survive, the text projects the
death of the letter-writer, and the end of the text is identified
with that death. Canacee's letter, one may remember, is
lodged in her lap, a point not lost on parodists of the poem,
who made the obvious connection with menstrual blood (or
'flowers' in Restoration slang). When Rochester invokes the
same connection, he does so to write *against* a woman,
Mistress Willis:

> Whom that I may describe throughout,
>     Assist me Bawdy Powers

> I'le write upon a double Clowt
> And dipp my Pen in Flowers.[23]
>
> (ll.5–8)

The 'pen' here is still his, however 'unfit' its use—to invoke both the 'Answer' and another of Rochester's poems on menstruation:

> By all *Loves* soft, yet mighty powers,
> It is a thing unfit,
> That *Men* shou'd Fuck in time of *Flow'rs*
> Or when the *Smock's* beshit.[24]
>
> (ll.1–4)

Betty/Canacee's appropriation of the pen is threatening as an emasculation within that set of associations, familiar from 'Artemiza to Chloe', of writing with combat and adventure—'. . . in Verse by your commande I write / Shortly you'l bid mee ride astride, and fight'. (ll.1–2). 'Weapons' and 'arms' provide still more explicit sexual connotation in 'The Earl of Rochester's Answer to a Paper of Verse, sent by L. B. Felton and taken out of the translation of Ovid's Epistles, 1680':

> Your Sex gains Conquest, by their Charms and Wit.
> Of writers slain I could with pleasure hear,
> Approve of Fights, o'er-joy'd to cause a Tear;
> So slain, I mean, that she should soon revive,
> Pleas'd in my Arms to find her self Alive.
>
> (ll.9–13)

On one level this could be read as sexualizing the act of writing in order to return the female writer to her proper sphere—that of sexual activity, albeit within the domain of an intelligence and power implied in 'charms and wit'. But Lady Betty—unlike the successfully defiant Artemiza—is not a writer, she is a performer of male authored texts, whom Rochester sees as having lost the skill, here required on the social stage of her intrusion into Rochester's party, to manipulate and angle those texts. Quite apart from this, Rochester is following Ovid and Dryden's sexualization of writing, but transforming it from the negative to the benign. Betty's lack of aplomb shows itself in taking the Ovidian pose too seriously. Her attempt to share in

the heroine's writing-herself-to-death is contradicted by the
material fact of the letter and its turning up in a quite
inapposite context, 'midst Pleasures of a Jovial Night' (l.3).
The letter is subsumed into a continuum of life (largely male
life, admittedly, as 'jovial' points up) in which the fixity, the
central placing of the subject, the self dramatization of the
genre—and above all its assumption that the subject and its
utterances are to be validated in an ultimate closure—are all a
nonsense.

Rochester's last two lines—'So slain, I mean, that she should
soon revive / Pleas'd in my Arms to find her self Alive' (ll.12–
13)—echo another lover's rebuke, when allusions to Ovid in
love-games have turned disconcertingly to the thought of
death.

> O, these I lack,
> To make you garlands of; and my sweet friend
> To strew him o'er and o'er!
>
> What, like a corpse?
>
> No, like a bank for love to lie and play on:
> Not like a corpse; or if—not to be buried,
> But quick, and in mine arms.[25]

The echo of Florizel and Perdita must be accidental—but
perhaps there is more in common between Shakespeare's
pastoral and Rochester's unrespectable language of the resi-
lient body than might at first appear. Rochester's pastoral too
can transform death and threat to life and pleasure. Though
Rochester abandons pastoral fairly early he shares with those
groups of his contemporaries who wrote to and about each
other under pastoral pseudonyms, the sense that writing is
more like belonging to a pastoral society than it is like
individual self-promotion, or like solitary suicide—that written
texts join together to create a social landscape, rather existing
as individual memorialization, as portraits or suicide notes.
The comic transformation to innocence and pleasure that the
Chloris of the pig-sty pastoral effects may not be available to
the later poems,[26] but Rochester still resists a writerly practise
that fixes the subject, renders it 'constant', self-defining, dead.

82	*Reading Rochester*

## NOTES

1. 'A Song'—*The Poems of John Wilmot, Earl of Rochester*, Keith Walker (Oxford, 1984), pp. 38–39. All subsequent quotations from this edition.

2. 'The mythologizing of Rochester's life and personality . . . was for the most part accomplished by people other than himself . . . in 'To the Post-boy' . . . he becomes a caricature of vice . . . Those orthodox values by which the wicked Earl of Rochester stands self-condemned are themselves mocked . . . Even more perplexing: what is the point at which one should separate this dramatic character, the subject of the lampoon, from the witty poet of the same name who stage-managed the incident in the first place and who controls in so complex a fashion the tone and language of his self present-ation?' Righter, 'John Wilmot Earl of Rochester', reprinted in *John Wilmot Earl of Rochester: Critical Essays*, ed. David M. Vieth (New York, 1988), pp. 5–8. Jeremy Treglown pin-points a similarly puzzling theatricality in the poem. 'It would be hard to name a writer who has contemplated his own moral and physical ruin with a more satisfied kind of horror . . . a real life adoption of the role of a villainous Renaissance stage malcontent.' (*Letters*, p. 2.)

3. Wilson, John Harold, 'Rochester's Buffoon conceit', *Modern Language Notes* 56, May 1941, p. 372–73.

4. See Wilson, as above.

5. Vieth's copy-text is B.M. Harley M.S. 6914, fol. 21r. In this collection of poems transcribed by different hands, the poem is headed 'To the Post Boy by Ld Rochester 1674'. It seems to be in the same hand as the table of contents. The poems in the collection are largely topical satires, and several of those ascribed to Rochester are clearly not his.

Righter simply transcribes the poem in the manuscript's largely unpunctu-ated form—one comma after 'scars' is the only pause in the poem's headlong rush, and indeed this seems apt. The full-stop which both Vieth and Walker introduce between 'Cardinals' and 'Witness' seems to me to be particularly disruptive—it destroys the sense that the scars are themselves witnesses to the activities described in the previous line, not simply that 'the boy / we are called on to 'Witness" (ll.6–7). John Harold Wilson's colon at this point seems more tactful. No-one uses the marginal note 'Cap'n Downs' which the transcriber adds to the left of the couplet that begins 'Frighted at my own mischiefes . . .' (ll.9–10).

6. 'The Mistress', pp. 29–30, l.32. But the same man mocks that attitude in others, as in his epilogue to Davenant's *Circe*;

> The Epilogue (to Circe)
> Poets and women have an Equal Right
> To hate the Dull, who Dead to all Delight
> Feel pain along, and have no Joy but spite.
> 'Twas impotence did first this Vice begin.
> (p. 58, ll.10–13)

7. A letter from Charles Hatton to his brother, 29 June 1676. Quoted in *John Wilmot Earl of Rochester, in the eyes of his contemporaries and in his own poetry and prose. 'The Debt to Pleasure'*, ed. John Adlard (Fyfield Books, 1974), p. 119.

This letter seems to dictate the terms in which Vieth and Treglown retell the story. There is another version in a letter by Andrew Marvell: *The Poems and Letters of Andrew Marvell*, ed. H. M. Margoliouth (1971) pp. 344–45. Though less vivid, this gives an intriguing sense of the potential political capital to be made of the incident.

8. See 'Love and Life' ('All my past life is mine noe more . . .'), l.1 (Walker, p. 44).

9. 'The Disabled Debauchee', pp. 97–99, ll.37–40; 'Song', p. 25, ll.15–16.

10. Adlard, p. 118.

11. 'To a Lady in a Letter', pp. 41–43, ll.29–32.

12. 'Song', p. 25, ll.1–5.

13. Walker entitles the poem 'Song' and prints underneath (by Sir Carr Scroope) 'The Mock Song' (p. 109–10).

14. *Female Poems* is one of the most enigmatic of anonymous seventeenth-century texts given in *Kissing the Rod : An anthology of Seventeenth-Century Women's Verse*, ed. Germaine Greer *et al.* (Virago, 1988), pp. 271–73. Greer, who does not seem to have contributed the 'Ephelia' section in this collection, suggests in her commentary on 'Ovid to Julia. A Letter by an Unknown Hand', in *The Uncollected Verse of Aphra Behn* (Stump Cross Books, 1989), that 'Ephelia both is and is not Cary Frazier' but that 'being red-haired she, i.e. Cary Frazier has every right to be called 'Ephelia' (the freckled one) and that this is the author of some, though not all the *Female Poems* . . .' (pp. 177–78). I suspect that there are enough clues in '*Female Poems* . . .'—given the initials of the male character involved in the voyage to Africa on which the 'love plot' depends, to allow a more exact identification, or at least a more carefully delimited field of possibilities.

15. 'The Preface to Ovid's *Epistles*' in *the Poems of John Dryden*, ed. James Kinsley (Oxford, 1958), Vol.I, p. 179, l.67.

16. Reprinted in *Motives of Woe; Shakespeare and Female Complaint, A Critical Anthology*, ed. John Kerrigan (Oxford, 1991), pp. 260–68.

17. *The Uncollected Verse of Aphra Behn*, pp. 18–21, commentary p. 174–75.

18. Dryden, Vol. I, p. 187.

19. Dryden, Vol. I, p. 186.

20. 'From Penelope to Ulysses', reprinted in extract in *Kissing the Rod*, pp. 291–92.

21. Vol. I, p. 180.

22. *Heroides V*, l.1, Translated by Grant Showerman (Loeb edition, 1947).

23. 'On Mistress Willis', pp. 44–45, ll.5–8.

24. 'Song', p. 45, ll.1–4.

25. Shakespeare, *The Winter's Tale*, ed. J. H. P. Pafford (Arden edition, 1966), IV, iv, ll.127–32, pp. 96–97.

26. 'Song', pp. 33–24, ll.39–40.

# Negativity and Affirmation in Rochester's Lyric Poetry

## SIMON DENTITH

In the following essay I seek to provide some context for the particular twists and inversions that characterize Rochester's lyric poetry. The context I suggest is not biographical, but social and therefore, ultimately, historical; that is, I seek to locate the various affirmations and debunkings that characterize these poems in the wider, class-marked discursive economy of the Restoration. But I attempt this act of location by attention to the tone of voice and shifts of register within the poetry, and to its differing rhetorical appeals. In this, my enterprise has a generally Bakhtinian inspiration; not so much the Bakhtin of the 'carnivalesque'—though he makes a brief appearance—but the Bakhtin who insists on the socially marked nature of all discourse.

I begin with a brief comment from an early nineteenth-century response to Rochester.

> Rochester's poetry is the poetry of wit combined with the love of pleasure, of thought with licentiousness. His extravagant heedless levity has a sort of passionate enthusiasm in it; his contempt for everything that others respect, almost amounts to sublimity.[1]

These remarks from Hazlitt's *Lectures on the English Poets* in 1818 are almost the sum total of his comments on Rochester; their paradoxical condensation nevertheless provides a way into the intense negativity of his lyrical poetry. It is above all that last phrase that I wish to explore; how can a 'contempt for everything that others respect' amount to 'sublimity'? Is Hazlitt perceiving Rochester as a Romantic hero of negation, sublime because of his contemptuous rejections of common-place values? Or is there a more complicated, even dialectical process at work, in which Rochester's passionate reductiveness emerges at the far side into its own and distinctive sublime?

There is no doubting the reductiveness. We need not go to the more famously satirical or obscene poems, but can look at an Anacreontic, which Rochester imitated from the French of Ronsard, 'Upon His Drinking a Bowl':

> *Vulcan* contrive me such a Cup,
>   As *Nestor* us'd of old;
> Shew all thy skill to trim it up,
>   Damask it round with *Gold*.
>
> Make it so large, that fill'd with *Sack*,
>   Up to the swelling brim,
> Vast Toasts, on the delicious *Lake*,
>   Like *Ships* at *Sea* may swim.
>
> Engrave no *Battail* on his Cheek,
>   With *War*, I've nought to do;
> I'm none of those that took *Mastrich*,
>   Nor *Yarmouth Leager* knew.
>
> Let it no name of *Planets* tell,
>   Fixt *Stars*, or *Consellations*;
> For I am no Sir *Sydrophell*,
>   Nor none of his *Relations*.
>
> But carve thereon a spreading *Vine*,
>   Then add Two lovely *Boys*;
> Their limbs in Amorous folds intwine,
>   The *Type* of future joys.
>
> *Cupid* and *Bacchus*, my Saints are:
>   May drink, and Love, still reign,
> With *Wine*, I wash away my cares,
>   And then to *Cunt* again.[2]

Rochester's immediate source for this is Ronsard, himself imitating Anacreon, though the 'Anacreonta' that both he and Rochester took as models were in fact Hellenic imitations.[3] So we have here an especially complex layering, in which successive poets have taken their predecessors' words and refashioned them, redirecting them and revaluing them as they do so. In this perspective, Rochester's loaded last line, though without precedent in either Ronsard or the Anacreonta, only continues a tradition of which the whole poem is itself a larger example.

Yet, on second thoughts, the extreme reductiveness of that last line, its crude defacing of the whole poem, marks an attempt to put a stop to the tradition embodied by the poem, of which Rochester has just proved himself the master. Its immediate target is that conventional vocabulary of love poetry briefly drawn on in the final stanza. By crudely and reductively insisting 'cunt', Rochester exposes as euphemism that elaborate language of courtship alluded to in 'Cupid and Bacchus, my Saints are / May drink, and Love, still reign'. In his book *Swearing*, Geoffrey Hughes remarks on the phenomenon of *dysphemisms*, 'startlingly direct and shockingly coarse violations of a taboo'. 'A great deal of swearing, foul language and profanity', he adds, 'is deliberately dysphemic'.[4] By deploying one vocabulary against another in this way, Rochester sets in motion what Bakhtin describes as the characteristic swing of grotesque realism, moving from the elevated to the 'lower bodily stratum' and in doing so effecting a brief carnivalesque inversion.

Yet, to complicate matters, the poem already has its own minor subversions, indeed its light anti-heroic tone is part of its point. It is, after all, 'only' an Anacreontic. So Rochester deftly and wittily—with 'extravagant heedless levity', to use Hazlitt's phrase—concocts a splendid hyperbolic invocation to Vulcan, and uses it to undermine the discourses of war and astrology. In this he is doing no more that Ronsard and the Hellenic poets had done before him, though of course he gives the poem immediate contemporary point with the references to Maastricht and the Yarmouth expeditionary force. But this whole construction is then undermined by the last line, showing just that 'contempt for everything that others respect' of which Hazlitt speaks.

How appropriate, though, is my invocation of Bakhtin in describing the inversion of values that Rochester effects? For Bakhtin, carnivalesque writing evinces 'gay relativity', so that the allusion to the body and the 'lower bodily stratum' is at once reductive and productive, a regenerative touching ground in otherwise stiff and etiolated discursive contexts. But Rochester's reductive gesture in this poem hardly has a regenerative aspect: rather it is an acerbic revelation in which the body is invoked in a simply negative register. To make this point is not to discount Bakhtin, for his thought about the carnivalesque was elaborated with respect to Rabelais and as part of a more general 'philosophical anthropology'. From a grand historical perspective, Bakhtin sees, in the centuries that follow Rabelais, the breakdown of that early Renaissance synthesis of the reductive and the regenerative. But the discursive manoeuvres of Rochester's lyrical poetry, the particular ways in which he opposes two vocabularies, two sets of values, require more precise historical location than Bakhtin's epochal formulations can suggest. To get a fuller sense of these manoeuvres we need to locate in social terms the language and attitudes that the poems embody.

Take, for example, the song beginning 'Love a Woman! Y'are an Ass!':

> Love a *Woman*! Y'are an *Ass*,
>     'Tis a most insipid Passion,
> To choose out for your happiness
>     The idlest part of *Gods Creation*!
>
> Let the *Porter*, and the *Groome*,
>     Things design'd for dirty *Slaves*,
> Drudge in fair *Aurelia's Womb*,
>     To get supplies for Age, and Graves.
>
> Farwell *Woman*, I intend,
>     Henceforth ev'ry *Night* to sit,
> With my lewd well natur'd *Friend*,
>     Drinking, to engender *Wit*.
>
> Then give me *Health*, *Wealth*, *Mirth*, and *Wine*,
>     And if busie *Love*, intrenches,
> There's a sweet soft *Page*, of mine,
>     Does the trick worth *Forty Wenches*.[5]

There is evident and self-conscious provocativeness in this. The misogyny above all, which gives point and direction to the whole poem, can perhaps best be understood as an example of that same debunking strategy which prompted the last line of 'Upon His Drinking a Bowl'. But Rochester combines this misogyny with a tone of aristocratic superiority, most evident in the second stanza, in which the sexual act becomes a drudgery to be performed by one's social inferiors. He thus produces a breath-taking nihilistic vision of the extreme inconsequence of the reproduction of the species—'to get supplies for age and graves'. The nihilism, in other words, emerges at the other side of the misogyny and the assumption of class superiority; these are a condition of that bracing perspective. If this is sublimity it is certainly not any familiar Romantic sublime.

It is worth emphasising that the aristocratic tone of this poem is indeed a tone of voice, one that can readily be adopted by such non-aristocratic writers as Oldham or Dryden ('When man on many multiplied his kind, / Ere one to one was cursedly confined'). So to allude to it is not necessarily to make any explanatory connection between the poem and Rochester's aristocratic status. But it is to recognize that the transformations that Rochester effects, the particular transvaluations of value he attempts, are made with discourses, words that carry social markings and take on their force in a highly stratified society. It may be, then, that these transformations are driven as much by social as by personal forces, or, better, that these forces are actually inextricable. At all events, Rochester commands, in this and other poems, a lyrical stance in which self-conscious provocativeness is articulated in a tone of aristocratic disdain for the petty concerns of morality, and it is this general stance which lends the poems their particular rhetorical attractions.

But quite what is conditional on what is hard to disentangle. My principal contention is this: in Rochester's lyrics we witness a transvaluation of values driven, not only by a body-based carnivalesque inversion, but by a social and political history which sets one discourse into conflict with another. In social and historical terms, Rochester may be seen as symptomatic of a wider crisis of authority, of the kind described by Susan Staves with respect to the Restoration theatre.[6] This crisis of authority manifests itself in a distrust of any secure language whatsoever, though this distrust is itself articulated in a tone of linguistic authority derived from the assumption of aristocratic ease. Most challengingly, however, the philosophi-

cal ambition of the poems, and their real humaneness, are
inseparable from, indeed produced by, this discourse of aristocratic assumption and half-serious misogyny.

This stance can be seen at its purest in a poem like 'Against
Constancy':

> Tell me no more of constancy,
>     that frivolous pretence,
> Of cold age, narrow jealousie,
>     disease and want of sence.
>
> Let duller fools on whom kind chance
>     some easy heart has thrown,
> Despairing higher to advance,
>     be kind to one alone.
>
> Old men and weak, whose idle flame,
>     their own defects discovers,
> Since changing can but spread their shame,
>     ought to be constant lovers;
>
> But we, whose heart do justly swell,
>     with no vain-glorious pride,
> Who know how we in love excell,
>     long to be often try'd.
>
> Then bring my Bath, and strew my bed,
>     as each kind night returns,
> Ile change a Mistress till i'me dead,
>     and fate change me for worms.[7]

The pleasure that this offers to its reader is of a momentary
suspension of the usual moral rules. It provocatively, but easily
and confidently, assigns constancy to the pretences of those
who have an interest in it from their own weakness. The poet
places himself superbly outside the usual constraints, by right
of his excellence as a lover. The poem takes the form of an
argument, like so much seventeenth-century lyrical poetry;
part of the reader's pleasure is to watch its 'turns', as the
various stages of the argument are propounded. This is not to
be taken in all seriousness, of course; the poem is an exercise in
virtuosity, where an outrageous conclusion is reached from an
outrageous premise. And this conclusion: 'Then bring my

Bath, and strew my bed, / As each kind night returns', is couched in a language of grand command the counterpart, perhaps, of that debunking 'cunt' of 'Upon His Drinking a Bowl'. This is not euphemism but a self-conscious dressing-up in grand language of what both poet and reader know to be self-justification (if not boasting). One of the principal pleasures that the poem offers is just this confident interchange of shared conscious knowledgeableness between poet and reader—provided that the reader is willing, of course, to enter into that exchange.

But the poem does not end with the ostensible conclusion to its 'argument', but with an altogether more dismal anticipation: 'Ile change a Mistress till i'me dead / and fate change me for worms'. Does this justify the self-glorifying hedonism of the poem, or does it undercut it? The first alternative is perhaps more consistent with Rochester's philosophical attitudes elsewhere, with his professed disbelief in the survival of the soul, and his insistence on the supreme value of the moment—an insistence that finds expression, in a similar context to the present one, in another lyric which 'argues' against constancy, 'Love and Life'. The second alternative, however—that the abrupt invocation of the prospect of death at the end of the poem undercuts the partly playful posturing that precedes it—seems more consistent with the experience of reading the poem. For the conclusion certainly effects a sharp change of register, in which suddenly a great deal more seems to be at stake than might have been anticipated. In this new perspective, the half-serious boastful hedonism of the poem appears both understandable and slightly pathetic. The reader who has enjoyed that knowing interchange with the poet is brought face to face with its conditions of existence—though this need not frighten her or him back into 'morality' but rather exact a painful admiration at the poet's willingness to entertain this level of self-consciousness.

'Against Constancy', then, provides an especially clear example of a provocative 'anti-love poem' couched in the language of social superiority, which requires of the reader a willingness to enter into a knowledgeable, socially loaded interchange, and concludes by forcing, inevitably, a confrontation with the conditions of its own knowledge and pleasure.

Here, Pope's 'mob of gentlemen who wrote with ease', comes to mind though, to judge from Pope's explicit comments on Rochester, his famous line was not as simply admiring as it might appear—or as simply dismissive either:

> *Pope*: He [Lord Dorset] and Lord Rochester should be considered as holiday writers—as gentlemen that diverted themselves now and then with poetry, rather than as poets.
>
> *Spence*: (This was said kindly of them, rather to excuse their defects than to lessen their characters.)[8]

Both here and in the more familiar characterization you can hear the voice of the professional poet, for whom 'correctness' is a kind of indication of craft status. By contrast, the 'ease', the deftness, the speed, the wit of those holiday writers is a crucial part of their social self-presentation, as much as the tying of Dorimant's cravat.

The question of self-presentation in Rochester's lyrics is thus intimately connected with the socially-marked skill with which he manipulates socially-marked discourses. This can be seen in 'To a Lady, in a Letter', the ease of which we know to have been achieved after at least some polishing, for it exists in different versions, and of the two that Vieth prints one is considerably more finished than the other. I shall discuss what Vieth calls the 'final version'.[9] The complexities of lyrical self-presentation in this poem are in fact considerable. Its basic premise is an assertion of equivalence between the poet's passion for wine and his mistress's sexual appetite. With apparent generosity, the poet offers to allow Chloris as many lovers as she wishes as long as she allows him as many bottles:

> Think not in this that I design
>     A treason 'gainst love's charms
> When, following the god of wine,
>     I leave my Chloris' arms,
>
> Since you have that, for all your haste
>     (At which I'll ne'er repine),
> Will take its liquor off as fast
>     As I can take off mine.
>                    (ll.9–16)

The generosity of this attitude is compromised by the elaborate but nevertheless wittily executed *double-entendre* of the second stanza quoted here. How sardonic is that allusion to ejaculation? Since the starting-point of the poem is the equivalence between drinking and sex, to describe both as 'taking liquor off' may be thought of as a self-justifying exercise in wit—and indeed, something like this may be what one finally says about the poem. On the other hand, the poem may be charged with an element of sexual disgust, so that 'take its liquor off' appears as a witty but reductive way of describing sex, especially when contrasted with now slightly parodic '. . . love's charms . . . Chloris' arms' of the previous stanza. And certainly, two stanzas later, the tone of the poem shifts strongly against Chloris:

> Nor do you think it worth your care
> How empty and how dull
> The heads of your admirers are
> So that their cods be full.
> (ll.21–24)

At this point, though the wit of the poem is maintained, it is no longer devoted to maintaining the equivalence between drinking and sex and has turned against Chloris. Yet a better balance is restored by the brilliant conclusion of the poem:

> All this you freely may confess,
> Yet we ne'er disagree,
> For did you love your pleasure less,
> You were no match for me.
>
> Whilst I, my pleasure to pursue,
> Whole nights am taking in
> The lusty juice of grapes, take you
> The juice of lusty men.
> (ll.25–32)

This striking chiasmus is, in a sense, the point of the poem. This is ultimately a kind of display poem in which the poet demonstrates his virtuosity by sustaining an unlikely or surprising topic—'Upon Nothing' is, of course, another example. In the last two lines of the poem, the wittily executed equivalence established once again between drinking and sex stands solely by *force majeure* of its wit and not by any force of logic. So the predominant tone of the poem finally becomes one in which the rakish generosity, undercut by suspicions of sexual disgust at Chloris, is subsumed by the virtuoso display of 'easy' poetic skill. The generosity of the poem lies not in its compromised attitude to Chloris but in the style with which it makes the gesture.

The dependence of philosophical insight upon the inversion of the conventional language of love-poetry can be seen in 'The Mistress',[10] often praised by the more sentimental admirers of Rochester who have not looked beyond its opening lines:

> An Age in her Embraces past,
>     Would seem a Winters day;
>         (ll.1–2)

The poem is indeed one of Rochester's fullest exercises in that conventional language, but he only ever occupies it provisionally. The poem is marked by a series of twists and inversions in which the silliness of the poetic discourse of love is alternately conceded and contested. The toughest part of the poem, however, lies in its conclusion, for it concedes the uncertainty of that vocabulary of love in all respects except when it is a vocabulary of suffering:

> Nor Censure us You who perceive
>     My best belov'd and me,
> Sigh and lament, Complain and grieve:
>     You think we disagree.
>
>   Alas! 'tis Sacred Jealousie,
>     Love rais'd to an Extream;
> The only Proof 'twixt her and me,
>     We love, and do not dream.
>
> Fantastick Fancies fondly move;
>     And in frail Joys believe:
> Taking false Pleasure for true Love;
>     But Pain can ne're deceive.
>
> Kind Jealous Doubts, tormenting Fears,
>     And Anxious Cares, when past;

> Prove our Hearts Treasure fixt and dear,
> And make us blest at last.

Rochester's pervasive scepticism extends to the vocabulary of love while it remains in its positive aspect, but can be abandoned when confronted by the torments of jealousy. The only certainty is provided by pain. This bleak perspective is another of Rochester's debunking manoeuvres, but unlike 'Upon His Drinking a Bowl' or 'Against Constancy' this is not the perspective that we are left with at the end of the poem. Instead, he returns from this unpleasant certainty to re-enter the traditional language of love poetry in the final stanza, and finds an untypically affirmative conclusion. In fact, in this last stanza there is a submerged allusion to Purgatory and salvation; the torments and fears of jealousy become a kind of preparation for the blessedness of the last line.

So in this poem Rochester juggles the discursive economy of the poem to produce a highly nuanced affirmation; it is a precarious performance in which he moves in and out of the poetic vocabulary of love, and both corrodes and sustains its epistemological legitimacy. If the affirmation is untypical, its manner certainly is not; it has the force of a paradox in which the only proof of future blessedness is current pain, though this religious conception is used wittily and in a wholly pragmatic way.

Rochester's lyrical poems, then, juggle with various discourses, stretching them and discarding them, only ever occupying them provisionally. Sometimes, as in the case of 'The Mistress', this juggling can lead to a fragilely affirmative conclusion; this is the case also with several other lyrics, though none shows an unproblematic affirmation or one unhedged about with caveats and ironies. 'A Song' ('Absent from thee, I languish still'), 'A Song of a Young Lady to Her Ancient Lover', and 'Love and Life', all hold out the tantalising possibility of an intimate sexuality as a value, and write of it in a register which, while sexually explicit, is not belligerently reductive.

Thus in 'A Song', the poem is marked by a simultaneous confession of reliance upon the addressee of the poem and an admission of the poet's liability to succumb to temptation:

1
Absent from thee I languish still,
　　Then ask me not, when I return?
The straying Fool 'twill plainly kill,
　　To wish all Day, all Night to Mourn.

2
*Dear*; from thine Arms then let me flie,
　　That my Fantastick mind may prove,
The Torments it deserves to try,
　　That tears my fixt Heart from my Love.

3
When wearied with a world of Woe,
　　To they safe Bosom I retire
Where Love and Peace and Truth does flow,
　　May I contented there expire.

4
Lest once more wandering from that Heav'n
　　I fall on some base heart unblest;
Faithless to thee, False, unforgiv'n,
　　And lose my Everlasting rest.[11]

The apparently unironic use of that language of affection in the
third stanza is uncharacteristically vulnerable for Rochester.
The extended use of the language of salvation also differs from
its more pragmatic use in 'The Mistress', because it seeks to
capture the affective charge of that religious language—there is
little suggestion, here, of the self-advertising capturing of that
language for secular purposes. Indeed, there may even be some
orthodox implications in the final stanza. Its primary sense, I
take it, is to use the language of religion metaphorically to track
putative possibilities of emotional betrayal and separation. But
the last two lines of the poem suggest that the religious
language may be taken in a more literal sense, so that in being
'faithless' and 'false' to his lover, the poet may indeed be risking
his eternal soul. Thus in drawing on different discursive
possibilities here, Rochester, as elsewhere, activates one language for and against another, but in this instance inflects the
poem in a way which is vulnerable, tender, and even hints at an

element of self-revelation ('That my Fantastick mind may prove / The Torments it deserves to try).

'A Song of a Young Lady to Her Ancient Lover' (see Chapter 1, pp. 6–19) similarly inflects a poetic vocabulary towards generosity and tenderness; towards just those emotional effects traditional in love poetry, which elsewhere Rochester debunks or entertains in only the most provisional way. There is surely some connection between this and the fact that the poem is more consciously fictional than his other lyrics, which all at least hint at a wealth of personal sexual experience. This fiction, moreover, is a male fantasy of female sexual generosity, in which sexual gratification lies more in the unexpected provocation than the enjoyment. This is a situation that does not require the language of euphemism ('love's charms'), and thus, for once, does not require to be debunked. 'Love and Life' is a more typically provisional affirmation of sexuality. In contrast to some of the poems discussed above, I do not think that the point of the poem is its own bravura manipulation of the forms of argument. Rather, it is a poem so balanced that its reading is especially unstable. It is not an 'impossible object', a work of art which logically self-cancels, for the logic of the poem is wholly consistent. But it is a poem which emotionally, or in terms of its tone, certainly does undo itself, for it presents a possibility of pathos and commitment which is then—partly or wholly—counteracted by a rakish conclusion.

In several poems, then, Rochester inflects the discursive possibilities of the poetry towards at least provisional affirmations. But they retain a suggestion of other possibilities, of other more reductive or negative ways of negotiating their material. In this they are consonant with the more directly negative poems that I discussed earlier. In all cases, the poems represent bravura manipulations of different discursive possibilities and shifts in register, inflected now this way, now that. It may be that Rochester never achieves the 'sublimity' to which he 'almost amounts', in Hazlitt's words. He certainly shows himself the master of multiple discursive inversions; indeed, I have argued that his display of mastery of the poetic forms available to him is often the point of the poem. But what perhaps is most challenging in some of his lyrical poetry is the dependence, not of the sublime but of whatever is positive or bracing, on just the most reductive and even rebarbative assertions. This is a paradox which contemporary frankness—our refusal to be shocked by the obscenity of the poetry—has done nothing to resolve.

And this, perhaps, is as it should be. For neither the frankness nor the obscenity of Rochester need repel us now, nor especially appeal; as contemporaries of Tony Harrison and Fiona Pitt-Kethley we are not impressed, after all, by the language in itself. What remains distinctive, and challenging, are the particular ways in which Rochester inflects the various poetic—and anti-poetic—languages available to him. Such are the ironies of historical distance, that it now seems extraordinary to hear, in the accents of easy aristocratic command, a kind of nihilism that can be bracing, generous, and even humane. It is the precise historical location of these accents, and their particular, non-generalizable complexity, that now give these poems their general force.

## NOTES

1. William Hazlitt, *Lectures on the English Poets. The Collected Works of William Hazlitt*, ed. A. R. Waller and Arnold Glover (London, 1902–06), V, p. 83.

2. *The Poems of John Wilmot, Earl of Rochester*, ed. Keith Walker (Oxford, 1984), pp. 37–38. Hereafter *Rochester's Poems*.

3. This history is conveniently traced in *Rochester's Poems*, pp. 246–48.

4. Geoffrey Hughes, *Swearing: A Social History of Foul Language, Oaths and Profanity in English* (Oxford, 1991), p. 10.

5. *Rochester's Poems*, p. 25.

6. Susan Staves, *Players' Sceptres: Fictions of Authority in the Restoration* (Lincoln, Nebraska, 1979).

7. *Rochester's Poems*, p. 42–43.

8. Quoted in *Rochester, The Critical Heritage*, ed. David Farley-Hills (London, 1972), p. 193.

9. *The Complete Poems of John Wilmot, Earl of Rochester*, ed. David M. Vieth (New Haven and London, 1968), pp. 84–85.

10. *Rochester's Poems*, pp. 29–30.

11. *Rochester's Poems*, pp. 38–39.

# 'Upon Nothing': Rochester and the Fear of Non-entity

## TONY BARLEY

Because of its knowing exhibitionism, because of its flair, because of its mock-solemn pride in its own achievement, Rochester's poem 'Upon Nothing' brushes aside the kind of readerly interrogation invited by similarly impressive metaphysical displays. If Donne's 'Lecture on the Shadow' or 'A Nocturnall upon S. Lucie's Day' or Marvell's 'Definition of Love', provide a recent generic pedigree for 'Upon Nothing', Rochester's salient improvisation on non-entity requires of its readership qualitatively less imaginative effort to succumb to its arguments and admire its paradoxes. 'Upon Nothing' asks, supposing it asks anything of its readers, for a take-it-or-leave-it sense of delightedly amused awe. The strength of its regal negligence acts to make the poem seemingly impregnable.

The conceptual game seems everything in 'Upon Nothing', which ostensibly delivers an extended descriptive definition of non-entity, but which couches the absolute with which it deals in terms of the dissolutions of a vigorously playful relativism. Knowing that his subject will of itself take the breath away, Rochester's title advertises and enacts what is to prove an unremitting sequence of dextrous disintegrations. What can be constructed upon nothing? Why, nothing, of course, and with that apodictic flourish, the poem proper begins, apostrophizing Nothing as personage, attracting Nothing's attention, engaging Nothing in one-sided dialogue, lauding Nothing with priest-like compliment, taking for granted its pre-eminent dominion over the universe.

Immediately, the absolute Nothing is conceived in terms of a relativism and a negativity which instantly destabilize much, though not all, of the sense of Nothing as a supreme idealist essence. Although Nothing can have no point of origin, Nothing is here historicized. Although Nothing necessarily lacks parentage, Nothing is here familial, fraternally related to the lesser nothing, Shade. Although Nothing extends its compass throughout an atemporal domain and is therefore 'well fixt', Nothing is here both exclusive of Time's parabola, and contradictorily, is in a contiguous relationship with Time's eternally travelling arrow:

> Nothing thou Elder Brother even to Shade
> Thou hadst a being ere the world was made
> And well fixt art alone of ending not afraid.
>                                    (ll. 1–3)[1]

Not the father, and not the eldest, but merely the 'elder brother' to the shadow that Something implicitly casts, or to the shade which cloaks death, Nothing pre-exists the world's formation not as a total state but as a curiously indefinite condition, with 'a' being, rather than being as such. By avoiding the superlative, the poet prevents the polarization that could give the reader fixed points of reference.

Because exempt from finality, Nothing cannot fear it; because non-existent, the threat of non-existence holds no terrors, but what might have been expressed as a positive disdain for closure is given here in the unsettling negative form ('not afraid'). In eschewing a specified opposite, the poet alludes to a vaguely circumscribed 'other' realm enjoying no discrete category. With similar effect, the noun-participle 'ending', which delays conclusion infinitely, undercuts Nothing's fearlessness by an indeterminacy which is already Nothing's own attribute. This first stanza then admits to solid ground even in commencement, the certainty of its tone establishing itself in contradiction to its ambiguously provisional sense. Such a tension holds, to a greater or lesser extent, throughout the following ten stanzas of the poem, in which Rochester rehearses his heretical cosmology and dismisses all denials of Nothing's omnipotence as pretentious.

David Vieth, in his edition of Rochester's poems, summarizes and contextualizes the poem's thesis as follows:

> Orthodox Christian theology holds that God created the universe out of nothing (the usual version) or chaos (the variation adopted by Milton in *Paradise Lost*). Hence,

according to a paradoxical tradition which developed as a corollary, this non-existent nothing is the source or unformed raw material of all things in the Creation, without which they could not exist.[2]

Having run the film of creation in reverse until it has spun off its reel, the poet steps back authoritatively into the absences of pre-existence, characterizing in a single disarming line the negative pre-conditions which pertained prior to substance and dimension: 'Ere Time and Place were, Time and Place were not', a statement of such necessary tautology that its bewildering resonance is offset by the persuasive force of its simple logic. The insistent combination of Time and Place, and the impossibility of imagining a time before Time and matter before Place, both governed by that seemingly artless 'Ere' (which, used quite unembarrassedly, demonstrates language's inability to convey non-existence), challengingly harks back of course to (Augustinian) theology's refusal to take interest in the absence 'before' creation, but also anticipates modern scientific myths of origin in which the problem of the ultimate anterior stubbornly remains.

It is interesting—though inevitable—that modern, popular-scientific accounts of cosmology encounter an identical incapacity to explain other than in notional abstractions the initial configurations that led to the formation of the universe. This, for example, is Stephen Hawking in his wryly titled *A Brief History of Time*:

> In order to predict how the universe should have started off, one needs laws that hold at the beginning of time. If the classical theory of general relativity was correct, the singularity theorems that Roger Penrose and I proved show that the beginning of time would have been a point of infinite density and infinite curvature of space-time. All the known laws of science would break down at such a point.[3] (p. 133)

> It was at the conference in the Vatican mentioned earlier that I first put forward the suggestion that maybe time and space together formed a surface that was infinite in size but did not have any boundary or edge.[4] (p. 136)

According to these characteristic accounts, the occurrence itself 'happens' in a zone of wordlessness; there is and was no beforehand, literally nothing preceded creation. The moment of origin moreover, is literally inconceivable: to grasp experientially what is proposed in the notions of 'a point of infinite density and curvature of space-time', or of a finite surface without boundary, is impossible. The concept of infinity here proves as teasingly elusive as Rochester's autonomous Nothing which in that one unspecified moment of '*When* . . . straight begott' Something, thus initiating Time; 'Then all proceeded from the great united what'. The *gravitas* is hardly straight-faced in this second stanza where the bizarrely abrupt 'What'—an explosive capitulation to non-sense—parodies the quiet disorientations carried by that governing preposition and those conjunctional adverbs 'Ere', 'When', and 'Then'; 'the known laws of science . . . break down' in this mockery of linear progression. The poet's amusement is barely contained (with Rochester sneering at 'the Something and Nothing of logicians' and punning obscenely on 'twat', as Dustin Griffin[5] suggests).

Rochester's playfulness in this first, cosmological section of the poem depends upon the promotion of a giddying sequence of mutually exclusive, but not self-cancelling, definitions of non-existence and theories of creation which the tone of self-aware panegyric winkingly pretends to find self-consistent. So Nothing features alternately as a positive and as a negative condition. The imagination has little problem picturing a positive nothing as an absence within and in opposition to which substance exists, the model for which might be that of an inverse vacuum. Negative nothing on the other hand, demands a fraction more sleight of mind in conceiving. Carl Sagan's attempt to describe such negative nothing in relation to the 'Big Bang' hypothesis of the origin of the universe is unsatisfying, but nonetheless helpful:

> In that titanic cosmic explosion, the universe began an expansion which has never ceased. It is misleading to describe the expansion of the universe as a sort of distending bubble viewed from the outside. By definition, nothing we can ever know about *was* outside. It is better

> to think of it from the inside, perhaps with grid lines—
> imagined to adhere to the moving fabric of space—
> expanding uniformly in all directions . . .[6]

It is particularly in the later parts of the poem that Nothing
comes increasingly to feature as pure non-entity. At the outset
however, negative Nothing is as yet a shadow of that other
multiple Nothing with its own 'being'—the 'primitive'
presence, the 'sole original', the 'fruitful Emptiness', the
begetter of a 'race' of 'offspring', the dark 'mighty power' ruling
a once 'peaceful realm'.

In his reading of the poem, Griffin rightly notes that it
proposes variant, mutually exclusive 'stories of creation':

> (1) Nothing begot Something, and from their incestuous
> union all else followed (st.2); (2) Something was severed
> or sundered from Nothing, as Eve was sundered from
> Adam's side, and subsequently severed or 'snatched' from
> Nothing's hand 'men, beasts', etc. (sts.3–4); (3) with
> terms now shifted from concrete to abstract, from 'Some-
> thing' to 'Matter', Matter is born of Nothing but frus-
> trates Nothing's desire for incestuous union, fleeing from
> its embrace, joining in rebellion against Nothing with
> Form, Light, Time, and Place (sts.5–6)[7] p. 270.

By transposing Rochester's mainly active formulations (stanza
3 excepted) into his own mainly passive account, Griffin avoids
the wheeling ambiguities of, for example, stanza 4, where the
possible syntactical reversal confuses subject and object, and
thus upsets all sense of the respective powers of Something and
Nothing:

> Yet Somthing did thy mighty power command
> And from thy fruitfull Emptinesses hand
> Snatcht, Men, Beasts, birds, fire, water, Ayre, and land.
> (ll.10–12)

If a God-like Something commands Nothing's 'mighty power',
equally, Nothing's 'mighty power' commands Something,
which proceeds thenceforth to its hyper-Promethean mission,
purloining from Nothing not only fire, but every other com-
ponent of being. Nonetheless, Griffin's inventory of the poet's

tales of creation illuminates what the poem pretends to
obscure, and the critic is persuasive in suspecting both that
Rochester is parodying 'the double account of man's creation
in Genesis' and is intentionally deploying 'discrepancies and
uncertainties in order to mock the process of explaining
origins'.

The jumbled, anti-linear catalogue which ends the stanza
quoted above, blasphemously jibes at the divine ordering
related in Genesis I, its repeated commas refuting hierarchy
and suggesting a chaotic equality. Moreover stanzas 3–6 tease
not only Cowley's 'Hymn to Light', but also, and more
obviously, the Miltonic gospel's narrative of Satan's rebellion
in *Paradise Lost*:

> Somthing, the generall Attribute of all
> Severed from thee its sole Originall,
> Into thy boundless selfe must undistinguished fall.
> (ll.7–9)

> Matter, the Wickedst offspring of thy Race
> By forme assisted flew from thy Embrace
> And Rebell-Light obscured thy Reverend dusky face.

> With forme and Matter, Time and Place did joyne
> Body thy foe with these did Leagues combine
> To spoyle thy Peaceful Realme and Ruine all thy Line.
> (ll.13–18)

The luck of history and social status precluded the imposition
of any Protestant *fatwah* on the writer of these Satanic Verses.
Something's predicted 'undistinguished fall' into a 'boundless'
future oblivion (Nothing's 'self') distends and twists the Angel
Satan's celebrated descent. Severed from the a-Deity Nothing,
which alone had particularity (as 'sole originall'), Something is
merely 'the *generall* attribute of all', hence 'undistinguished'
from the outset. The mass rebellion of the alliance of the
implicitly God-given abstractions, qualities, components and
conditions of existence turns the world of Miltonic morality
and the Biblical 'good' upside down. The revolt provides a
compendium of all possible modes of immoral and unnatural
challenge to rightful, established authority: the ungrateful
'Wickedst' betrayal of a loved child ('Matter'), the cowardly

treachery of that 'offspring' in accepting the assistance of an outsider ('Form') and ignominiously fleeing the parental 'Embrace', the deliberate, murderous deceit of 'Rebell-Light' in obliterating Nothing's 'Reverend dusky face'. In the obscurity provided by Light, the confederacy of Form, Matter, Time, Place and Body hatch a military conspiracy, motivated it seems, by nothing more than envy: 'To spoyle thy Peaceful Realme and Ruine all thy Line' (l.18).

The fact that Nothing's 'Line' comprises none other than the aforementioned confederates makes for a very quiet irony that passes almost unnoticed. But the following stanza (7) underscores the joke as, when all seems quite lost for Nothing, Nothing finds the decisive counter-stroke:

> But Turncote-time assists the foe in vayne
> And brib'd by thee destroyes their short liv'd Reign
> And to thy hungry wombe drives back thy slaves again.
>
> (ll.19–21)

Nothing's victory in this epic conflict is soon assured—not only because one of the conspirators is the inevitable 'Turncote', but because utterly malleable, Nothing can outdo its enemies in policy, bribing Time to destroy their brief tenure on power, re-enslaving this would-be independence movement in the 'hungry womb' of a new female Nothing which begat it in the first place. Once masculine, now feminine, the munificent womb greedily ingests and absorbs; the once creative space becomes a place of constriction and retention.

The two comparatively restrained stanzas which ensue (8–9) function almost in parenthesis as a kind of unintended ruminative digression. They show the poem beginning to stray a little into a less ambiguous modest and serious mode, where for once the wit serves a subordinate role, very nearly integrated with the thought—until now suppressed—that Nothing's 'truth' is a mystery:

> Though Misteries are barr'd from Laick Eyes
> And the Divine alone with warrant pries
> Into thy Bosome, where thy truth in private lyes.
>
> Yet this of thee the wise may truly say
> Thou from the virtuous Nothing doest delay

And to be part of thee the wicked wisely pray.
(ll.22–27)

The voice here is unassuming. The extended play on the right of the divine to pry into Nothing's privacy to find 'the truth' which 'lies', for once does not dominate, and if it causes a double-take on the reader's part, the result is not more than a smile, which does not detract from the reader's straightforward assent with the primary sense of Nothing's inviolable mystery. Similarly with stanza 9. Nothing takes nothing away from the virtuous, Nothing delays the final end of the virtuous which is to become nothing; in contrast, the wish for oblivion is the wise prayer of the wicked.

If stanzas 8 and 9 arise unexpectedly, and in a different key, as though another more subdued and solemn-wise meditation might be emerging in counterpoint, they also serve to mark the poem's place of transition from cosmological philosophy to social satire. Stoic wisdom, the judicious acknowledgement of the limitations of human knowledge, and of its paltry pretensions, is the transitional theme. The wicked may be wise but the wise are less wicked than laughably pathetic: 'Great Negative' (the tone of ironical assurance returns):

how vainly would the wise
Enquire, define, distinguish, teach, devise,
Didst Thou not stand to poynt their blind Phylosophies.
(ll.28–30)

Here the irony is engagingly obvious. Being blind, the wise do in fact see nothing, do 'vainly . . . Enquire, define, distinguish, teach, devise' despite Nothing's standing point, pricking all such bubbles of pretension. And again obviously, the catalogue of the vanities of the wise erases in dismissive self-parody the entire preceding science of Nothing which the poem has until now so sympathetically recorded.

Why is Rochester writing 'Upon Nothing'—and which of the poem's two main perspectives interests him more: the dazzling, all-embracing maze of cosmology we have so far been led (by the nose) through, or the gleefully contemptuous assault against a civilization in which every element of social dignity, social achievement and social virtue is shown to have as much

substance as the new clothes of the fairytale Emperor? Does
the poem's process enact a diminution, as has been suggested,
or is that first part an extended, delaying prelude to a position
which finds more excitement in the real absurdities of social
organization than in mythological speculation? So well
balanced is the poem that to suggest an answer favouring
either of these alternatives might well seem inappropriate.
Indeed, it practically becomes a matter of taste as to whether
or not the pyrotechnic brilliance of the first half's epic
metaphysics seems of greater moment than the second half's
slow-growing crescendo of satirical invective. Yet the very
extent of the shift of attention in the poem keeps such questions
naggingly alive.

When the metaphysics of cosmology are to all intents and
purposes done with, the substantial world of social (mis)be-
haviour remains. And here experience can be pinned down and
named for what it is. Exaggerated political, national and
sexual stereotypes mask their basis in the truths such clichés
typically inscribe. This grimly funny, utterly enjoyable
humour tells the world's whole story from the perspective of
the satirist so persuasively as to gainsay all and any challenge
to it, all and any detraction or contradiction or qualification:

> Is or is not, the two great Ends of ffate
> And true or false the Subject of debate
> That perfect or destroy the vast designes of State-
>
> When they have wrackt the Politicians Brest
> Within thy Bosome most Securely rest
> And when reduc't to thee are least unsafe and best
>
> But (Nothing) why does Something still permitt
> That Sacred Monarchs should at Councell sitt
> With persons highly thought, at best for nothing fitt,
>
> Whilst weighty Somthing modestly abstaynes
> ffrom Princes Coffers and from Statesmens braines
> And nothing there like Stately nothing reignes?
>
> Nothing who dwell'st with fooles in grave disguise
> ffor whom they Reverend Shapes and formes devise
> Lawn-sleeves and ffurs and Gowns, when they like
>      thee looke wise:

ffrench Truth, Dutch Prowess, Brittish policy
Hibernian Learning, Scotch Civility
Spaniards Dispatch, Danes witt, are Mainly seen in thee;

The Great mans Gratitude to his best freind
Kings promises, Whors vowes towards thee they bend
fflow Swiftly into thee, and in thee ever end.

(ll.31–51)

Four stanzas (11–14) attend quasi-discreetly to the state and government, indicting the hollowness of political programmes and social administration in alternately objective, delicate and quizzical tones, but with an increasingly venomous off-handedness and a noticeable increase in acceleration. They are followed by three driving stanzas of uncompromisingly overt invective, one speedily ridiculing and dismissing the clergy, the next reeling off scornfully a varied handful of national inadequacies (15–16), the last, an abruptly halted coda (17), that is a chilling judgement on what is promised, owed and delivered in relationships between people: this being the only stanza of the poem to broach the subject of *personal* interaction—or rather its absence. The momentum of the second part of 'Upon Nothing' suddenly brakes in this concluding stanza, and the poem stops short—and dead.

It takes only a moment of reflection to realize that Rochester is attaching precious little weight to the observations which make up his social critique, notwithstanding the validity of many of those self-same observations. The poet entertains no thought whatsoever of political or ecclesiastical reform, indulges no wish to remedy deficiencies in 'national character': any impulse towards correction would instance yet another of Nothing's gestures. At the same time, the inevitability of a state of affairs in which 'the vast designs of state' reduce to nothing, because treasuries are always empty and counsellors always empty-headed, is matter merely for perennial enjoyment. The ironical anger which underpins this whole section does not come from a stance of unheeded, malcontent worldly-wisdom, nor is it actually directed against its ostensible targets which are merely butts for the sparkling, mischievous humour overlying that anger. The bathos of stanzas 11 and 12 in which questions of Fate and Truth are the context for the 'vast

designes of State' over which politicians 'wrack' their breasts (!)
teases without griping, without outrage, while the puzzled-
pained confusions of 13 and 14 do likewise, with the joke
depending throughout on those simple-sarcastic qualifiers:
'highly thought, at best', 'weighty', 'modestly', 'stately'.

To be sure, all trace of the jovial seems instantly to vanish in
the explosive scorn of stanza 15 where Nothing is found at
home with clerical 'fooles in grave disguise' who flatter and
mimic it, appearing 'wise' by devising and donning an amor-
phous array of 'reverend' paraphernalia which both expresses
and cloaks their folly. But here too, the dismissive contempt
acts as if in excess of its stated referent, as though it were either
a gratuitous outburst, or had been transferred from some other
unnamed source. This same feeling is induced in the brilliant,
and lighter, penultimate stanza which rapidly counts off and
discounts 'ffrench Truth, Brittish policy, Hibernian Learning'
and the rest in an apparently self-generating list. Again, the
unsettling combination of show-off playfulness and antagonism jars on, as much as it excites, the reader, suggesting that
the poet's game has an ulterior function, one that is actually
careless of national fallibilities. One suspects that the more
wide-rangingly Rochester the sportsman pursues this Nothing,
the more his quarry is actually hounding him.

It is the final stanza which perhaps provides a psychological
key to the discrepancy between the tone of the assumed voice of
'Upon Nothing' and the oddly disturbing effect the poem
intermittently produces. The suspicion that there is an individual identity present at some remove from the poetic persona
periodically arises, and never more so than in this concluding
stanza. The notion that the poem comprises a masterly set-
piece exercise, is a demonstration of the playful possibilities
inherent in the paradoxes of the conventional topos 'nothing',
is one which the poet would like to have us believe yet does not
ever quite believe himself: the satisfactions of closure are
withheld or unattained. A sense of personal disappointment
and personal hurt dominates the last stanza in those masochis-
tically selected instances of unfulfilled expectation and
betrayal. 'The great mans Gratitude to his best freind, / Kings
promises, Whors vowes'. The very occlusion of the personal,
the child-like transference of hurt onto blamed hurtful others

who thereby represent an entire world of failed personal interaction (already defensively mediated by obstructive incompatibilities of status and role: 'great man', 'King', 'Whors'), suggests that the experience of emptiness is here Rochester's own, and that the moments of anger in the poem express the flip-side of the poet's own hurt. The indefinite nature of the poem's sudden closing thought, in which gratitude, promises and vows bend towards nothing, flow swiftly into nothing, and ever end in nothing, confirms this feeling—the on-going tendency *towards* nothingness in all such arrested interpersonal transactions inscribes a pathetic, rueful condition, despite the formal adroitness of these final lines.

What I am suggesting here is that 'Upon Nothing' consists of a series of defensive strategies through which the poet tentatively touches upon his own sense of non-identity. The external nothings of the poem are projections of a feared internal non-entity. The pressure exerted by a feeling of personal non-being occasions the poem but the poem itself seeks to resist that pressure by any means that it can find at its disposal. Neither the parodic philosophical game of the first half, nor the tongue-in-cheek social satire of the second encapsulates the dominant interest since the choice of subject matter and its treatment throughout the poem are primarily functional.

To protect himself from Nothing, the poet begins by juggling with the notional components of an external (idealist, original, ultimate) Nothing, ventriloquising the languages we use in the ultimately fruitless attempt to comprehend what is (apparently) outside of experience. Rochester assumes the existence of no positive absolute, no secure ontological frame or fabric which might effectively combat the Nothing which Being impotently interrupts. The perception of non-being that seems external proves continually to threaten the real world of experience and, more than that, to invade it. Thus, even while it is affecting to speak directly to Nothing, or to be speaking on Nothing's behalf, the poetic voice is unable to maintain completely its assurance. For all that the poet-persona takes pride in, and enjoys, the easy skill of rhetorical argument, the conceptual virtuosity, the witty humour, the capriciousness, these cannot be sustained, and the assured tone is finally a posture, a temporary stand against the overwhelming sense of negation.

In the first part of the poem the moments of slippage where the mask of the speaker, Nothing's eulogist, is slyly allowed to drop while Rochester draws attention to his own ingenuity, act to confirm the poet's self-confidence. In such moments the reader is let in on the parodic in-jokes and is tantalized with a sense of shared participation, with being offered the possibility of identification with the poet. But at the same time, the poet maintains the comedian's distance by fluidly re-emerging with his persona, refusing full identification, denying the reader security, and thereby manages temporarily to bolster his own sense of stability.

In the heady world of metaphysics, such defence mechanisms can work for a time but the process of the poem cannot put off for ever the need to attend to the real world, and Nothing's presence therein. So the social, and the personal which the social implicitly forms, come to dominate the later stages, thus offering insight into the poem's private motive. The humour is deeper, more assimilated here, and the reader has no effort to make in recognizing the truth of the poet's knowing social critique. But the changes in tome during the poem's final movement are more marked, and the coy, inflated, sweeping, knowing, jibing, inventively abandoned social observations which appear with such cavalier effortlessness throughout the resolution hint at an anarchic flair symptomatic of near breakdown. The posture of careless flourish fails to withstand the unlocated anger beneath it; the stubborn residue of what seem specific past frustrations and disappointments suggest a feared loss of control on the poet's part, with potential exhausted collapse just an arm's length away.

'Upon Nothing' is not about Death, or the fear of death unlike Rochester's other (later) foray onto that thematic terrain—his translation of the Chorus of Act II of Seneca's *Troades*:

> After Death, nothing is, and nothing, Death,
> The utmost Limit of a gaspe of Breath;
>
> (ll.1–2)

From beginning to end, Rochester's version is concerned with common-sense deflation and demystification, adopting an attitude which is level-headedly pedagogic. As nothing, death should hold no terrors whatsoever, any dread of non-existence is invented, is fantasy. 'Dead, wee become the Lumber of the World', nothing more, and if 'Devouring tyme swallows us whole' we should simply accept that 'impartial' fate:

> For Hell, and the foule Fiend that Rules
> Gods everlasting fiery Jayles
> (Devis'd by Rogues, dreaded by Fooles),
> With his grim, griezly Dogg, that keepes the Doore,
> Are senselesse Storyes, idle Tales,
> Dreames, Whimseys, and noe more.
>
> (ll.13–18)

The tone of the piece is completely self-consistent; no fractures or fissures interrupt it. Whether pagan or Christian, all 'devised' myths of *post mortem* retribution should be discounted *en masse*. Straightforward, unshakeable conviction is the key-note here, the assurance is real and unassailable but in no way dogmatic or strained—there is no need to insist. Rather amused by all the fuss, the speaking voice simply sets the record to rights.

The comparative complexities of 'Upon Nothing' might well lead to the deduction that without Seneca's guidance, Rochester is far less sanguine about reaching 'The utmost limit' of the last 'gasp of breath'. In his *Self and Others*, the psychiatrist R. D. Laing addresses the pathology initially associated with the fear of non-entity in terms of the following:

> Tillich (1952) speaks of the possibilities of non-being in the three directions of ultimate meaninglessness, ultimate condemnation, and ultimate annihilation in death. In those three directions man as a spiritual being, as a moral being, as a biological being, faces the possibility of his own annihilation, or non-being.[8]

Yet it is not the apprehension of these three 'ultimate' possibilities which is disturbing in Rochester's poem. The future as such occupies little of the poet's attention, the awareness is not of awaiting the eventual arrival of self-*annihilation*. The anxiety expressed in 'Upon Nothing' is already contained in, and centred in, the immediacies of the present.

Referring to his earlier study *The Divided Self*, Laing

advances a supplementary category of disintegration experienced by the individual:

> The ontological insecurity described in The *Divided Self*
> is a fourth possibility. Here, man as a person, encounters
> non-being, in a preliminary form, as a partial loss of the
> synthetic unity of self, concurrently with a partial loss of
> relatedness with the other, and in an ultimate form, in the
> hypothetical state of *chaotic nonentity*, total loss of related-
> ness with self and other.

It is this fourth possibility which applies most nearly to
Rochester's composition. The strategies employed by the poet
to erect and fortify a structure of personal security in the face of
what seems a total loss of relatedness with the world outside
the self are compellingly desperate. The witty playfulness, the
poised elusiveness, together with all the varied voices and
changing perspectives displayed in 'Upon Nothing', indicate
the poet at some deep level operating neurotically against that
invasive chaos of non-entity which mirrors his own internal
sense of imminent disintegration from within.

Perhaps it is significant that the extreme expression of
contempt in the poem occurs in stanza 15, the stanza which
attacks the clergy, but more important in this context, the
stanza which deals most explicitly with the pretences of
deception and disguise. A case of both transference and
projection, one might think. Rochester feels he knows inside
out what is crucially at stake in the adoption of disguises, or of
personae. In his Introduction to *The Complete Poems*, Vieth
makes especial note of the fact that the 'male speakers in
Rochester's poems can be ranged on a spectrum of identities'
(*Introduction*, xli), and he goes a step further in exploring the
attendant implications by drawing attention to the poet's 'real-
life' predilection for varying his own identities:

> Augmenting this multiplication of identities was the
> real-life Rochester's practice of disguises. As Burnet
> relates,
>
> > He took pleasure to disguise himself, as a *Porter*, or as a
> > *Beggar*; sometimes to follow some mean Amours,
> > which, for the variety of them, he affected; At other

times, meerly for diversion, he would go about in odd shapes, in which he acted his part so naturally, that even those who were on the secret, and saw him in these shapes, could perceive nothing by which he might be discovered.

The outstanding instance, of course, was the affair of Alexander Bendo, in which 'he disguised himself, so that his nearest Friends could not have known him . . .'

(*Introduction*, xlii)

'Upon Nothing' affects to be just such a pleasurable diversion but its dependence upon changing identities, acted so naturally, betrays anxious compulsion underlying its play. Disguised as Nothing's friendly advocate, Rochester seeks to distance and distinguish himself from non-entity; with the poem's concluding stanza this operation finally proves to fail.

## NOTES

1. Quotations from 'Upon Nothing' are from Keith Walker's edition: *The Poems of John Wilmot, Earl of Rochester* (Oxford, 1984), pp. 62–64.

2. David M. Vieth's edition: *The Complete Poems of John Wilmot, Earl of Rochester* (New Haven and London, 1974), p. 118.

3. Stephen W. Hawking, *A Brief History of Time: from the Big Bang to Black Holes* (London, 1988), p. 133.

4. *Ibid.*, p. 136.

5. Dustin H. Griffin, *Satires Against Man: the Poems of Rochester*, (Berkeley, 1973), p. 271.

6. Carl Sagan, *Cosmos: the story of cosmic evolution, science and civilisation* (London, 1983), p. 279.

7. Griffin, *op.cit.*, p. 270.

8. R. D. Laing, *Self and Others* (rev. edition Harmondsworth, 1971), p. 51.

# On Not Being a Very Punctual Subject: Rochester and the Invention of Modernity

NICK DAVIS

Rochester's slightly older contemporary, Antony à Wood, makes a distinctive claim about Rochester's commitment to study of the classics:

> He was a person of most rare parts, and his natural talent was excellent, much improved by learning and industry, being thoroughly acquainted with the classic authors, both Greek and Latin; a thing very rare (if not peculiar to him) among those of his quality.[1]

Samuel Johnson, coming across the claim in Wood's standard reference work and feeling obliged to do something with it, has recourse to sarcasm: 'He read what is considered as polite learning so much, that he is mentioned by Wood as the greatest scholar of all the nobility'.[2] It is instructive to assess the damage that would be done to Johnson's case against Rochester if Johnson were obliged to concede that, even in this one instance, Rochester might have been capable of defining and sustaining a valid intellectual project (Johnson characterizes Rochester's life as a series of moral and intellectual *evasions*). Nevertheless, the judgement of Rochester that Wood's testimony implies may be the more accurate of the two. As I shall try to show, Rochester engaged in—consistently and in all earnestness, if by unorthodox means—some of the more important debates of his time, and ones that have considerable modern resonance. His poetic writing, while not for the most part philosophical in the usual sense, is notable for its capacity to make intellectual 'clearings', or broach areas of perception where reflective thought is called into play. (In this he seems quite unlike Donne or Dryden, say, but shows a certain affinity with Marvell and the Cavaliers.) One of Rochester's principal concerns was with the nature of Reason itself, an issue much to the fore in the intellectual battles of the period; some of Rochester's growing readability—an observable phenomenon of recent times—probably has to do with the reopening of questions about Reason which Johnson and his contemporaries tended to treat as settled. This essay examines the proposition that his poems are written, in part but characteristically, out of engagement with an intellectual politics of general cultural significance.

## I

In Rochester's most mainstream-philosophical poem, 'Satyr', wheeled on stage in the role of adversary is a churchman who professes astonishment at the choice of targets of denunciation. This 'formal Band and Beard' (1.46)[3] can muster some eloquence in the defence of Mankind, and of Reason. His set-piece intervention concludes by apostrophizing the highest human aim or faculty thus:

> Reason, by whose aspiring influence,
> We take a flight beyond material sense,
> Dive into Mysteries, then soaring pierce,
> The flaming limits of the Universe,
> Search Heav'n and Hell, find out what's acted there,
> And give the World true grounds of hope and fear.
> (ll.66–71)

In a complex reply which makes up the body of the poem (ll.72–173) the satirist re-examines the churchman's premises of speaking, declared and unconscious, setting a more viable concept of Reason against the one that has been advanced ('Tis not true Reason I despise but yours', l.111), and giving more concrete form to his argument about human inferiority to the animals. Here as elsewhere Rochester defends and, more crucially, *defines* his project of writing (thoroughly intertwined with a project of living) against the ideals projected by an intellectual group and tendency attaining no small social influence in the Restoration period. As David Trotter has shown,[4] the chosen interlocutor of the 'Satyr' can be identified

without too much historical reductivism as a representative
Church of England Latitudinarian. By choice and circumstance (they were prominent at court), Rochester's embroil-
ment with the Latitudinarians seems to have been a continuing
one. In February 1675 Edward Stillingfleet, royal chaplain
and future Bishop of Worcester, attacked him, as the author of
the 'Satyr', in a sermon preached before the King—presumably as a response to his own appearance in line 74; it seems
probable that the poem's 'Epilogue' (ll.174–221) was written
by way of retort to the sermon. In the line that offended
Stillingfleet the 'Satyr' also makes slighting reference to one of
the works of the prolific Simon Patrick (future Bishop of Ely).
The most vituperative passages of Joseph Glanville's (anony-
mously printed) *Character of a Coffee-House, with the Symptomes of
a Town-Wit* (1673) are levelled at a wit figure in the style of
Rochester, and could be read as an entirely personalized attack
on him.[5] As doesn't seem to have been noted in this connection,
at some point in his career Rochester had a memorable face-
out, implying continuing mutual hostility, with Isaac Barrow.[6]
Eventually, at the time of his final collapse and illness,
Rochester came to value another Latitudinarian divine,
Gilbert Burnet, 'above all the Churchmen I know',[7] having
already placed churchmen above all other living people; it
coheres with other features of his life that Rochester's chosen
capitulation should have been to a member of this particular
party.

Trotter offers an explanation of why there should have been
endemic antagonism between Rochester, as notorious 'wit' at
court, and the Latitudinarians: concerned with social stability
in a country recently at war, they were opposed specifically to
challenging, provocative forms of language (though Glanville's
invective would, it should be said, scarcely fit the principle),
and opposed generally to the upsetting or questioning of their
society's most widely-held orthodoxies (though Trotter makes
less of this than he might, they had also decided what their
society's leading orthodoxies of purpose should be; more of
that presently). This explanation has some value, but I shall
suggest that there were more essential reasons why Rochester
should have been concerned with the Latitudinarians, as well
as they with him. I can point to an area worth exploring by

briefly considering one of the more bizarre incidents of Rochester's life—at first sight this has no direct bearing on his quarrels with liberal Anglican divines.

The object illustrated in the frontispiece to this book— described by John Aubrey, somewhat at a loss for words, as resembling 'a . . . of candlesticks'[8]—stood in Charles' Privy Garden at Whitehall. In June 1675 Rochester smashed it: coming in late one night with friends, and shouting (according to Aubrey) 'What! doest thou stand her to [fuck] time?', he seems to have led the attack. A drunken prank, no doubt (as the biographers say), and one which may have cost Rochester a period of exile from court; but Rochester seems seldom to have been intellectually incapacitated by drink, and here probably knew what he was attacking. The object, basically a very complex multiple sun-dial, is described by its designer (one Francis Line, a Jesuit based at Liège, who tactfully blames its destruction on winter snow and ice) as causing the sun's movement to show the hour, and also to show the differentness of hour around the globe, in as many different ways as human ingenuity has hitherto devised.[9] (The Jesuits were, it would seem, attempting to woo the English establishment as they were currently wooing the Chinese one, *via* sophisticated cosmological reckoning.) To Rochester, drink-crazed or not, this curious object represented, I would suggest, a nightmare of universalizing time-delineation and time-measurement—as, more pervasively and not in a form that could be readily smashed, did the programme for the reform of consciousness advanced by the Latitudinarians.

For immediate bearings on members of the Latitudinarian grouping, it may be noted that their interests, and to some extent their personnel, overlapped with those of the Cambridge Platonists, and of the Royal Society.[10] As Trotter explains, their 'aim was to promote a rational religion favourable to the increase of trade, empire and science'.[11] It is worth juxtaposing the nearest thing to a group manifesto, Simon Patrick's *A Brief Account of the new Sect of Latitude-Men; Together with some reflections upon the New Philosophy* (London, 1662), with Rochester's counter-definition of 'right reason' in the 'Satyr', written a decade later. 'Right reason' for Rochester, drawing on the Aristotelian tradition (its the equivalent for scholastic *recta ratio*, making for the realization of *prudentia/phronesis*), connects ratiocination equably with the practical needs of life. It is:

> That *Reason* that distinguishes by sense,
> And gives us *Rules*, of good, and ill from thence:
> That bounds desires, with a reforming Will,
> To keep 'em more in vigour, not to kill.
> Your *Reason* hinders, mine helps t'enjoy,
> Renewing Appetites, yours wou'd destroy.
> My Reason is my *Friend*, yours is a *Cheat*,
> Hunger call's out, my Reason bids me eat;
> Perversly yours, your Appetite does mock,
> This asks for Food, that answers what's a Clock?
>                                        (ll.100—09)

Delusive Reason, on the other hand, is a 'supernatural gift, that makes a *Myte-* / Think he's the Image of the Infinite' (ll.76–77). The satirist's interlocutor has, we may recall, spoken of piercing 'the flaming limits of the universe' (l.69) (i.e. the outer layers of the cosmic sphere), and of coming to know Heaven and Hell beyond, with Reason's aid. In a manner somewhat reminiscent of Pascal, Rochester is playing off his era's enhanced, thoroughly disconcerting, sense of human partici- pation in infinity (cf. the intellectual tradition of Galileo) against its more callow optimism about enlarged human powers of cognition, in the sense of powers to objectify.

Simon Patrick had written, conversely, of a Reason that can take human beings everywhere.[12] The 'Latitude-Men', in his characterization (they show 'latitude' in the sense of conform- ing to the dictates of authority and of being unwilling to enter into dispute about points of liturgy and doctrine) proceed with this enabling confidence because they already know the sort of thing that they are going to find when Reason encounters its objects. Most conspicuously, the 'atomicall Philosophy' or 'hypothesis' (the specific reference is to Descartes)—it and the ridiculing of scholasticism take up a good half of the *Brief Account*—is already known (i.e. considered, pre-emptively) to *work* with respect to physical space and the objects that occupy it. Accordingly, 'it must be the Office of Philosophy to find out the processes of this Divine Art in the great automation of the world'; after all, physicians are already doing the like with 'those little watches . . ., the bodies of animals' (p. 19). Suddenly, Philosophy has a massive but *realizable* project before it, releasing unquenchable longing for such clearly guaranteed returns:

> There is an infinite desire of knowledge broken forth in the world, and men may as well hope to stop the tide, or bind the Ocean with chains, as hinder free *Philosophy* from overflowing. (p. 23)

If churchmen swim with this tide, which is in any case irresistible, they will even be able to 'encounter with the witts (as they are called) of the age, that assault Religion with new kind of weapons' (p. 24).

Isaac Barrow can show us more about the reorganization of subjectivity that pursuit of this overwhelmingly-attractive cognitive project must presuppose. In the *Geometrical Lectures* of 1670 Barrow achieved, to his own satisfaction, a perfect mapping of temporality—i.e. all potential forms of motion (and so of activity) 'in' time—on to stable Euclidean geometrical space. This led him to a startling *aperçu* concerning the utter homogeneity of time:

> Time does not imply motion, so far as its absolute and intrinsic nature is concerned; not any more than it implies rest; whether things move or are still, whether we sleep or wake, Time pursues the even tenour of his way.

G. J. Whitrow explains that Barrow 'regarded time as essentially a mathematical concept that has many analogies with a line'. As Barrow expressed it, 'Time hath length alone, is similar in all its parts and can be looked upon as constituted from a simple addition of successive instants or a continuous flow of one instant' (cf. his pupil Newton's conception of 'absolute, true and mathematical time', whose linear course can be charted independently of any particular events and processes).[13] One of the attractions of this way of looking at things is that one can—as a psychological figment and despite *Quaker Oats*-packet paradoxes of self-inclusion—imagine one's own observing position (the apex of the 'cone of vision') as being definitively locatable as a point on the same already-given spatial-temporal co-ordinates.[14] To be a 'punctual subject', in the terms of this essay, is systematically to represent oneself in such an apparently stable point of mental 'vision', thus showing the entire potential space of motion, action and thought opened up by anticipation to knowing sight (as by the co-ordinate grid of a map). The 'Latitude-Men', *au fait* with a number of the period's more imposing intellectual developments, could present powerful arguments for the advantages— spiritual, practical, material—of developing such a mode of consciousness. Rochester, described by Antony à Wood as having been turned by the intellectual society of the court into 'a perfect *Hobbist*',[15] was sufficiently aligned with his era's vanguard Rationalism to enter into significant dialogue with the Latitudinarians. Nevertheless, he devoted a great deal of energy to defining, in these contemporaries' terms, what it was *not* to be, in these contemporaries' terms, a very punctual subject.

Does this attitude have its own counter-rationale? For our own era Martin Heidegger, going behind Kant's sense of the absoluteness ('transcendental necessity') of Newtonian categories of experience, has probably done most to define and explore a contrary set of mind. Heidegger indicates a good deal of what is at stake in characterizing early modernity as a threshold of transition to 'the age of the world-picture (*Weltbild*)'.[16] Previous ages made diverse picturings of the world, but only in the modern age has it become the norm to project, under the aegis of mathematics, the space of a single homogeneous picture of the world in which all possible 'subjective' picturings ought to find their rational coherence (there was no medieval or 'Elizabethan' world-picture, contrary to received academic belief—only picturings in indefinite non- or partial correspondence). Coherence is thus attributed to the human subject (Heidegger recalls the fact that Latin *subiectum* translates Greek *hypokeimenon*, meaning 'that-which-lies-before', p. 128) as the imagined beholder of an 'objective' representation whose internal coherence has already been mathematically established:

> 'We get the picture' (the German is more like, 'We are in the picture', but the English expression also suits the argument) concerning something does not mean only that what is, is set before us, is represented to us—in all that

belongs to it and all that stands together in it—as a system. 'To get the picture' throbs with being acquainted with something, with being equipped and prepared for it. Where the world becomes picture, what is, in its entirety, is juxtaposed as that for which man is prepared and which, correspondingly, he therefore intends to bring before himself and have before himself, and consequently intends in a decisive sense to set in place before himself. Hence 'world picture', when understood essentially, does not mean a picture of the world but the world conceived and grasped as picture. What is, in its entirety, is now taken in such a way that it first is in being, and only is in being to the extent that it is set up by man, who represents and sets forth (*durch den vorstellenden-herstellenden Menschen gestellt ist*). (pp. 129–30)

It is rather as if the distinctive form of the will to know has disappeared into the certainty of the objectifying vision; for Rochester, on the other hand, the will to know always presents itself in a recognizable form, and moreover one that requires recognition. To set a 'world picture' before oneself is silently to posit what Heidegger calls an 'anthropology':

> What is decisive is that man himself expressly takes up this position (*vis-a-vis* what the individual represents to him/herself as the guaranteed field of 'objectivity') as one constituted by himself, and that he makes it secure as the solid footing for a possible development of humanity. Now for the first time is there any such thing as a 'position' of man. (p. 132)

The drawback of an 'anthropology', in Heidegger's sense, is that it is an 'interpretation of man that already knows fundamentally what man is and hence can never ask who he might be' (p. 153). The disruptive question is thus this question of 'Who?', and it is very precisely the one that Rochester goes on asking.

## II

As modern commentators often point out, Rochester's poetry stands in a revisionary relationship to the 'conceited' poetry of the earlier seventeenth century. I wish to stress the more aggressive (or Bloomian-'strong') aspects of this relationship, particularly apparent in Rochester's very thorough reworking of his predecessors' handling of temporality. Poetry in the 'school of Donne' often produces a kind of hypertrophy of the imagined moment, where examination/exploration of time's dilatability for consciousness is set against some recognition of the inexorability of cosmological time; this cosmological time extends to clock-time and ordinary behavioural time, for many purposes, since mechanical clocks, rapidly improving in design, were conceived as small constructed imitations of the cosmic motions, and patterns of human time-keeping were modified by their development. Sometimes Donne pits the mind's capacity to explore its own sense of time against the aspiration to quit time altogether: 'The Extasie', 'The Good-Morrow', and the 'Hymne to God my God, in my sicknesse' are explorations of the idea from differing rhetorical standpoints. Marvell presents this motif with characteristic succinctness and availability for scrutiny in his 'Thus, though we cannot make our Sun / Stand still, yet we will make him run'. The most obvious written context for the remark is *Joshua* x 12–14, where God, at the prophet's request, arrests the motion of the sun so that the Israelites can complete a revenge on their enemies. The only slightly less obvious written context, and one that the argument of Marvell's poem very positively calls into play, is a passage from the key Augustinian treatment of human temporality, Book XI of the *Confessions*, where citation of the biblical event defines the turning-point of the enquiry.

Augustine's philosophical predecessors, with the authority of Plato looming behind them, had derived the human sense of time from the diurnal rotation of the visible cosmic bodies—in Plato's view this was the creator-god's first purpose in endowing human being with eyes (see *Timaeus* 46E–47C; *Genesis* 1:14 might be understood as endorsing the Platonic view). Augustine, however, is not satisfied with this position, and cites Joshua's battle in order to prove that the human time-sense must have a surer, more intimate experiential basis than cosmological time delineation:

I cannot therefore accept the suggestion that time is
constituted by the movement of heavenly bodies, because
although the sun once stood still in answer to a man's
prayer, so that he could fight on until victory was his, the
sun indeed stood still but time continued to pass.

(Book Xi 23; p. 272)

The capacity to measure time and compare units of time must
therefore be innate to the human soul: our time-reckoning
comes from within. Marvell's lines can be seen as hesitating
nicely between the claims of 'phenomenological'[17] intimacy
with time—in effect, the ordination of time through human
mental activity—and acknowledgement of temporal process as
imposed externality (it should be emphasized that these are not
views which can be *logically* reconciled). The necessary point of
slippage is, of course, the wordplay on 'Sun'/'Son': 'Temporal
process is ordained from outside us by the humanly-unaccoun-
table movements of cosmic bodies, most obvious in the sun's
daily rotation' / 'We can bring temporal process under a sort of
equivocal human control by going about the pleasurable,
though also risky, business of human reproduction', where the
son to be set in motion carries over some of the aura of the
divinely-created sun.

One could say that rationalism in the style of the 'Latitude-
men' pre-emptively reconciles phenomenological and cosmological time; or—a better critical handle on the position—offers
cosmological time in an absolute representation as the *a priori*
ground of all possible time-experience. For Rochester, this is to
concede far too much to sheer externality, including externality in the familiarized form of the man-made timepiece ('This
asks for Food, that answers what's a Clock?'). Although
Rochester admired Marvell, the Marvellian tactic of reconci-
liation by semantic sleight of hand is not in his style (in fact,
even by post-Civil War standards, his position on verbal
ambiguity seems to have been decidedly chaste). Rochester,
who in certain respects probably was 'a perfect *Hobbist*', does
not deny externality and mechanism as possible ways of
thinking about the human relation to time. His poetry takes,
however, a determinedly 'phenomenological'—that is, 'from
the inside looking out'—view of processes that may well be

Hobbesian-mechanistic in nature, while at the same time withholding the imaginary satisfactions of a pure phenomenology (a perspicuous mind's entire view of itself). It does this surprisingly by entering, when we set it beside Marvell's lines, into a still more complex relation with their Augustinian intertext.

'Love and Life' (for a text of the poem, see p. 44 in Walker's edition of Rochester's poem) sets up a sort of imaginary conversation between Hobbes and Augustine, where the still more pertinacious 'extremist' (Everett) logic of the libertine speaker has the final word. Hobbes and Augustine as delicately invoked here have, in the first place, a certain amount in common. In *Leviathan* the first had declared, taking his stand on the mechanical philosophy, that 'the *present* only has a being in Nature; things past have being in the memory only, but things to come have no being at all'[19]; and that memory 'is nothing but *decaying sense*'[20]—which helps to underwrite the idea that having one past life located 'in memory alone' is a desperately limiting condition. But Rochester's lines still don't quite read like Hobbes in paraphrase, and for some intimation of the wider spaces for thought that the poem opens up I would suggest turning to Book XI of the *Confessions*. Augustine also powerfully denies mind-external, objective status to past and future (unlike many of his contemporaries, and indeed unlike Hobbes, he is detached from the monumental past and organized future of the *urbs*), but in the interests of an entirely different argument. A large sweep of enquiry into the human experience of time begins by establishing the elusiveness of the temporal present as conceptual object ('If, therefore, the present is time only by reason of the fact that it moves on to become the past, how can we say that even the present *is*, when the reason why it *is* is that it is *not to be*.' XI, 14; p. 264), but offsetting this with the indubitable fact that 'we are aware of periods of time' (16; p. 266)—i.e. we must be capable, somehow, of measuring a time whose instants slip away as we try to focus our attention on them. The answer to the conundrum is, as one is beginning to suspect, that there must be something wrong with the proposedly unifying conception of time as instantaneous or punctual, and of time as objectifiable: Augustine will offer to resolve the status of the present, paradoxically, by asking 'where' past and future—entities that one would normally distinguish from it by definition—are to be found. Both are, as it turns out, aspects of time present (as Ricoeur notes, *praesentia* in the plural, implying an internal multiplicity), given that the soul has the special power to make the past 'present' through memory, and the future 'present' through expectation, and so to make of time itself a fundamentally intra-mental form of experience:

> It might [thus] be correct to say that there are three times, a present of past things, a present of present things, and a present of future things. Some such different times do exist in the mind, but nowhere else that I can see.

The soul apprehends time through 'distention' of itself—it is inherently and *sans* reference to cosmic time stretched out to encompass its past, its present, its future—and the time-experience *is* a continuing, necessarily somewhat imperfect synthesis of the three heterogeneous presences of time within. The potentiality of present time is enormously deepened, accordingly, through acceptance of the loss of what had seemed to be its one inalienable feature, the status of determinate instant set apart from other determinate instants through the logical dissection of time as linear progression. Rochester for his part seems considerably further from Donne or Marvell, say, than from Augustinian 'phenomenology', in his constant refusal to link time in any authentic, constitutive sense with the plottable movement of bodies in space.

We have not, however, quite reached the nub of the Augustinian argument about temporality in its bearing on Rochester's poem, since Augustine still wishes to explain how non-instantaneous time might 'feel' and be practically handled by the soul distended between memory, attention to the present and anticipation. His solution is to familiarize a complex but entirely commonplace form of experience by referring to any speaker's shifting comparison between what has been, what is being and what will be recited. The example is, moreover, a highly suggestive one in that the soul handling a verse-form (the reference is to quantitative verse, composed of short and long syllables) shows its capacity to measure time as non-instantaneous, exercising the capacity not in spite of but *because of* the empirical fact that the sounds of two syllables cannot both be present simultaneously as they are compared for processes of measurement. But this everyday achievement is also that of human beings stretched out across history, finding their way through a massive poem or song of God's devising (see 26–28, pp. 274–78). Rochester offers a parallel solution, seemingly arrived at through a radicalizing interpretation of Augustine that leads towards quite different philosophical territory. For Rochester it is precisely *in* discourse, *and nowhere else*, that the mind makes its imperfect synthesis of presents, constitutive of its sense of time. Accepting a premise of this sort, we can see that 'Love and Life', as a brief, shapely lyric poem, displays and operates the mechanisms of imperfect synthesis with shocking clarity: it is its own 'livelong minute'— approximately the time that its saying or singing will take— and then it stops. Augustine had already linked the human sense of temporality, in an example with multiple implication, to the experience of speaking something already set down for memory. Some of Rochester's best writing offers to go with the grain of an intimate temporality by absolutely foregrounding the duration in *différence* of linguistic utterance, consisting of whatever sense of time human beings might have.

That this is a space of *différence*, not mappable onto homogeneous Euclidean space, is shown clearly enough by Rochester's penchant for self-citation (in the just-cited poem, 'this livelong Minute' would of course count as an example) as an indefinitely extendable gambit of poetic writing. Reading of Donne's 'The Extasie'—for purposes of comparison—calls for the paying of close attention to the poem's writerly *Gestalt*: the argument as blocked out in the stanza sequence defines a closed, symmetrical pattern of statement; 3 + 4 + 5 + 4 + 3. Rochester, composing 'The Mistress' partly as Bloomian strong revision of 'The Extasie', cultivates a writerly effect of quite a different kind. At the fourth stanza the poem begins explicitly to comment on itself, from a new vantage point where the effusions of stanza three may also count as 'Heaven knows what;' but this is far from being the auto-destruction of the poem's project, in that the 'wiser men' imagined as interlocutors are drawn back by stanza five into the psychological-philosophical predicament (also nameable as the *madness*) of the speaker, before being given mocking proof that they cannot, but absolutely should, correctly interpret the observed quarrels of poet and mistress as demonstrating the Platonic-ecstatic nature of their love (stanzas six to nine). Discursive 'space', so understood, can be intricately and, in principle, endlessly interwoven with itself. Rochester's interest in the practice, and the limitless opportunity for switching between discursive levels which it opens up, apparently has to do with the making of a decisive theoretical commitment to the *sociality* of discourse: the originating subject of 'The Mistress' is not the expansive-defensive ego, à la Donne, but something not at all readily locatable at a single speaking position. Several dis-courses—spoken, gestural—of poet, mistress, and 'wiser men' are carefully co-ordinated in this poem, but it would be an odd reading that made them intersect at a single conclusive point.

Since approval of resistance to closure has become a conventional enough formula in contemporary criticism, I shall try to give the last comment sharper form with the help of 'The Disabled Debauchee'. The poem develops, patently enough, as a densely-choreographed movement between the threefold 'present moments' of anticipation, attention and retrospection. Rather less obviously this is a self-infolded movement, in that its most elaborately plotted correlation of future, present and past (the drinking-bout where the speaker plays detached statesman, stanzas five to eleven) rides on the back of an elision of the present through confident anticipation of future impotence, establishing the entire scene of the poem as one of vicarious action (stanzas one to four). When the speaking present enters as an empirical object of concern, it is in the scarcely recognizable form of this future's own retros-pection: what speaks in the poem can be hailed only as 'the ghost of my departed vice', a mode of address that doesn't solicit an answer. The visual space of the poem strongly evokes that of the memory as pre-modern thought conceived it, with manipulable 'fleets of glasses' and the wine-inspired conver-sation that issues from them ('volleys of wit') jocosely standing in for, respectively, the 'places' and memory-provoking images (*imagines agents*) of the traditional mnemonic Art.[21] The ex-debauchee *can* only look at the glasses; they are no more than memory 'places' to him. Nevertheless, these 'places' will

multiply as the buyer assembles fleets of them to do battle with
and deepen the vertigo of drink. By means of a carefully-
disposed *imago agens*, the all-purpose arousing image of an
erotic contest to fuck/be fucked by the link-boy, the 'statesman'
supplies the interlocutors with the sense of direction that he
has down for them. We are in—also looking at—what is
essentially a public space of theoretical persuasion (aggressive
persuasion and persuasion to aggression, sustaining the metaphors of battle), identical on its smaller scale with the one that
statesmen as such command through their adroitness (stanza
twelve). The poem co-ordinates several discourses—again, we
may take these to be as much gestural as linguistic—of admiral
present and past, of speaker future and present, of future
drinkers, of wise statesman. These discourses take their origin-
ators precisely nowhere: the drinkers' stated intentions are
negated, by drink and talk, and with the effect that they are
assigned someone else's; the speaker communing with his
future chums is pretty much like the admiral communing with
himself; the statesman in fact *wants* inaction for himself, the
condition under which he can enjoy his own wisdom. Closure
is available for these discourses, and so for the poem as their
assemblage—in the socially-approved form of battle, in the less
socially-approved form of firing 'some Antient Church' (an
interesting putting-together, it seems, of the depredations of
Cromwellian armies with the idea of giving some pious matron
the pox), or simply by going on fighting and thereby losing the
battle with drink. Closure, however, is always *for others* (it is
even as 'you' who goes on buying in the drink), diverting an
onlooker positioned somewhere else entirely. To be 'wise', to
think from the vantage-point of the whole poem, is to make—
though this is also scarcely a matter of choice—closure the
business of others.

## III

Or, more exactly, the business of the psychoanalytic 'other'.
Freud initiated modern investigation of transitivism, or those
many aspects of mental functioning which at some level imply
effective non-differentiation of self and other (see in particular
the 1919 paper 'A Child Is Being Beaten'). The term was

supplied by Charlotte Bühler on the basis of researches carried out in the 1930s (Lacan, summarizing: 'The child who hits says he/she has been hit, the child who sees another fall starts crying . . .'[22]), and the idea is a common factor in Lacan's shifting accounts of the formation of the human subject. I invoke it not in order to co-opt the masterly authority of Lacan, still less with a view to psychoanalysing Rochester (if one accepts the value of the concept at all, transitivism is a universal of mental functioning and not an individual psychic oddity), but on the grounds that Freudian thought represents our own century's most convincing attempt to unthink the classic modern position on the subject, and re-establish contrapunctal conceptions of selfhood. We can get to transitivism very quickly by asking, rather as Augustine asks of times past and future, 'where' the subject in 'The Disabled Debauchee' is to be found—the answer being, in its compelling objects, where the 'its' somehow becomes elided, passing into what is there to mirror (it). In a simplistic reading the 'brave admiral' finds himself as he wishes to be in his remembered youthful self. In a reading rather more adequate to the poem's logic the projected youthful self finds him, in an action that involves 'his' necessary disappearance into it. The relation between ego and ego's compulsive other is characterized (as classical epic or Ovid's *Metamorphoses* would tell us plainly enough if Freud didn't) by identification and aggression in forms that can readily and unpredictably swap places,[23] a movement recurrently tracked in Rochester's poems. It would be hard to think of another body of poetry where the phenomenon of transitivism, precarious basis of the social bond, is so strongly foregrounded; though one might also say that Ben Jonson's plays, in their different medium, issue out of a similar preoccupation.

In Rochester reflection on transitivism is, in a way that marks him off from Jonson, indissolubly bound up with reflection on the discursive fashioning of gender. If, by and large, Rochester's female *actants* explore the alternatives of abjection, ferocious or titanic potency, and masquerade, 'A Letter from Artemiza in the Towne to Chloe in the Countrey' exuberantly takes up the possibilities of an all-encompassing female performance. This is perhaps the most brilliantly coordinated of Rochester's larger-scale poems; in conceptual design it is more like 'The Disabled Debauchee' than it may look at first sight, in that it tracks relations of transitivism for the implied benefit of an observer who, in so far as he/she attempts to occupy this perhaps impossible position, will thereby be placed 'somewhere else'. Artemiza is not, patently and by her own self-account, this 'wise' observer—on the contrary, she hurtles along whatever tracks she finds with the huntress-abandon signalled in her name. The poem is structured as a sequence of disappearances (flights or headlong pursuits) into ego's compelling counterpart to ego, on the principle that social desire (we might say 'socialized' desire, which for the Freudian tradition desire always already is) consists of accession to the desire of the other; this calls into play a relationship of aggressivity towards an other whose attitude to 'self' one has somehow to take on without having the remotest chance of displacing it—'it' is where 'you' find yourself having to be.

The poem's chain of substitutive pursuit begins with Artemiza's accession to Chloe's wish to have the Town written for her; this already propels Artemiza as newly-created writer into the place of 'wit' as Chloe must be assumed to imagine it, since that is the place (such is the definitiveness of the outsider's knowledge, privileging/exposing the 'inside' knower) from which any valid verse written about the Town would have to originate. Artemiza declares the impossibility of occupying this position—she's the wrong sex (in the process she imagines a wiser letter that someone else might have written to her: 'Deare Artemiza, poetry's a snare . . .')—and then occupies it in any case on the contradictory basis of being an 'arrant woman' (i.e. 'Woman's' state is that of self-contradiction). This carries with it the suggestion that she may be able to appease men already in the place of 'wit' by flirting with them (cf. Chaucer's Wife of Bath's manner of crashing into spaces of discourse which men customarily occupy). Looking to shed the contingently-found character of 'arrant woman' (by 1.69 women have become a 'they', bearers of socially-compelled 'want' who don't understand what they 'like'), Artemiza produces an idealizing oration on love, which in its turn produces disparagement of all those people in the 'Lewd Towne', especially women, who lack such a vantage-point and such a vision. This will become funnier in relation to abject/ potent Corinna's later oratory on love and railing against 'the lewdnesse of the town' (l.236) with an entirely specified end in view: her destined victim has, we are told, never 'seen / A Creature looke soe gay, or talke soe fine' (l.241).

Artemiza's place is now, however (while we wonder what she's leading up to), taken by the woman she calls on to the scene in order to bear out the point about women that she's just made. This 'fine lady' who talks with such hateful fluency about the Town is in a sense what Chloe want—she gets the rest of the poem—and so also, in an available hostile slanting, Chloe, possessing the sort of would-be-insider knowledge to which only someone from the shires would lay claim, meanwhile ludicrously poses as a figure of pastoral innocence (an untaught Indian queen, no less). But she is at the same time and more compellingly Artemiza, aping her possible *arrivisme* (Artemiza goes politely 'visiting', this other is a base and appalling intruder), pushing men around with more adroitness than Artemiza seems able to muster on her own account (the 'lady's' husband purely and perhaps unknowingly acts out her will, finally by exiting from the poem for good). Succeeding as a rhetorician through force of shamelessness, bearing the knowledge of the Town that Artemiza won't speak in her own voice, compulsive masquerader (cf. the 'fifty Antique postures') who knows everything on the condition that she herself doesn't know where she stands, picking up the baton charmingly dropped by Artemiza in order to stage the more aggressive side of the Wife of Bath's social performance. Artemiza has the chance to observe and comment on her counterpart-plaything for a while, as this counterpart becomes briefly absorbed in her own compulsive plaything, the monkey (fantasized as a more acceptable version of a husband: 'Oh I could live and die with thee'). But the 'fine lady' recovers for long enough to disappear more completely into her own butt and heroine, Corinna, who very comprehensively acts out Artemiza's fears about 'wits' (compare Corinna's dumping, ll.194–208, with Artemiza's stated fears about courting scorn from these 'ill-humour'd' people), before tackling her selected male 'fool' with a ruthlessness of purpose which the 'lady' holds up for naked admiration within a frame of disavowal and

professed pity. Part of the attraction of female protagonists for
Rochester seems to be that they can be shown as propelling
themselves into society as masquerade in a way that the 'wit'
figure by self-definition cannot. I have offered a crude and
summary map of the poem, but one intended to suggest
something of its various discourses' very thorough imbrication
with one another, and at the same time something of the
complexity of 'being Artemiza'.

'Artemiza to Chloe' opens up an intriguing theatre of social
desire. However, this is a theatre, if we attempt to visualize it,
possessed of disconcerting spatial properties. As in Freud's
1919 paper on the position of the subject in common sado-
masochistic fantasies, ego is on the stage, utterly gripped by its
own performance in the place of the other; and with equal
psychic reality ego is watching this performance as an other's
aggressor and victim, occupying identical spaces when we
attempt to assign it/them to a fixed position in an optical
scheme. In terms of narrative presentation (*szujhet*) the poem is
a story about a sexual encounter, where a project of seduction
masks an absolute will to destroy and supplant. But this
proposed relation of included and including doesn't entirely
stand up to scrutiny, since the theatre of social desire is
gendered in its very constitution. (Freud will, of course, view
desire for knowledge as a mask worn, though generally with
benign consequences, by inveterate human curiosity about
sexuality and sexual difference: 'Y' expect att least, to heare,
what loves have past / In this Lewd Towne, synce you, and I
mett last', ll.32–33). This is not a space where desire—'social'
or 'sexual'—is seen; desire happens, for Rochester much as for
Freud, on the condition that absolute fixity in the representation *of* desire, *for* the subject, is unattainable. (Genuine desire
is not the narcissistic yearning of the male voice in the 'Mock-
Song': desire in its proper form, as the female voice in that
poem explains, can relish the wish to have its eyes fucked out,
as opposed to the wish to see its own completion.) Artemiza's
writing is made out of necessarily inconclusive encounters with
spaces and persons gendered as male, in relation to which its
imaginable originator is insistently gendered as female.
Freud's paper, in pursuit of its own wider argument, derives
representations of 'subject' and 'object' in the fantasies in

question from conflicts experienced in negotiation of the Oedipus and castration complexes, which impose a differentiation of perceived and self-perceived sexual identities. In Jacqueline Rose's summary, 'what (the paper) could be said to reveal is the splitting of subjectivity in the process of being held to a sexual representation (male *or* female), a representation without which it has no place.'[24]

It is worth looking closely at the opening moves of the poem, by virtue of which this writhing act becomes a 'woman's':

> Chloe, in Verse by yor commande I write;
> Shortly you'l bid mee ride astride, and fight.
> (ll.1–2)

—overtly a representation of the male scene of war, and the obvious unwisdom of a woman's attempting to enter it; not very covertly a 'women on top' joke which would, if explored, evoke a scenario of female sexual revenge on men who have been rendered passive. It is, however, important that the writing should mime its lack of full control over the joke: this would represent accession to *another* woman's wish; the lines ostensibly recommend decorous restraint. In other words, the joke remains covert, functioning only as a concealed link between the opening statement and the lines that follow. These allude to, by denying, a wish to be 'on top of' men, as a woman, and by means more socially perilous than ordinary sexual warfare:

> These Talents [which?] better with our sexe agree,
> Then lofty flights of dang'rous poetry.
> Amongst the Men (I meane) the Men of Witt
> (At least they passt for such, before they writt).
> (ll.3–6)

Artemiza abrogates the all-seeing position which ought to be the product of successful Daedalian flight; the ensuing mode of activity, self-unseeing but uncomfortably seen, is defined in contradistinction to but also in a state of endemic rivalry with that attributable to the wit-figure. Corinna's story will thus count as the extreme realization of conflicts about who is placed 'on top' and who is placed 'underneath' through aggression conducted in discourse, conflicts which have been set in place from the start. Corinna starts in the paradoxical position of one whose social currency as woman has disappeared through no action or inaction of her own whatsoever, but entirely through the placing self-removal of another, the 'Man of Witt' who 'Made his ill-natur'd Jest, and went away' (ll.199–200). By the end Corinna, self-recharactered, will on the other hand have placed a selected male in the 'fool' position with a comprehensiveness that no wit-figure could approach. Artemiza's 'huntress' position—in society, in writing—is an entirely imaginable and viable one which involves the acting out of well-realized contradictions. The wit remains a wit, however, through unremitting aspiration to be 'somewhere else', the self-disengaging displayer and manipulator of processes by which what is experienced as subjecthood comes into being.

## NOTES

1. *Athenae Oxonienses*, 4 vols (London, 1813–20), III, p. 1229.

2. *Lives of the Poets*, 2 vols (London, 1906), I, p. 149.

3. References are to *The Poems of John Wilmot, Earl of Rochester*, ed. Keith Walker (Oxford, 1984), which has been compared with *The Complete Poems of John Wilmot, Earl of Rochester*, ed. David M. Vieth (New Haven and London, 1968).

4. See 'Wanton Expressions', in Jeremy Treglown, ed., *Spirit of Wit: Reconsiderations of Rochester* (Oxford, 1983), pp. 111–32.

5. Here is a representative extract:

> (On the 'Town-Wit':) He is too often the *stain* of a good Family, and by his debaucht life blots the noble *Coat* of his Ancestors. (. . .) The School had no sooner '*dued* him with a few superficial besprinklings, but his *Mothers indulgence* posted him to Town for *Genteeler breeding*, where three or four wilde *Companions*, half a dozen bottles of *Burgundy*, two leaves of *Leviathan*, a briske encounter with his *Landlords Glassewindowes*, the charms of a little *Miss*, and the sight of a new play dub'd him at once both a *Wit* and a *Hero*, ever since he values himself mainly for *understanding the Town*.

6. For this anecdote, see John Adlard, ed., *The Debt to Pleasure* (Manchester, 1974), p. 33:

> As a proof of his [i.e. Barrow's] wit, the following is recorded: Meeting Lord Rochester one day at court his lordship, by way of banter, thus accosted him: 'Doctor, I am yours to my shoe tie.' Barrow, seeing his aim, returned his salute as obsequiously, with 'My Lord, I am yours to the ground.' Rochester, improving his blow, quickly returned it with

'Doctor, I am yours to the centre'; which was as smartly followed by
Barrow, with 'My Lord, I am yours to the antipodes': upon which
Rochester, scorning to be foiled by a musty old piece of divinity (as he
used to call him), exclaimed, 'Doctor, I am yours to the lowest pit of
hell!' on which Barrow, turning on his heel, answered, '*There*, my lord,
I leave you.'

7. Jeremy Treglown, ed., *The Letters of John Wilmot, Earl of Rochester*
(Oxford, 1980), p. 244.

8. Adlard, *op. cit.*, p. 78.

9. See Francis Hall (*alias* Line), S.J., Professor of Mathematics, *An
Explication of the Diall sett up in the Kings Garden at London, an. 1669* (In which
very many sorts of Dyalls are conteined; by which, besides the Houres of all
kinds diversly expressed, many things also belonging to Geography, Astrology, and Astronomy, are by the Sunnes shadow made visible to the eye)
(Liège, 1673); the *Explication* was also issued in Latin. In 1671 the Jesuit
Kircher printed a branching diagram of similar shape which attempts to
display, for purposes of comparison, the time and length of day in all the
major countries of the world. It is reproduced in Joscelyn Godwin, *Athanasius
Kircher* (London, 1979), p. 79.

10. For the intellectual character of the group, see in particular Barbara J.
Shapiro, 'Latitudinarianism and Science in Seventeenth-Century England'
in Charles Webster, ed., *The Intellectual Revolution of the Seventeenth Century*
(London, 1974), pp. 286–316.

11. *Op. cit.*, p. 113.

12. 'Reason is that faculty whereby a man must judge of every thing, nor
can a man believe any thing except he have some reason for it, whether that
reason be a deduction from the light of nature, and those principles which are
the candle of the Lord, set up in the soul of every man that hath not wilfully
extinguished it; or a branch of divine revelation in the oracles of holy
Scripture; or the general interpretation of genuine antiquity, or the proposal
of our own Church consentaneous therto, or lastly the result of some or all of
these; for he that will rightly make use of his Reason, must take all that is
reasonable into consideration. And it is admirable to consider how the same
conclusions do naturally flow from all these several principles.' (p. 10)

13. For all these citations and a valuable discussion, see Whitrow, *Time in
History* (Oxford, 1988), pp. 128–29.

14. See Michel Foucault's discussion of seventeenth-century rationalist
philosophies of representation in *The Order of Things* (London, 1970), Ch. 3.

15. *Loc. cit.*

16. See the essay of that name in *The Question Concerning Technology*, ed. and
trans. William Lovitt (New York, 1977), pp. 115–54.

17. I am much indebted to the interpretative unpacking of Augustine's
enquiry into time provided by Paul Ricoeur in *Time and Narrative*, 3 vols
(Chicago, 1984–88), Vol. 1, Ch. 1.

18. If I read him aright, he is taking Dryden to task in 'Timon' (see ll. 143–
50) for not having got semantic slippage under sufficient control in the
quoted couplet from *The Indian Emperor*—which fits in with the poem's

establishment of 'mine host's' old-fashioned tastes. The lines are, 'As if our Old World, modestly withdrew, / And here in private had brought forth a New.' The problem judging from Rochester's comment, is with 'a New'/ 'anew', indistinguishable as spoken. 'Upon Nothing' is, it might be said, a bottomless pit of semantic slippage; nevertheless, 'nothing' can be read as having a clear, distinct and single meaning at every instance of its occurrence, which has a good deal to do with the poem's power.

19. In an excellent critical essay Barbara Everett points out the relevance of this passage to the Rochester poem; see 'The Sense of Nothing' in Treglown, *op. cit.*, pp. 1–41, p. 8. I am generally indebted to Everett's reading of the poem.

20. C. B. Macpherson, ed. (Harmondsworth, 1968), pp. 97, 88.

21. Frances Yates' classic study, *The Art of Memory* (London, 1966), brings out the importance, for pre-modern conceptions of memory in general, of the *Ad Herennium*'s instructions for the cultivation of memory through a visual establishment of 'places' containing *imagines agentes*.

22. 'L'aggressivité en psychanalyse', in *Écrits* (Paris, 1966), pp. 101–24, p. 113.

23. Mikkel Borch-Jacobsen helpfully comments: 'As the Kleinian school has shown, envy is inscribed in a two-sided relation, not a triangle. It does not arise out of competition for the object (the loved, desired object); it focuses instead on a double (and not a third party), an interloper who is increasingly hated as the subject puts herself in the other's place and finds herself deprived of what then becomes *her* place'; *The Freudian Subject*, trans. Catherine Porter (Stanford, 1988), p. 36.

24. *Sexuality in the Field of Vision* (London, 1986), p. 210.

# From 'Nothing' to 'Silence': Rochester and Pope

## PAUL BAINES

In 1739 Alexander Pope, during the course of a 'ramble', stayed for one night at the Duke of Argyle's house at Adderbury. The house had belonged to the Earl of Rochester, and the legend is that Pope was given Rochester's bed. The occasion was celebrated in a poem ascribed to Pope and printed in three monthly magazines in August and September.

> With no poetick ardors fir'd,
>     I press the bed where *Wilmot* lay:
> That here he lov'd or here expir'd,
>     Begets no numbers grave or gay.[1]

What it begot instead was a rather starchy compliment to the patriotism and familial benevolence of his host—truly a father of his country. Rochester's famous bedroom prowess, and his still more spectacular deathbed repentance, are not the stuff of 'poetick ardors' for the mature and respectable poet, and Rochester is cited as a potential poetic forbear only to be effaced by a moral and political one.

Not all Pope's references to Rochester are so strait laced; there are a few approving citations in the poems, some fairly even criticism in anecdotes to Spence, some conscious reworking of lines from Rochester's poems and a number of echoes and memories. But Pope's biggest gesture towards the earlier poet was to publish (and continue publishing) 'On Silence', a juvenile imitation of Rochester's 'Upon Nothing'. Insisting on the youthfulness of the piece, Pope presented Rochester's influence as formative, even fatherly. Because Rochester's poem is itself about the nature of origins, poetic ones amongst others, I want to contrast these two poems, each a version of a trope of procreation (which Pope toys with in commemorating his stay in Rochester's bed) and thereby focus on some of the critical differences between the two poets.

I

Pope names Rochester's poem as his source, but 'Upon Nothing' is itself highly allusive. Rochester cannot have known the riddling 'Farai un vers de dreit nien', written around 1106 by the much-excommunicated Guillaume de Poitiers (another aristocrat-poet with a reputation for levity, blasphemy and debauchery); and in Middle English 'nothing' is used mainly as a modifier—'nothing loth', 'nothing offended', and so on.[2] But during the Renaissance the relatively neutral and uncomplicated word takes on a new urgency. Rosalie Colie has described how paradoxes of the time often revolve around concepts of nothingness, both as a reflection of God's creation *ex nihilo* and as a more threatening perception of physical or existential void. Seventeenth-century scientists had to describe and respond to the physics of the vacuum, so long declared philosophically and theologically impossible; theologians to cope with the potential blasphemy of giving a name to something which does not exist.[3] Brian Rotman has further examined the semiotic and iconographic impact of the mercantile adoption of the circular sign 'zero' in late medieval arithmetic.[4] In English the prime mover of this shift is Shakespeare, who may be said to have given 'to airy nothing / A local habitation and a name', as his repeated pluralizing and characterization of 'nothing' gives the word a disturbing new currency. Repetitions and palindromic oppositions render the word curiously vital, linguistically alive and kicking.[5] It is not merely the word-play which allows the Queen and Bushy to spin 'nothing/something' conceits in *Richard II*; 'nothing' is also a focus for the tragic ranting of Leontes, and for Hamlet's brutalization of Ophelia: the mythological 'womb' of nothingness reduced to the earthly and human vagina or 'nothing', the locus of birth and 'dying', fascinated desire and *horror vacui*.[6] *Lear* insistently iterates the nothingness of procreation in a world in which both love and language are split apart by a duplicitous arithmetic zero. The language of nothing is here both enormously inventive and tragically reductive; teemingly fertile in ideas, but in the end describing only death and absence.[7]

Donne inherits both this fertility ('some lovely glorious

nothing') and a more orthodox *contemptus mundi* which sees the world as 'nothing' but which also grabs at metaphysical truths precisely by compounding verbal impossibilities (so Christ can be 'nothing twice at once, who is all').[8] The theological imperative is here also a poetic one; 'A Nocturnall upon S. Lucie's Day' insists upon death in such a way as to reaffirm both the identity of the lover and the validity of poetry:

> For I am every dead thing,
> In whom love wrought new alchemy.
> For his art did express
> A quintessence even from nothingness,
> From dull privations, and lean emptiness
> He ruined me, and I am re-begot
> Of absence, darkness, death; things which are not.

This dense hyper-negation, underpinned by the quasi-theological creativity of love's art, proves to be a self-confirming model of poetic construction. Appropriately enough, this is the first recorded use of the word 'nothingness'—a new coinage in a poem which concentrates a whole lexicon of negation into a tail-in-mouth poetic autobiography.

Donne installs a poet-God to formulate and marshall the fructifying creativity of the nothing-symbol. Most of his successors follow him in rendering the difficult term part of orthodox theology, the void out of which God created everything, the necessary antecedent to definition of universal origin. The Bible gives us a God who 'stretcheth out the North over the empty place, and hangeth the earth upon nothing'.[9] In consequence, being made of nothing, we retain a kind of worthlessness: 'all nations before him are as nothing; and they are counted to him less than nothing, and vanity'.[10] This is a 'nothing' which actually entails presence and plenitude. God's ability to make something out of nothing was much stressed as a counter to Epicurean materialism, one of the few philosophies to accept the vacuum. Edward Benlowes's *Theophila, Or Loves Sacrifice* (1652) shows:

> Praise but doth *Inexpressables* expresse:
> Soul, Th'Architect of Wonder blesse;
> Whose All-creating WORD embirth'd a Nothingnesse.

> Who brooding on the Deep, Production
> Dispos'd, then call'd out *Light*, which on
> The formless Worlds rude *Face* was all dispers'dly
> thrown.[11]

Several other contemporary accounts envision the world as 'son' or 'daughter' of a feminized vacuum, 'the womb of *fertile Nothing*'; life itself becomes '*nothings younger Brother*'.[12] Traherne encourages us to become 'intimately acquainted with that shady nothing out of which the world was made', to look for 'that obscure, shady face' of nothingness from which the individual (and the world) is created.[13] 'Mother *Nothing*', the absence which God fills with presence, becomes a respectable pious figure.[14]

Another way of dealing with the problem of 'nothing' is to turn paradox into encomium. H. K. Miller has provided a history and list of Renaissance panegyrics on small or unworthy objects (fleas, poverty, pox, madness).[15] Encomia upon 'nothing' provide a special subset of such whimsies because of the conceptual and verbal difficulties involved.[16] The best known example is *Nihil*, by the Paris academic Jean Passerat.[17] The senses of 'nothing' are 'confounded' (Johnson's complaint in citing the poem as a source for Rochester), in that its neutral and logical meaning is, by repetition, distorted into a positive name for an all-powerful being. So 'NIHIL est gemmis, NIHIL est pretiosus auro'; and 'nothing' is safe in war, 'nothing' can walk without legs. The inflation of logic into ontology, marked by the capitalization, causes a semantic stoppage; but only a temporary one. The sentences read perfectly straight, and are of course actually platitudes; to chide your friend for being ignorant of 'nothing' ('NIHIL ignorare') offers no more than a momentary shock before it becomes 'learned in all thing'.[18] It is more serious to say:

> Tange NIHIL, dicesque NIHIL sine corpore tangi.
> Cerne NIHIL, cerni dices NIHIL absque colore.

But this is mere talk ('dices'); in the end nothing (not NOTHING) *is* more eminent ('praestantius') than virtue or greater ('majus') than Jove; 'Dilique NIHIL metuunt', the Gods don't fear anything. The blasphemous suggestion that we should raise altars to nothing (we shouldn't raise any altars at all) is erased partly by its own verbal play and partly by the untouched theological gravamen that creation was from nothing, by omnipotence.

Passerat's poem was much reprinted and imitated in Latin anthologies. It was translated into English heroic couplets by Sir William Cornwallis in *Essayes Of Certaine Paradoxes* (1616), with a much-expanded account of God's creativity ('Nothing but *Nothing* had the *All-creator*') and a more aristocratic politics, both of which offer a secure vantage point for essentially safe verbal play. A travesty version, published in 1653, reduced the paradox to a completely formless series of contingent examples with an almost authentically blasphemous disregard for order; God's creativity becomes just another syntactic accident amidst trivial satirical targets.[19] This is almost the world of the street ballad, and there are a couple of broadsides loosely in this vein. *The praise of nothing* (1635?) is a repetitive attack on women and marriage which hardly uses the potential of 'nothing' at all, reducing itself to conventional masculine morality.[20] A more interesting ballad is *Much A-do about Nothing*, originally issued around 1660 in broadside form, but much anthologized and expanded over the next 70 years.[21] At its most extended it contains 28 stanzas of jaunty four-foot triplets, again apparently unconcerned with form or order: the catchphrase 'nothing' forms a precarious unity. The verbal shifts between 'nothing' as logical place-holder and conceptual entity are entirely unpredictable. It mixes familiar moral truisms (in war it's best to have nothing, all great princes come to nothing in the end) with discreet units of contemporary social satire: gallants (who have nothing), lawyers (who can say nothing in their own defence), and whores (who are nothing). Politically, the ballad is an anti-Puritan celebration of the 'nothing' to which Cromwell, his son and his cronies are all reduced. The 'nothing' about which most ado is made, however, is a sexual one; the ballad invokes the Elizabethan euphemism for the vagina:

> What one man loves is another mans loathing,
> This blade loves a quick thing, that loves a slow thing;
> And both do in the conclusion love Nothing.

But if this is the focus of desire, it is also the site of creation, and here the ballad sets itself against all the traditional paradoxes by completely excluding the metaphysical agency of God:

> Fire, Air, Earth, and water, Beasts, Birds, Fish and silly men,
> Did start out of Nothing, a Chaos, a Den;
> And all things shall turn into nothing agen.
> . . .
>
> When first by the ears we together did fall,
> Then something got Nothing, and Nothing got all;
> From Nothing it came, and to Nothing it shall.

This is hardly existential angst; but it does evince a comic disregard for traditional pieties which most other 'nothing' paradoxes tend to confirm. Technically this is more radical than Lucretius, who at least asserts the eternity of matter (atoms are forever); here everything just 'starts' out of nothing.

In the main, however, though some of these paradoxes use 'nothing' to flirt with heterodoxy, the end result can be curiously circular and comforting: the problem is only verbal or academic. Mother Nothing can still be worshipped as God's consort. Nicholas Billingsley's verse 'praise of nothing' proposed that if God made the world from nothing, nothing should be reverenced.[22]

> Shal thee, from whence all things a being have,
> Lye dead, and buried, in oblivious grave?

Billingsley allows Nothing to speak for herself—she is very definitely female, and stresses her role in mothering her daughter (through the love of God) 'All-things' who has treacherously usurped her place:

> All Birds, Beasts, Fishes, rarest gems rich mines,
> From out my fruitful loynes, derive their lines.

Towards the end Billingsley reverts to logical misuse (nothing is so merciful as God, 'Nothing but grace, conducteth into glory') and moralistic warnings about the fate of princes and cities. But it is nonetheless an attempt to personalize the concept of nothingness, to make a genuine, if whimsical, encomium on Nothing. With these two poles of 'nothing' paradox, the comic equation of void and vagina and the orthodox tribute to the fatherly creativity of God, we can begin to speak of Rochester's poem.

## II

The critics of Rochester's 'Upon Nothing' divide into two camps: those who see it as *empty*—a tissue of commonplaces, mere wit or parody—and those who see it as *full*—a serious expression of nihilistic horror. Rochester's speculative discussions with Blount, Burnet and Parsons have all been rifled to provide a kind of existential key to Rochester's confrontation with the cosmos.[23] Equally, however, the parodic and intertextual quality of the poem has been stressed by Dustin Griffin and David Farley-Hills, in useful correctives to those views which simply turn the poem into Rochester's pre-conversion testament. These readings distance 'statement' into a commentary on the way in which language is used to address metaphysical questions. For Griffin, the poem draws on the tradition of 'nihil' encomia as a means of subverting creation narratives. So Rochester mocks and inverts the generative and sexual language of creation accounts in Cowley and Milton, while at the same time questioning the validity of *any* verbal account or intellectual study of the non-physical world.[24] David Farley-Hills, while broadly agreeing with this reading, tries to find a deeper artistic unity in the poem than 'the continuous current of negative feelings', which is all Griffin can discover.[25] 'Nothing' constitutes 'a metaphor to describe the ultimate meaninglessness of the world with which man has to deal'; accounts of the universe are revealed in their figurality and dependence on metaphor as mere projections of human desires and compulsions. I want to consider this kind of radical reading in terms of what it implies about Rochester's sense of poetic tradition.

'Upon Nothing' is situated at the convergence of the several interdependent literary traditions discussed above: the creation narrative, the 'nihil' paradox, the poetic sign of Shakespeare and Donne. All of these may be analogues rather than direct sources. Of the encomia, the two Rochester is most likely to have read, (because they were easily available), are Passerat's *Nihil*, and *Much A-do about Nothing*; Rochester's poem (also originally published as a broadside, in triplets) was placed alongside the latter as 'The New Nothing' in one anthology.[26] It is easy to find both general and close verbal resemblances: the later poem can come to seem like an echo-chamber, a vortex which absorbs and implicates all such speculative writing. Rochester's mix of an 'ex nihilo' creation narrative and political satire, the apocalyptic return to nothingness, the end of leaders in nothingness and the nothingness of philosophical study can all be found in earlier poems. Even the personification of and address to Nothing are achieved by Billingsley.

But the aplomb of the poem suggests a map of deliberate misreading rather than a problematic anxiety of influence. The gravity of the poem has shifted towards a balance between the universe and the world, the metaphysical and the physical: the two realms easily collapsed by paradoxical ecomiasts are here poised in formal opposition. They are linked as inverse metaphors of each other: the political world is concerned with problems of existence, while creation is inherently a political struggle. Rochester makes political use of 'nothing', in a far more critical way than the (mostly) authoritarian paradoxists. 'British policy' is equivalent to 'nothing', 'the Great mans Gratitude to his best friend' (1.49) and 'Kings promises' come to 'nothing', there is 'nothing' in the treasury or in 'Statesmens braines'. Theological study of nothingness (the pivot between this world and the world of spirit) is a matter for someone's rules: only the clergyman can 'with warrant' search into mysteries, there is a political structure even here. And just as politics is saturated with a problematic ontology (the politician worries about 'Is or is not' and 'True or false'), so the ontological section of the poem (stanzas 1–7) actually records a political struggle.

Rochester (parodying Cowley and Beaumont) makes 'Nothing' an 'Elder Brother even to Shade', with all the inherited power and privilege that suggests.[27] Creation is not some orderly hierarchization of the world's material by divine omnipotence but an impious and chaotic psychomachia.[28]

Nothing's 'mighty power' is 'commanded' by 'Somthing', obscured by 'Rebell-Light' and the victim of conspiracy:

> With forme and Matter, Time and Place did joyne
> Body thy foe with these did Leagues combine
> To spoyle thy Peaceful Realme and Ruine all thy Line.[29]
>
> (ll.16–18)

Rochester is picking up not only the military and political metaphors which Milton uses to envisage the opposition between God and Satan, but also the way in which the family is used as a model of the universe: in *Paradise Lost*, Chaos is married to Night and they have a 'realm' to 'reign' over; darkness's 'old possession' is an ancient claim to power.[30] The abstract conditions of existence are rendered concrete as the aspiring self-creators of Milton's Hell, not the ordered hypostases of God's plan. Nothing's revenge against Something is not the justified punishment by an all-seeing God of the 'Rebell-Light' Satan, but a cunning and secret manipulation of the same Machiavellian techniques:

> But Turncote-time assists the foes in vayne
> And brib'd by thee destroyes their short liv'd Reign
> And to thy hungry wombe drives back thy slaves again.
>
> (ll.19–21)

Spenser had described 'wicked *Time*' as the 'Great enimy' to life, and also envisaged life as a kind of political struggle between womb-like Chaos, which 'supplies' matter, and live things which 'borrow' it and 'invade / The state of life'.[31] Love (as in Donne, a metaphor for God) makes form out of chaos, 'whose sundrie parts he from them selues did seuer'. Matter is rebellious; 'with contrary forces to conspyre / Each against other, by all meanes they may, / Threatning their owne confusion and decay'.[32] But in Spenser these metaphors are themselves contingent, pointers to some extra-human dimension. Rochester extends the metaphor into conceit, playing out its implications and turning it into a self-contradictory form which cannot be redeemed by the process of finding new metaphors or by reference to God.

The family is a family at war, without a convincing

patriarch. If God is in the poem at all, it is as a sort of demiurge, the 'Something' who perniciously disturbs the reverential silence before him. Poetic accounts of creation normally use a generative model; Billingsley makes Nothing remember the emergence of 'skys, stars, earth, trees, fruit, animals' from her 'fruitful loynes'. Cowley sexualizes 'nothing' as a fertile womb for God's creation: in the odes he makes Light the 'First born of *Chaos*, who so fair didst come / From the old *Negro's* darksome womb!'; 'she' becomes 'the worlds beauteous Bride, the lusty Bridegroom He!'[33] Milton consistently envisages creation in terms of a seminal God and a teeming, pregnant chaos.[34] God does not so much create as procreate, bequeathing (as a metonym of the original creative act) idealized coition, Eve as the mother of mankind, and finally the 'wondrous birth' of Christ to the Virgin Mary.[35] But Milton also envisages *uncreation*, the absence of God, in these terms: the 'wide womb of uncreated Night', 'Th' intractable abyss, plunged in the womb / Of unoriginal Night and Chaos wild' where some fairly nasty copulation thrives.[36] Just as the devils 'create' Pandemonium out of matter in parody of God's creation, so Satan claims autochthonous status, 'begets' Sin out of himself, Death by incestuous union with Sin, and a whole race of verminous progeny proceed from continuing incest.[37]

Rochester confounds both models. His own compact check-list of creation, reduced (perhaps significantly) to seven items, inverts the traditional order retained even in *Much A-do* by placing men first and the elements last and making the whole a kind of rape, a cross-breeding of God's creativity with Satan's:

> Yet Somthing did thy mighty power command
> And from the fruitfull Emptinesses hand
> Snatcht, Men, Beasts, birds, fire, water, Ayre, and land.
> (ll.10–12)

Though Rochester uses the sexual metaphor for creation as procreation, it is not here God begetting the world from mother Nothing so much as a bizarre series of accidental sexual metamorphoses which undermine descriptions of our relations with God and reveal them as fictions projected from human behaviour; God's metonym become Man's metaphor. Nothing

is, to begin with, an elder brother who begets out of himself
(again like Milton's Satan):

> When Primitive Nothing, somthing straight begott
> Then all proceeded from the great united what -
>
> (ll.5–6)

This is perhaps 'begot something straight away' but also 'begot
something which was straight', unlikely to need much of a gloss
to readers of Rochester. The 'great united what', if we follow
Paulson's reading, puns on 'great united twat', thus connecting
Nothing (in the obscene sense) with the image of the original
vagina and exfoliating the decorous eroticism of creation
accounts into a sniggering pun.[38] 'Fruitfull Emptinesses hand'
also suggests a kind of feminine expertise, while Nothing is said
to possess a 'Bosome' which can be pried into for its private
truths (l.24) or rested on in peace after a struggle (l.35).[39]
Nothing's embrace can be fled (l.14) but time 'to thy hungry
wombe drives back thy slaves again' (l.21).

Rochester avoids the crass misogyny of the 'nothing' ballads
but generates instead a more profound disquiet about the fused
lover-mother with male characteristics.[40] This is not an erotic
account of creation, despite Rochester's work on Lucretius,
who also uses 'seed' and 'mother' to describe creation processes. But then Rochester's poems, for all their unabashed and
sometimes brutal account of sexuality, rarely mention offspring, and when they do the terms recall those of 'Upon
Nothing'.[41] Procreation is more often a mistake, adulterous or
illicit, as in the comic nightmare miscegenations of 'A Ramble
in St James's Parke'.[42] The lack of procreativity is figured here
by the drying up of the imagery itself; it seems to lack fruit and
power as the poem develops, producing only the feeblest of
echoes in the final stanza where 'Kings promises' stand in
even-toned apposition to 'Whors vowes' and both possible
parent figures are dismissed as liars, creations of their own
untruth.

The legibility of 'united what' as 'united twat' suggests that
we all emerge not so much from the vagina as from a slip of
tongue (or lips), the space between words—especially abstract
and interrogative ones. The substitution of the interrogative
particle 'what' for the expected substantial noun indicates the

anacoluthic autonomy of language; there are no references, just questions. The poem's oddly paratactic feel and its deceptively meandering syntax suggest verbal ambiguity even within apparent form. It is noticeable that Rochester parodies Genesis (the creation of the world), rather than the Gospel of John (the creation of the word); this is definitely *not* Rochester's 'hymn to the logos'.[43] The only references to language as such in the poem come in 'Kings promises, Whors vowes'—hardly very auspicious utterances. The use of language in study appears delusive; Rochester omits the positive sense of 'knowing nothing' as a kind of wisdom, whose exemplar, Socrates, is mentioned by most paradoxists. Instead we have:

> Great Negative how vainly would the wise
> Enquire, define, distinguish, teach, devise,
> Didst Thou not stand to poynt their blind Phylosophies.
> (ll.28–30)

The succession of modifying distinctions in academic endeavour comes to be just an atomic and disordered cloud, powerless against final nothingness. Rochester has already demonstrated the autonomy of verbal concepts in attempting to deal with ontology: form, matter, time, place and body, all loosely connoting an Aristotelian physics, here combine in merely political union, voluntarily, demonstrating not only the perniciousness of creation but the generation of the world from false and untrustworthy language. The same relation is inverted in the worldly part of the poem:

> Is or is not, the two great Ends of fate
> And true or false the Subject of debate
> That perfect or destroy the vast designes of State -
>
> When they have wrackt the Politicians Brest
> Within thy Bosome most Securely rest . . .
> (ll.31–35)

The questions have a catachrestic freedom, a lack of syntactical connection, beyond any substance they might be held to refer to; Rochester's phrasing foregrounds *words* as the problem which builds or ruins the state and harasses the politician. Rochester suggest that we do not use language to talk about substance but endow it with the substance missing from reality.

Rochester's own use of the devious and paradoxical language of 'nothing' is praised by Johnson for its separation of positive and negative senses; of all the paradoxes his seems the most consistent attempt to use 'nothing' in a single sense.[44] By making the stance of the poem vocative rather than indicative, Rochester eliminates most of the merely logical play; no 'nothing is more x than y' sentences here. There is a kind of wholeness about the conception:

> Nothing who dwell'st with fooles in grave disguise
> for whom they Reverend Shapes and formes devise
> Lawn-sleeves and ffurs and Gowns, when they like thee
> looke wise:
> (ll.43–45)

Rochester's apprehension of a surface masking emptiness is hollowed out into a perfect bubble, a verbal construct which leaves nothing when decoded. Worldly success is an art of design, of wearing the right clothes, of signs which can never deliver substance. Rochester's stanzas are themselves models of transformation: out goes the logical 'nothing', so easily translated into orthodox acceptability, and instead we have a consistent perception of emptiness, inflated into whole units, like a vacuum in a series of chemical flasks.

Tone, then, is much more consistent than in the paradoxes, and there is a much greater sense of formal and rhythmic largeness. Rochester's triplets are not the quick-fire jollities of *Much A-do*, and his use of an Alexandrine as the concluding line of each (basically iambic) stanza gives the poem a kind of elegiac pause. The poem can't run on forever, like most of our examples; it begins with 'Nothing!' and ends with 'end'. But the precision of tone and form also make this heterodox demythologization more subversive than Passerat's ramshackle but basically orthodox logic-chopping, and the subjects of its mockery must finally include poetry as well. Its euhemeristic skill in elegantly unpicking the mythopoeic or 'poetic' character of the speculative mentality cannot actually end up spiritualizing it in spite of itself (in the way that Blount claimed when commenting on Rochester's baldly materialist

translation of a chorus on death from Seneca).[45] Farley-Hills
tries to make a case for seeing the poetic form itself as a kind of
redemption form nothingness, evincing 'the triumphant ring of
creation out of recalcitrant material'; but while coherence may
well be contrived 'out of the very material of chaos', this doesn't
mean that Rochester believed his own poetry had special
status. While Griffin's reading of the heavy metre as a kind of
'heroic chaos' seems bizarre, Farley-Hills's determination to
exempt the poem from the ironies it discovers in the formative
figuring of other poetic 'creations' seems contradictory.[46] The
poem demonstrates the generation of exact pictures of emptiness; but its beauty does not validate or privilege poetry so
much as mimic poetry's pretensions. Poetry has done this: it
has produced a visible vacuum, just as it can transform the
sexual organs to independent mechanisms or render a dildo a
live 'Signior'. It can make a paradigm of the world not just out
of chaos but out of *nothing at all*, except words. Poetry does not
escape the fundamental flaws of language; it actually embodies
them, as the purest form of an inherently metaphorical and
anthropomorphic system.

It would have been very easy, indeed normal, for a paradox-
ist of nothing to mimic God, the creator-poet. Every one of the
'nothing' poems I have considered makes some reference of this
kind; Guillaume de Poitiers announces 'Farai un vers de dreit
nien', making verse out of nothing as well as about it;
Billingsley thinks 'nothing' is 'A Theam, more fit for *Homer*,
then for me'. Passerat (followed by Cornwallis) begins by
looking for a poetic subject, and finding 'nothing': 'Invenit mea
Musa NIHIL, ne despice munus'. *Much A-do* celebrates its own
poetics of nothing:

> I'le Sing you a Sonnet that ne'er was in Print,
> 'Tis truly and newly come out of the Mint,
> I'le tell you before-hand, you'l find Nothing in't.

All the eighteenth-century derivatives of the 'nothing' theme
(and there are many) have at least the concept that a modern
writer habitually writes from or about 'nothing'.[47] There is
always some hint, however debased, of the poet as replicating
God's original act in imagining and giving form to that which
did not exist previously. It is a powerful metaphysic of literary

creation, and Colie quotes examples from Puttenham, Herbert, Browne and others.[48] Cowley's expansion of the Genesis narrative of creation is given not directly but reflexively, as an example of devout Jewish poetry, and his equation of the 'godlike *Poets* fertile *Mind*' and the '*eternal Minds poetique Thought*' is ornately explicit.[49] As the Son is the creative Word, so the Father is 'the world's great Author', a title not beyond the aspiration of 'the Author John Milton' whose situation as the recording poet is vividly foregrounded in several books.[50]

If 'Upon Nothing' is a parody which hooks itself into and sabotages its sources, effacing them or rendering them contingent, if it suggests that the world is not authored or engendered by the transcendent significations of God, that there is no haven outside the chaos of accident and figure, no reassuring presence (male or female), we can also see that any positive commentary on poetry is reduced to literally nothing, a speaking absence in Rochester's poem. 'Upon Nothing' is finally a self-ironizing test which inflates an old logical joke into a complete meta-poem which renders creative language (and the artist) conspicuously self-annihilating. It is a tissue of quotations, rearranged as graffiti; the saboteur remains anonymous.

## III

Rochester's poem was copied into a very large number of manuscripts and enjoyed much esteem during the Augustan period.[51] This may be partly, as Griffin suggests, through sublimation and misreading. The cool Addison provides a typical reference in *Spectator* no.305 (19 February 1712, the same year in which Pope's poem was first published).

> *French* Truth and *British* Policy make a Conspicuous Figure *in* NOTHING, as the Earl of *Rochester* has very well observed in his admirable Poem upon that Barren Subject.

But in an access of counter-subversion, Addison turns Rochester's criticism of British political inaction into praise of its lack of Machiavellian intrigue. Pope's 'reading' of the poem into a formal imitation also domesticates it politically, as well as sexually. Pope had a good deal of compensatory rakishness (a less familiar debt to Rochester), and was himself not above making dubious parodies of the Lord's Prayer. He 'played the rake' in writing to ladies, and wrote racily about Rochester's daughter.[52] 'On Silence' annuls or controls an instinct which Pope recognized well, placing a Hellenistic decorum on Rochester's art of graffiti. But there is also a much greater sense of having to accommodate the mischievous potential of 'Upon Nothing' as a model of anti-poetry; the very fact of imitation comes to prove the unintentional creativity of the original.

Pope reproduces Rochester's basic metre exactly (if more smoothly), and the opening clearly marks out the allusion to 'Upon Nothing' by encapsulating it:

> Silence! Coeval with Eternity;
> Thou wert e'er Nature's self began to be,
> 'Twas one vast Nothing, All, and All slept fast in thee.

Pope goes on to provide a version of the creation narrative (somewhat elucidated) and includes many verbal echoes; but the imitation is not actually a close translation. Pope was experimenting with satire at the time this poem was written; it was first published alongside his first clear satire, an imitation of Dorset.[53] 'On Silence' is a miniature satiric prospect of society, replacing the political burden of Rochester with a series of satiric class types. Rochester's politics of creation is toned down: the 'sway' of silence constitutes a 'gentle Reign' to which Silence's foes and rebels eventually return in a movement which recalls Rochester's but does not equal its bizarre intensity. Similarly, the worldly politics is more even-handed:

> The Country Wit, Religion of the Town,
> The Courtier's Learning, Policy o' th' Gown,
> Are best by thee express'd, and shine in thee alone.

Both court and country are equally vacuous in a stanza which comes as close as any to replicating the riddling technique of 'nothing' encomia. Pope brings the triplet into a kind of couplet form, with positive and negative aspects; he finds a number of inventive differential ways of using 'silence' as a category to define types of behaviour, but he cannot use the logical 'nothing' joke any more. 'Nothing' combined neutral logical functions within a sentence, a disturbing ontological connotation of the void, and a threat to the stability of language. 'Silence' does not function in this way; though it denotes the absence of speech (or of noise), it is not a word about words in the way 'nothing' is, nor can it participate in any similar unstable verbal play. The substance of Pope's poem is already something rather than nothing, a shaded category not an absolute one. 'Silence' has its ambiguities, but they register in terms of degree rather than totality, and its history is not based on verbal incongruity and logic-chopping. The Greek *euphemia* can be (negatively) the avoidance of blasphemy, or (positively) a holy silence, reverent speech, or even panegyric, and reverential silence can be the subject of straight encomium (as in a poem by Richard Flecknoe which may well have some bearing on Pope's).[54] Poets commonly envision silence as a personified abstraction with more or less divine status, and there is a whole range of doctrinal and poetic usage which celebrates 'sacred silence' in a positive way.[55]

Yet its associations with night and death do not render silence unambiguously beneficial. Silence can also be sad, sullen and gloomy, a mark of threatening stealth, separation from God, the emptiness of space, even hell.[56] 'To silence' emerges as a verb in Shakespeare and is often used to denote censorship (not to mention political assassination) in the seventeenth century.[57] *The Dumb Divine Speaker, Or: Dumbe Speaker of Divinity*, which describes itself as 'a learned and excellent Treatise, in praise of Silence' seems often more interested in avoiding the 'defects of the Tongue' (lying, flattery, 'murmuring', hypocrisy, blasphemy) than in the reverential aspects of silence.[58] This more chequered history is perhaps reflected in Pope's rather indecisive placing of silence in satiric context, at once a force for a darkly counter-subversive elimination of state enemies and a corpulent inactivity in the face of injustice:

> But could'st thou seize some Tongues that now are
> free,
> How Church and State should be oblig'd to thee!
> At Senate, and at Bar, how welcome woulds't thou be!

> Yet *Speech*, ev'n there, submissively withdraws
> From *Rights* of *Subjects*, and the *Poor Man's Cause*;
> Then pompous *Silence* reigns, and stills the noisie Laws.

Equally, silence is (ostensibly) good because it acts in the manner of a benevolent ruler, offering oblivion to confused mentality: 'Rebel Wit' ends up seeking 'a surer State' in silence's 'gentle Reign'; and

> Afflicted *Sense* thou kindly dost set free,
> Oppress'd with Argumental Tyranny,
> And routed *Reason* finds a safe Retreat in thee.

But this kind of political amnesty can also look suspect: silence is a way out of argument, a failure of reason. And silence also offers a false reputation to knaves and whores—it is a 'Varnisher of *Fools*, and Cheat of all the *Wise*'.[59] Both folly and wisdom must end, indiscriminately, in silence.

Yet this is not scepticism. By adopting a conditional rather than a pure negative, Pope has opened up the discussion of language implicit in Rochester. *The Dumb Divine Speaker* offers an intensely documented discussion of the uses of silence both to avoid error, lying and blasphemy and to give more weight to true and reverent speech. Similarly, Pope's poem is really about the use and abuse of language, reason and thought, whereas Rochester refuses to adopt this kind of balance. Pope has also shifted the creation narrative closer to the Gospel of John, which offers a mystical but reassuring account of the origin of all things in the *word*, the metaphorical and mystical union of language and flesh in the son of God; the problem of anteriority, of a referential world which will be safe for metaphor, is solved by God *speaking* the world.[60] Pope moves away from the sheer activity of creation towards a creation by thought which itself demands a much more intellectual engagement than the action-centred Genesis. On this basis Pope can restore the traditional and decorous eroticism of poetic accounts of creation:

> Thine was the Sway, e'er Heaven was form'd or
> Earth,
> E'er fruitful *Thought* conceiv'd Creation's Birth,
> Or Midwife *Word* gave Aid, and spoke the Infant forth.

This *is* a 'hymn to the logos'. Poetic 'fruit' is back, and yet personal sexuality is veiled in conceit; no elder brothers for Pope, silence is 'Coeval with Eternity'. And no punning on slang terms for vagina: one of the abuses of language is the dirty pun one finds in Rochester, the 'Lord's Quibble' that Pope sinks with a series of other verbal corruptions in the final stanza. The end of the poem is silence, but not *aporia*. Here the exclusion of direct reference to poetry seems designed rather to leave it out of ambiguity than to engage it in a self-destructive viral loop. The earliest version shows Pope struggling to reconcile the speech of poetry with the silence it celebrates; in the end he 'silenced' the problem by excision.[61] Blasphemy is translated into *euphemia*.

## IV

In the opening of *Davideis* Cowley plays on Christ as the progenitor of the poet-king David (paradoxically his own ancestor, as Jesus) in begging inspiration for his 'vestal' Muse. God is of course the father of the Word as well as the World. In Rochester this mythologizing idea of the 'issue of the brain', the progenitive connection between author and text, tends to be subverted, its coy sexuality framed and mocked.[62] Otherwise, writing is associated with sex only illicitly—rhyming for your pintle's sake, drinking to engender wit, the poetess as whore— or in grossly debased terms, with excrement.[63] Just as 'Upon Nothing' renders all origins, parentage and creation dubious, so Rochester disfigures this powerful metaphor for creative activity.

The metaphor is rejuvenated by Pope, however, both in the abortive and embryonic spawning of the hacks in *The Dunciad* and in its positive form: we began with Pope's denial that lying in Rochester's bed had 'begotten' any numbers. However, 'On Silence', with its celebration of a 'poetic' father-god, is offered by Pope as a kind of poetic filiation, a point of origin (as well as difference and departure). And, of course, Rochester's influence on Pope lasts much longer than the juvenile moment: 'Nothing' and 'Silence' raise issues which occupy Pope for the rest of his career. The association of silence and 'dulness' (stanza 7), reminds us that images of vacuity, of absence of definition, of the great Mother (Dullness), of noise, of the uncreating world and the phantom 'nothing' poet form the central anti-logic of that other paradoxical encomium, *The Dunciad*, while the fullness of creation from infinity down to 'nothing' is the argument of the genuinely ecomiastic *An Essay on Man*.[64] Rochester remains an important reference.[65]

Pope read his copy of Rochester thoroughly, marking, emending and comparing Rochester's imitations of Latin poems with the originals. Rochester's 'Allusion to Horace' formed a model for Pope's manner of Horatian engagement with the contemporary literary scene.[66] This process of comparison itself suggests Pope's own mode of ironic allusion, where the original acts as a moral and aesthetic standard and a necessary part of the reading of the 'imitation'. Pope displayed his imitation by printing parallel texts (which only happened to Rochester's 'Allusion' in the eighteenth century). 'Imitation' now includes originality—the original shows a point of aspiration, but also leads us to identify what is new. Origin and originality can be separated, defined. Pope's practice makes a formal issue of the imitation/plagiarism divide, and this comes to affect criticism of Rochester: Johnson, who starts to list the sources of 'Upon Nothing' and who identifies Rochester as the first Horatian imitator (the original imitator, as it were) is merely tart about derivations from Boileau in 'A Satyr'.[67] Under a new 'professional' code, the institution of copyright, so expertly utilized by Pope, cements the idea of intellectual as well as legal property, and its concomitant devices of individual style and signature.

Pope makes this 'self' public property, his whole poetic career homogenous with his own life, depending on his identity and integrity as a man. Pope was 14 when he wrote the first version of 'On Silence'; we know the dating because Pope tells us.[68] It was his first attributed imitation, published while still a young man in 1712, placed in the self-summary *Works* of 1717, and given a final revised form in the late career with a set of other imitations (Cowley, Spenser, Chaucer, Waller) 'done by the author in his youth' (1736). As the poet matures, so the notion of origin becomes more prominent. Pope evidently did surround himself with poetic models, and as his own status grew he published these versions, partly to show deference, partly to indicate a serious apprenticeship in a range of verse forms, and partly to subsume and efface them. Pope lisp'd in numbers, for the numbers came; but various poetic and political fathers encouraged him (one of them was 'mitr'd Rochester', the bishop—Francis Atterbury—who shared a name with Rochester's house).[69] We are brought back to a point of origin which almost deifies the poet; so many anointing fathers, presiding over a new creative force.

But fathers are there to be outgrown, acknowledged from an adult point of view; Pope publishes the imitations when he no longer needs to imitate for technical practice. In effect, Pope cites sources to open textual history up to a certain point, to acknowledge allusion, to gather respectable backers, and to indicate his own differential presence. We are not meant to look any further back than Rochester; Pope is not interested in opening up an endless train of intertextuality. Each poem mirrors the creativity of God in being an original creation, and Pope's care of the form is implicit in his control of all aspects of textual reproduction. If there are sources, this is just an acknowledgement of a poetic father, a worldly God with his own independence, now replaced by a new seminality. The text comes increasingly to represent 'his' self. Pope's unprecedented economic and typographical control of textual matters led to a series of self-confirming publications: the first *Works* at the age of 29, the construction of a self-edited 'corpus', the complaints when booksellers ascribed hack-work to him, the edition of the *Letters* (with all their promise of personal intimacy): a composite textual legacy of copyright and manuscript. Pope envisages a private individual to be found behind the text, with a secret biography which could authenticate the public verse: a poet with a history, with a process of composition. The assertion of a unified public and personal identity marks the emergence of a desire for an original, personal, speaking voice. For all its public stance, Pope's is a culture of the original moment, the inside story and the lure of inception.

The kind of research invited by such authorial display may take us beyond the organized tour and the printed instructions. The textual history of 'On Silence' is almost too neat: we prize the early holograph, not only because it is about the first poetical manuscript of Pope's that we possess but because it differs quite substantially from the published version and thus shows the steps in Pope's thought and practice (as well as allowing us to see that the poem published in 1736 was not actually the poem written in 1702). We hoard up the variants from another early transcript (this time, regrettably, not in Pope's hand).[70] We recover the small variants between the 1712 text and the 1736 version. Further, we read the marginalia in Pope's copy of Rochester, trying to decipher and interpret the smallest pen-flick against a poem.[71] Somewhere we hope to redeem a true creative origin from the disputed possessions of different figures in the tradition (not to mention the whole ground of language), replicating Pope's myth of original authority even in the act of dismantling the very poetic autobiography which gave rise to it.

Text and self cannot be identified and distinguished in this way in the case of Rochester. There is, of course, only too much public image in action, rumour, and disguise.[72] Even Rochester's dying body was turned into a public anatomy of repentance. But the poetic self—whether persona or not—makes no pretence of integrity or psychological order or private morality. For all the exposition (or exhibition) of self there is no autobiographical chronology; Vieth's editorial divisions look increasingly like fiction. Even the letters often cannot be dated. There is no organized oeuvre; printing is accidental and anonymous. In *Timon* the speaker is presented with a libel falsely ascribed to himself, and protests: but in the end lets it go round the town. Rochester's poetry, like Popes's, is a poetry of allusion, but without the same concept of fixity in reference and difference that Pope espouses. Origins are less in particular poems than in series of poems and in the wider realm of language. Early critics stressed Rochester's originality and style as if it were beginning to matter: Parsons, for example, declares that Rochester avoided 'sordid imitation'—'tho he has lent to many others, yet he has borrowed of none'; he always improved his sources.[73] For Samuel Woodford, Rochester had 'all his Father-Poets . . . outgon'.[74] But when Rochester himself speaks of unmistakeable personal style ('soe to write, as none ere writ before') we cannot tell whether he means it or is ascribing it to his conceited enemy Mulgrave.[75]

Rochester's notoriety encouraged multiple ascriptions and a

massive bibliographical problem. Burnet records that 'when any thing extraordinary that way came out, as a Child is fathered sometimes by its Resemblance, so was it laid at his Door as its Parent and Author'.[76] The 1680 *Poems* continued the cumulative scribal tradition in collecting any 'fathered' piece, and well into the eighteenth century 'new' material continued to be marketed as Rochester's. Tonson's 'respectable' edition of 1691 took Rochester from the spawning private textuality of the scribes and pirates and placed him within the confines of the printed and proof-read book; this edition began the work of canon-formation and critical and biographical estimation (as well as bowdlerization, trimming to an acceptable norm). In the absence of an integral parentage, Rochester's 'progeny' could be multiplied or 'castrated', the canon stretched or squeezed to yield a biographical image.[77] Divergent textual traditions both represented a kind of nostalgia for an 'authentic' personal Rochester—the true poetic wit, or the fantastic libertine hero.

The revolution in textual studies of Rochester brought about by the work of David Vieth has made possible some kind of history of this at once expanding and contracting universe. 'Upon Nothing', which we have so far treated as more or less unitary, was 'published' in manuscript form, and in a couple of 'unauthorized' broadsides during Rochester's lifetime; there are some 32 'primary' texts for consideration. They do not line up neatly; the variants in the manuscripts and early printed copies occupy more space in Walker's edition than the final text does. Harold Love's thorough and impressive attempt to schematize a directional 'genealogy' of the versions rests on the thesis that there must have been an original 'ancestor', a polished holograph designed as a kind of inner publication to a circle of court wits.[78] Love opts for qualitative assessment of variants as evidence of 'genetic relationships' between texts, arguing for the plausibility of a single point of origin (rather than trying to construct a non-directional stemma showing relationships but not source). The reasoning focuses on a reading which he takes to be non-authorial but which is nonetheless present in most of the versions and which should therefore descend from a unitary but defective text. This cannot, of course, rule out a multi-ancestor tradition, or successive (or careless) 'authorial' versions, or independent duplication of errors; as Love admits, this family must remain hypothetical. It seems peculiarly poignant that a poem which mocks the theogonic but error-prone fecundity of the word should receive such genealogical recuperation, and that such reconstruction should itself be based on an ancestral slip— 'nothing' for 'something', 1.42—from the 'fair copy'.

This is not to say that the text is chaos; its popularity may have stimulated an oral tradition which itself contaminated scribal copies, and its verbal sophistry actively promoted textual misunderstanding and clumsy emendation; but it is nonetheless more formally consistent than, say, the cheerfully anonymous and ever-expanding *Much A-do*. Even so, it is still hard to speak of a definitive authorial version, and the poem remains indeterminate by comparison with Pope's carefully arranged stanza-format, typographical emphases and note on date; here, even the variant holograph and transcript just serve to confirm the normality of apparatus, as a perfect 'vertical' model of text-formation. Walker's semi-diplomatic rendering of Rochester gives us a much more vivid sense of a poem, which does not in the end (or the beginning) need to care about form or transmission, than Vieth's tidy modernization, which extracts form and hierarchy from textual diversification—and in so doing, subjugates some of the poem's essentially 'horizontal' allegiances and references. Bibliographical study of textual transmission is, of course, vital in producing practical reading versions, but even more so in demonstrating the breadth, and limits, of possible texts. We must avoid making a Pope of Rochester, a bio-bibliographical entity out of a broadcast dissemination. 'Upon Nothing' and 'On Silence' present opposite accounts of the poetic and theological idea of origin; they are also themselves ontologically opposite, dividing accident from author in their very mode of existence.

## NOTES

1. 'On lying in the Earl of Rochester's Bed at Atterbury'; *The Twickenham Edition of the Poems of Alexander Pope*, ed. John Butt, 11 vols, (London and New Haven, 1939–1969), VI, 380–382. For the authenticity see Norman Ault, *New Light on Pope* (London, 1949), pp. 182–85.

2. See *The Poetry of William VII, Count of Poitiers, IX Duke of Aquitaine*, ed. Gerald A. Bond (New York and London, 1982), pp. lxix, 15–16, 63–64.

3. Rosalie L. Colie, *Paradoxia Epidemica: The Renaissance Tradition of Paradox* (Princeton, 1966); see especially 219–51 and 252–72.

4. Brian Rotman, *Signifying Nothing: The Semiotics of Zero* (London, 1987).

5. For examples see *The Merchant of Venice*, I.i.114 and III.ii.257; *All's Well That Ends Well*, II.i.95, iv.23–28 and v.34; *Coriolanus*, II.ii.80–82; *Cymbeline*, III.iv.135, IV.ii.300, and 367–68; *Troilus and Cressida*, III.ii.195–96, IV.v.78–81; references are to *The Complete Works of William Shakespeare*, ed. W. J. Craig (London, 1911).

6. *Richard II*, II.ii.32–37; *Winter's Tale*, I.ii.284–95. See also Colie, *Paradoxia Epidemica*, pp. 232–51.

7. Colie, *Paradoxia Epidemica*, pp. 463–81; Rotman, *Signifying Nothing*, pp. 79–86.

8. 'Air and Angels', 6; 'Upon the Annunciation', 7. For theological uses see also 'A Litany', final line; 'A Valediction: of the book', 53; 'The First Anniversary', 155–58, 171. For secular and metaphorical uses see 'A Valediction: Of Weeping', 9; Elegy, 20, 'Love's War', 41; 'Negative Love', 16. Quotations are from *The Complete English Poems*, ed. A. J. Smith (Harmondsworth, 1971).

9. Job 26.7; biblical references are to the King James version.

10. Isaiah 40.17; see also Daniel 4.35; Psalms 39.5; Proverbs 13.7; 1 Timothy 6.7; 2 Corinthians 6.10.

11. Canto II, stanzas VI–VIII, p. 24.

12. 'Davideis', bk. I., in *Poems*, ed. A. R. Waller (Cambridge, 1905), p. 251; 'Life and Fame', ibid. pp. 201–02; Joseph Beaumont, *Psyche: Or, Loves Mysterie* (London, 1648), Canto VI, st.102–03, pp. 82–83.

13. 'The First Century', no.30; *Selected Writings*, ed. Dick Davis (Manchester, 1980), p. 75. See also 'The Salutation', 'Insatiableness', and 'Third Century', no.1, ibid. pp. 19, 66, 84; and Colie, *Paradoxia Epidemica*, pp. 145–68.

14. See further Beaumont, *Psyche*, Canto VII, st. cclxviii, p. 115; Sir Kenelm Digby, *Two Treatises* (Paris, 1658), p. 498; Sir Thomas Browne, *Christian Morals*, second edition (London, 1756), p. 122; William Beveridge, *Private Thoughts: In Two Parts Compleat*, tenth edition (London, 1720), pp. 8, 99.

15. 'The Paradoxical Encomium with special reference to its vogue in England, 1600–1800', *Modern Philology*, 53 (London, 1956), pp. 145–79.

16. For philosophical problems with 'nothing' as a term, see Aristotle, *Metaphysica*, IV.v.4–7, and Hobbes, *Leviathan*, Part I, Chapter Four; ed. C. B. Macpherson (Harmondsworth, 1968), p. 108.

17. The original text is dated Paris, 1587. I use the text given in Johnson's life of Rochester: *Lives of the English Poets*, ed. G. Birkbeck Hill, 3 Vols (Oxford 1905), I, pp. 227–28.

18. But Passerat's joke that 'nothing' is better than the doctor to cure illness may be serious: the point is made as a devout conceit in Beaumont, *Psyche*, Canto IX, st.83–84, p. 143.

19. 'S.S.', *Paradoxes or Encomions In the Praise Of . . . Nothing . . ..*

20. A lightly 'corrected' text is in *A Book of Roxburghe Ballads*, ed. John Payne Collier (London, 1847), pp. 147–52.

21. I use the text from *Merry Drollery Compleat*, ed. J. Woodfall Ebsworth, (Boston, Lincs, 1875), pp. 66–69, where its title is 'A Song of Nothing'.

22. In *Kosmobrephia, Or The Infancy Of The World* (London, 1658). A similar line is taken in the anonymous *The prayse of Nothing* (London, 1585).

23. Reba Wilcoxon, 'Rochester's Philosophical Premises: A Case for Consistency', *Eighteenth-Century Studies*, 8:2 (Winter 1974–75), pp. 183–201; K. E. Robinson, 'Rochester's Dilemma', *Durham University Journal*, LXXI (n.s. XL) no. 2 (June 1979), pp. 223–31; Marianne Thormahlen, 'Rochester and *The Fall: The Roots Of Discontent*', *English Studies* 69:5 (1988), pp. 396–409.

24. Griffin, *Satires against Man: The Poems of Rochester* (Berkeley, 1973), pp. 269–80. Two articles by Jeremy Treglown place this kind of technique in a wider context: 'The Satirical Inversion Of Some English Sources In Rochester's Poetry', *Review of English Studies*, n.s. 24 (1973), pp. 42–48; 'Scepticism and Parody in the Restoration', *Modern Language Review*, 75 (1980), pp. 18–47.

25. David Farley-Hills, *Rochester's Poetry* (Ottowa and London, 1978), pp. 173–78.

26. See Johnson, *Lives of the English Poets*, I, 228n. After several appearances in the drolleries, *Much A-do* was printed in *Wit and Mirth: Or Pills To Purge Melancholy*, 6 vols (London, 1719–1720), III, pp. 138–40. In *The London Magazine*, VI (April 1737), p. 218 appears 'A Ballad on Nothing' in the same triplet form and metre and with the same tune. For scholarship on the relationship to Rochester see Gillian Manning, 'Rochester and *Much A-do about Nothing*', *Notes and Queries*, vol. 33 (December 1986), pp. 479–80 and Paul Hammond, 'Rochester and *Much A-do about Nothing* again', *Notes and Queries*, vol. 35 (June 1988), p. 171.

27. Perhaps a shade of Edmund-Edgar in *Lear*, or the 'patrimony' of Satan in *Paradise Lost*, X.818, which themselves allude to biblical models.

28. Compare this with Cowley's reference to the 'Elements League' in 'Davideis' I; *Poems*, ed. Waller, p. 251.

29. References to Rochester's poems are from *The Poems of John Wilmot, Earl of Rochester*, ed. Keith Walker (Oxford, 1984); 'Upon Nothing' is at pp. 62–64.

30. II.962, 971; IV.665–66; V.576–78 (references are to *Milton: Poetical Works*, ed. Douglas Bush (Oxford, 1966). For images which combine sexual and political metaphors, see Rochester's 'Fragment of a Satire on Men', 27–30, and Rochester to Savile, August–September 1674, *The Letters of John Wilmot Earl of Rochester*, ed. Jeremy Treglown (Oxford, 1980), p. 107.

31. *The Faerie Queene*, III.vi.36–39; *Spenser: Poetical Works*, ed. J. C. Smith and E. De Selincourt (London, 1912), p. 175.

32. 'An Hymne In Honour Of Love', 76–84; *Poetical Works*, p. 587.

33. 'Hymn. To Light'; *Poems*, p. 444.

34. For example see *Paradise Lost*, I.22, III.1, V.180–81, VII.276–82, 453–55, VIII.150.

35. *Paradise Lost*, IV.750, V.388, VIII.520, IX.273, XII.368–85. See also Spenser, 'An Hymne Of Heavenly Love', 22–35.

36. II.150, 624–28; X.476–77. See also Beaumont, *Psyche*, canto VI, st.103, p. 83.

37. *Paradise Lost*, II.746–810.

38. Kristoffer Paulson, 'Pun Intended: Rochester's "Upon Nothing" ', *English Language Notes*, 9, (1971), pp. 118–21.

39. For similar uses of 'hand' by Rochester, see 'A Song of a young Lady, 19; 'The Imperfect Enjoyment', 31; 'A Satire on Charles II', 30; for peace on the breast, see 'Absent from thee', and 'A Ramble', 129–30.

40. Griffin's reading psychoanalyzes these images with reference to the whole oeuvre and personality.

41. See the recurrence of 'slaves' and 'womb' in *'Song'* ('Love a *Woman!*').

42. See 'Tunbridge Wells', 136–60; 'Satyr', 205–09; 'A letter from Artemiza . . .', 248–51; 'A Ramble', 11–32. 'Upon his leaving his mistress' affords a different perspective.

43. Ronald Berman, 'Rochester and the Defeat of the Senses', *Kenyon Review*, XXVI:2 (Spring 1964), pp. 354–68, at p.359.

44. For a close reading of the poem in these terms, see Stuart Silverman, 'Upon Rochester's "Upon Nothing" ', *Enlightenment Essays*, 2 (1971), pp. 190–200.

45. To Rochester, 7 February 1680, *Letters of Rochester*, p. 234.

46. See Griffin, *Satires Against Man*, pp. 278–79; Farley-Hills, *Rochester's Poetry*, pp. 177–78.

47. Swift, *A Tale of a Tub*, ed. A. C. Guthkelch and D. Nichol Smith (Oxford, 1920), p. 208. See also Fenton to Broome, 7 August 1726, *The Correspondence of Alexander Pope*, ed. George Sherburn, 5 Vols (Oxford, 1956), II, 385; Henry Fielding, 'An Essay on Nothing', in *Miscellanies, Volume One*, ed. H. K. Miller (Oxford, 1972), pp. 179–90; 'T. Trifler', *The Elogy of Nothing* (London, 1742), pp. 18–19.

48. *Paradoxia Epidemica*, pp. 61–62, 182, 194, 198, 300, 424.

49. 'Davideis', bk.1, *Poems*, p. 253; see also pp. 261–63 and the first of Cowley's notes to this book (p. 266). For Milton's less explicit use of the trope see *Paradise Lost*, III.380–413; also I.8–10, IV.680–85, V.144–209, VII.557–74 and 594–634.

50. V.188, and title page. For God as 'author' see also III.374, VII.591, VIII.317 and 360 and for Milton's self-implication, the openings of I, III, VII and IX. Satan is also an 'author' (II.864, VI.262, X.236), as is Adam (III.122, IV.635).

51. For the manuscripts see Walker's edition, p. 173; see also *Rochester: The Critical Heritage*, ed. David Farley-Hills (1972), p. 7; and Johnson, 'Rochester', in *Lives of the English Poets*, I, pp. 219–28, at p. 224.

52. See James A. Winn, 'Pope Plays the Rake: His Letters to Ladies and making of the *Eloisa*', in *The Art of Alexander Pope*, ed. Howard Erskine-Hill and Anne Smith (1979), pp. 89–118; Pope to Martha Blount, 6 October 1714, *Correspondence of Pope*, I, 261.

53. *Twickenham Edition*, VI, 15–19.

54. Originally in *Miscellanea* (London, 1653); reprinted in *Seventeenth-Century Lyrics From the Original Texts*, ed. Norman Ault, second edition (New York, 1950), p. 285. An adapted version was placed in the context of a

reverent vow in *Love's Kingdom* (London, 1664). See also Horace, *Carmina* 3.2.25 and Hildebrand Jacob, *Hymn to the Goddess of Silence* (London, 1734).

55. For personifications, see Statius, *Thebaid*, X, 89–94; Spenser, *Faerie Queen*, IV.x.51; Milton, *Paradise Lost*, IV.600–04; Beaumont, *Psyche*, canto VI, st.174, p. 88. For religious uses, see Psalm 39:2; Proverbs 10:19 and 11:12; *Paradise Lost*, V.557, VII.106 and 594; Dryden, *Hind and the Panther*, pt.3, 1.1171; Andrew Gray, *The Spiritual Warfare* (London, 1670); John Chappelow, *Silence a Christian's Duty* (London, 1710); Traherne, 'Dumbness' and 'Silence'; Cowley, 'Silence'; Henry Vaughan, 'Silence, and Stealth of Days'.

56. Virgil, *Aeneid*, II.255; Statius, *Thebaid*, I.368, 4.448; Sidney, *Astrophel and Stella*, xcvi.5; Shakespeare, *Midsummer Night's Dream*, IV.i.101; Pope, 'Eloisa to Abelard', 166; Blaise Pascal, *Pensées*, trans. A. J. Krailsheimer (Harmondsworth, 1966), p. 95; *Paradise Lost*, I.83, VI.308; *Paradise Regained*, IV.22.

57. Sidney, 'The Second Eclogues', no. 28, 1.15; Shakespeare, *Julius Caesar*, I.ii.290; Donne, *Progress of the Soul*, 250.

58. 'Written in Italian, by 'Fra. Giacomo Assinati d'Acuto Romano' and translated by Anthony Munday (London, 1605).

59. For the biblical wisdom of which this is a parody, see Proverbs 17.28; and for the satiric point, Horace, *Sat.*, 2.6.58.

60. See *Paradise Lost*, III.169–70, VII.163, 210.

61. See *Twickenham Edition*, VI, 463–64.

62. See Bernard Beatty's remarks elsewhere in this volume on the 'brave *Midwife*' jibe against Dryden's lines on Creation in 'Timon', 147–50.

63. 'Timon', 22; 'Song' ('Love a *Woman!*'), 12; 'Letter from Artemiza', 26–27; 'My Lord All-Pride', 7–12; 'An Epistolary Essay', 40–43. See Farley-Hills, *Rochester's Poetry*, p. 43, and Griffin, *Satires Against Man*, pp. 69–72, for readings of this metaphor.

64. See John Sitter, *The Poetry of Pope's Dunciad* (Minneapolis, 1971), pp. 112–14; Don Lowell Erickson, ' "The Progress of Dulness": Imagery of Nothing and Negation In The Satire Of Rochester, Dryden, Swift, and Pope', Ph.D., Washington University, 1975; John M. Aden, *Pope's Once and Future Kings* (Knoxville, 1978), pp. 58–61.

65. See Griffin, *Satires against Man*, pp. 257–66; Aden, *Pope's Once and Future Kings*, pp. 44–45; George Fraser, *Alexander Pope* (London, 1978), pp. 100–01; Joseph Spence, *Observations, Anecdotes and Characters of Books and Men*, ed. James M. Osborn, 2 Vols (Oxford, 1966), nos. 86, 469–73.

66. See Maynard Mack, *Collected in Himself* (Newark, NJ, 1982), pp. 437–38, and Michael Phillips, 'The Composition of Pope's *Imitation of Horace*, Satire II, i,' in *Alexander Pope: essays for the tercentenary*, ed. Colin Nicholson (Aberdeen, 1988), pp. 171–94.

67. *Lives of the English Poets*, I, 224, 226; see also III, 176.

68. For a biographical reading of the poem, see George Sherburn, *The Early Career of Alexander Pope* (Oxford, 1934), pp. 98–99.

69. *Epistle to Dr. Arbuthnot*, 135–140.

70. Howard Erskine-Hill, 'Alexander Pope at Fifteen: A New Manuscript', *Review of English Studies*, n.s.XVII, no.67 (1966), pp. 268–77.

71. For Pope's marginalia to 'Upon Nothing', see Mack, *Collected in Himself*, p. 438.

72. For Rochester's sporadic concern about or interest in this see *Letters of Rochester*, pp. 99, 114, 157; Gilbert Burnet's *Some Passages of the Life and Death of the Right Honourable John Earl of Rochester* (London, 1680) and Robert Parson's *A Sermon preached at the Earl of Rochester's Funeral* (London, 1680). Both give the deathbed view of Rochester's self-parody.

73. The comment is repeated, without acknowledgement, by Giles Jacob. See *Rochester: The Critical Heritage*, pp. 46, 189–90; for similar comments see 142 (Robert Wolseley), 166–69 (Thomas Rymer), and 170 (Anthony à Wood). Rochester makes a brief statement on imitation in 'Allusion to Horace', 30–36, and repeats the customary charge against Dryden that his rhymes were 'stoln' (2).

74. *Rochester: The Critical Heritage*, p. 118.

75. 'An Epistolary Essay', 44–49.

76. *Some Passages*, p. 14. See also *Rochester: The Critical Heritage*, pp. 172, 188, 202, and Johnson, *Lives of the English Poets*, I, 223.

77. For 'castration' of the poems see *Boswell's Life of Johnson*, ed. G. B. Hill, revised by L. F. Powell, 6 Vols (1934–1951), III, 191.

78. *The Text of Rochester's 'Upon Nothing'* (Clayton, Vic., 1985). I am very grateful to Professor Love for making this paper available to me.

# 'An Allusion to Horace', Jonson's Ghost, and the Second Poets' War

## BREAN S. HAMMOND

Post-Romantic conceptions of originality make it difficult for us to regard as other than paradoxical the claim that 'An Allusion to Horace', the poem in which Rochester is most indebted to a precursor, is also one of his most original contributions to English poetry. If Rochester was not quite the first English poet to press a Roman satire into the service of his own times, he was the first to appreciate that this could be done systematically over the length of an entire poem, to wit Horace's *Satire* 1.10.[1] Doubtless, Rochester did not intuit the full potential of this new medium. That would come, not so much through the greater poetic genius of Alexander Pope, as through Pope's more developed understanding of the pheno-menology of reading the 'imitation'. As soon as you cease to rely on your reader's hazy memory of the original Latin, and print it in juxtaposition to your own English, using typography when necessary to call attention to your own especially felicitous adaptations, knowing departures and virtuoso puns, you achieve effects that were not possible for Rochester.[2] Where, for instance, Rochester could simply omit an Horatian passage that he did not see as having any relevance to contemporary circumstances (such as that commencing 'scili-cet oblitus patriaeque', in which Horace condemns that practice of adulterating the native satiric strain with Greek words), later satirists like Pope and Johnson, fearing that the reader would construe this as a 'cop-out', would invest far more effort in inventing parallel circumstances. In Pope's hands, the Horatian imitation offers the reader a pleasure analogous to that of the musical 'variations on a theme of . . .'—extreme formal constraint, from which every departure is experienced as a glorious freedom.[3] Rochester's poem is not such a triumph of the Baroque, but its relative lack of polish offers an opportunity to observe certain aspects of contemporary cultural debate—in particular, the fight for possession of Ben Jonson, which at this time was a struggle even more active than the perennial contest over Shakespeare—and the gradually assembling rhetoric of plagiarism.

In general terms, the reasons for Rochester's mounting an overt attack on Dryden in 1675 are well enough understood. At a time of rapidly polarising politics, Dryden was known to be in the Duke of York's camp, whereas Rochester was a supporter of Buckingham. Mapped onto incipient Tory/Whig political divisions, however, were more volatile and nebulous conflicts over the status of the writer in society. Dryden's failed play *The Assignation: or, Love in a Nunnery* was published in 1673 with a dedication to the court wit Sedley, in which the writer made a bold bid for acceptance into Sedley's inner circle. Celebrating the close friendship of the Roman poets, Dryden had the temerity to describe, from the insider's viewpoint and for the benefit of those who have exaggerated their licentiousness, the typical behaviour of the aristocratic epicureans:

> We have . . . our Genial Night; where our discourse is neither too serious, nor too light; but alwayes pleasant, and for the most part instructive: the raillery neither too sharp upon the present, nor too censorious on the absent; and the Cups, onely such as will raise the Conversation of the Night, without disturbing the business of the Morrow. And thus far not only the Philosophers, but the Fathers of the Church have gone, without lessening their Reputation of good Manners, or of Piety. For this reason I have often Laugh'd at the ignorant and ridiculous Descriptions, which some Pedants have given of the Wits (as they are pleas'd to call them:) which are a Generation of Men as unknown to them, as the People of Tartary or the *Terra Australis* are to us . . . Such wits as they describe, I have never been so unfortunate to meet in your Company: but have often heard much better Reasoning at your Table, than I have encounter'd in their Books. The Wits they describe, are the Fops we banish: for

> Blasphemy and Atheism, if they were neither Sin nor Ill
> Manners, are subjects so very common, and worn so
> Threadbare, that people who have sence avoid them, for
> fear of being suspected to have none.

Later in the dedication, Dryden rebuts the charge that he has
habitually disparaged the achievement of earlier authors—Ben
Jonson in particular—by citing as a precedent Horace's tactic
in the *Satires*, wherein the Roman poet certainly criticized his
eminent predecessor Lucilius, but also gave him credit where
credit was due:

> I am made a Detractor from my Predecessors, whom I
> confess to have been my Master in the Art. But this latter
> was the accusation of the best Judge, and almost the best
> Poet in the *Latine* Tongue. You find *Horace* complaining,
> that for taxing some Verses in *Lucilius*, he himself was
> blamed by others, though his Design was no other than
> mine now, to improve the knowledge of Poetry: and it was
> no defence to him, amongst his Enemies, any more than it
> is for me, that he Prais'd Lucilius where he deserv'd it:
> *Pagina laudatur eadem.*[4]

It must have been particularly painful, then, for Dryden to
discover that Rochester had probably picked up the germ of
the idea of applying Horace's *Satire* 1.10 from him, and had
used it to accuse *Dryden* of plagiarism! Worse still, in the
cruellest lines in the poem, entirely unlicensed by Horace,
Rochester mocks Dryden's clodhopping attempts to talk
bawdy, ridiculing his claim to be intimate with the aristocratic
libertines, whose light touch he entirely lacks:

> Dryden, in vaine, try'd this nice way of Witt,
> For he, to be a tearing Blade thought fit,
> But when he wou'd be sharp, he still was blunt,
> To friske his frollique fancy, hed cry Cunt;
> (ll.71–74)[5]

Ironic that Dryden, whose most famous characterization of his
satiric art in the *Discourse concerning Satire* (1692) would stress a
razor sharpness that separates the head from the body, and
leaves it standing in its place, is in Rochester's lines banished
as a mere dull fop. The depth of feeling engendered by

Rochester's public repudiation of him can be measured by his preface to the published edition of *All For Love* (1678) in which, in total contrast to the in-crowd intimacies of the Sedley dedication, Dryden makes a withering irony out of accepting himself as a mere venal professional:

> We who write, if we want the Talent, yet have the excuse that we do it for a poor subsistence; but what can be urg'd in their defence, who not having the Vocation of Poverty to scribble, out of meer wantonness take pains to make themselves ridiculous?[6]

Rochester's tactic in the 'Allusion' is to contrast crowd-pleasing, ill-considered popular entertainment, hastily composed and thrown together, with writing that is carefully constructed and submitted only to those whose rank and education puts them in the best position to judge (ll.12–17; 93–97; 104–09 *versus* ll.20–29; 98–103; 110–14; 120–24). Practical criticism of specific writers designed to exemplify these broadly contrasting attitudes to composition occupies most of the remainder. The caste or status-group basis of Rochester's attack on Dryden in 'An Allusion to Horace' is explicitly enunciated in the final lines:

> I loath the Rabble, 'tis enough for me,
> If Sidley, Shadwell, Shepherd, Witcherley,
> Godolphin, Buttler, Buckhurst, Buckingham,
> And some few more, whom I omit to name
> Approve my Sense, I count their Censure Fame.
>                           (ll.120–24)

Line 120 underwrites its memorability by alluding to one of Horace's most famous lines from the *Odes*—'Odi profanum vulgus et arceo'. Even more sharply, though, the posture struck by Rochester with regard to 'the false Judgement of an Audience / Of Clapping-Fooles' (ll.13–14) recalls Ben Jonson's various attempts to educate, cajole and browbeat his audience into acceptance of his comic genius, finally, in the 'Ode to Himself' written after the failure of *The New Inn*, expressing a Timonesque resolution not to waste his sweetness on the desert air that was the contemporary Caroline audience.[7] Dryden must have read 'An Allusion to Horace' as a public commitment of Rochester's power to Shadwell's side in the struggle, now some

seven or eight years old, for possession of Ben Jonson's comic
mantle, even though Rochester's praise of Shadwell is qualified
in important ways. Yet for the modern reader poring over the
precise terms of Rochester's sponsorship, the difference
between the two rivals is elusive. Those terms are as follows:

| *Shadwell* | *Dryden* |
|---|---|
| Shadwells unfinisht workes doe yet impart, | But does not Dryden find ev'n Johnson dull? |
| Great proofes of force of Nature, none of Art. | Fletcher, and Beaumont, uncorrect, and full |
| With just bold Stroakes, he dashes here and there, | Of Lewd lines as he calls 'em? Shakespeares Stile |
| Shewing great Mastery with little care; | Stiffe, and Affected? To his owne the while |
| And scornes to varnish his good touches o're, | Allowing all the justnesse that his Pride, |
| To make the Fooles, and Women, praise 'em more. | Soe Arrogantly, had to these denyd? |
| (11.44–49) | And may not I, have leave Impartially |
| | To search, and Censure, Drydens workes, and try, |
| | If those grosse faults, his Choyce Pen does Commit |
| | Proceed from want of Judgment, or of Witt. |
| | Or if his lumpish fancy does refuse, |
| | Spirit, and grace to his loose slatterne Muse? |
| | (ll. 81–92) |

On the basis of the key critical terms here—'nature', 'art', the
painting metaphor applied to Shadwell's work, 'judgement',
'wit', 'fancy', 'spirit' and 'grace'—it is difficult for the modern
reader to understand exactly what was at issue between the
two writers. Even if we look beyond the poem to those
statements made by Dryden about his attitudes to earlier
writers, to which Rochester's passage alludes, there is some
difficulty in extrapolating from them the theatrical practices

involved. Typical of the exchanges between the two writers over Jonson's merit as a comic dramatist was Dryden's preface to *An Evening's Love* (1671), to which Shadwell responded in his preface to *The Humorists* in the same year. Dryden writes:

> To make men appear pleasantly ridiculous on the Stage was . . . [Jonson's] talent: and in this he needed not the acumen of wit, but that of judgement. For the characters and representations of folly are only the effects of observation; and observation is an effect of judgement. Some ingenious men, for whom I have a particular esteem, have thought I have much injur'd *Ben Johnson* when I have not allow'd his wit to be extraordinary: but they confound the notion of what is witty with what is pleasant. That *Ben Johnson*'s Playes were pleasant he must want reason who denyes: But that pleasantness was not properly wit, or the sharpness of conceit; but the natural imitation of folly: which I confess to be excellent in it's kind, but not to be of that kind which they pretend (italics reversed).[8]

Shadwell construes this as an attack on comedy of 'humours' and thus responds:

> I cannot be of their opinion who think he wanted wit . . . Nor can I think, to the writing of his humors (which were not only the follies, but vices and subtleties of men) that wit was not required, but judgement; where, by the way, they speak as if judgement were less a thing than wit. But certainly it was meant otherwise by nature, who subjected wit to the government of judgement, which is the noblest faculty of the mind. Fancy rough-draws, but judgement smooths and finishes, nay judgement does in deed comprehend wit, for no man can have that who has not wit.[9]

Shadwell goes on to deny Dryden's argument that Jonsonian comedy of humours is essentially a mimetic art, requiring no imaginative heightening. Applying the categories of faculty psychology, playing and re-playing the counters of 'wit' and 'judgement', the disputants never quite develop a language adequate to analyse dramatic performance, or exemplify the differing comic effects that they strove to achieve. It may be of some critical service, therefore, to try to elucidate this matter, and demonstrate its importance to the cultural status of Rochester's poem.

Rochester, in 'An Allusion', wants to cut a wide swathe between those poets, like Settle, Otway and Lee, who are working dramatists, professional writers ekeing out a living by marketing their writing talents; and those like Waller, Buckhurst and Sedley who, by virtue of their social rank and court connections, can obey gentlemanly aesthetic prescriptions like those expressed in ll.20–29, which are then said to be the characteristic excellences of Shakespeare and Jonson (ll.30–31). Waller is the great panegyrist, Buckhurst the satirist extraordinaire, and Sedley a master of the erotic capable of releasing desire so subliminal that it seeps up through cultural barriers:

> For Songs, and Verses, Mannerly Obscene,
> That can stirr Nature up, by Springs unseene,
> And without forceing blushes, warme the Queene:
> Sidley, has that prevailing gentle Art
> 
> (ll.61–64)

There are four writers whose work defies this easy typology, and whose work it is the poem's major task to evaluate: Etherege, Wycherley, Shadwell and Dryden. The Etherege problem is solved by making him *sui generis*: 'refin'd Etheridge, Coppys not all, / But is himself a Sheere Originall' (ll.32–34). Wycherley is a thorough, painstaking artist (ll.50–54). The reputations of Shadwell and Dryden are the most fluid; both are antitypes: one said to be a natural writer whose creative energy overrides his attention to detail, the other to have a 'lumpish fancy'. Permitting ourselves to move out of the confines of the neo-classical critical vocabulary, let us try to examine what is at stake here.

Essentially, the difference between Dryden's comedy of 'wit' and Shadwell's comedy of 'humours' is that between a theatre dominated by its spoken text (Dryden) and one dominated by dramatic action, situation and gesture (Shadwell). Shadwell's *The Sullen Lovers* and Dryden's *An Evening's Love* were produced within one month of each other in May and June 1668; and although it is clear that both plays owe a debt to Jonson, it is clear that Shadwell is the writer who really understands Jonsonian stagecraft and wishes it to form the basis of a reinvigorated comedy. In Dryden's play, Bellamy's servant Maskall makes him out to be an astrologer in order to explain how he has come by certain knowledge about his inamorata Theodosia's love life. Thereafter, Bellamy is consulted by various individuals, including Theodosia's father Don Alonzo, who wish to benefit from his mystery, rather in the way that Jonson's alchemist Subtle is approached by the various gulls. Don Alonzo knows a good deal of occult lore, and Bellamy's attempts to improvise the language while also satisfying the demands of various clients for clairvoyance are reminiscent of Jonsonian situation management. Act 3.1 comes to a recognizably Jonsonian crescendo of farcical babble when Don Lopez attempts to inform Don Alonzo that another young gallant is in love with his daughter, but Alonzo, priding himself on the gift of foreknowledge, insists on completing all his sentences for him:

> *Alon.* Why, when do you begin, Sir? how long must a man wait for you? pray make an end of what you have to say quickly, that I may speak in my turn too.
> *Lop.* This Cavalier is in Love.
> *Alon.* You told me that before, Sir; Do you speak Oracles that you require this strict attention? either let me share the talk with you or I am gone.
> *Lop.* Why, Sir, I am almost mad to tell you, and you will not suffer me.
> *Alon.* Will you never have done, Sir? I must tell you, Sir, you have tatled long enough; and 'tis now good Manners to hear me speak. Here's a Torrent of words indeed; a very *impetus dicendi*; Will you never have done?
> *Lop.* I will be heard in spight of you.
>
> *This next Speech of* Lopez, *and the next of* Alonzo's, *with both their Replies, are to be spoken at one time; both raising their voices by little and little, till they baul, and come up close to shoulder one another.*
>
> *Lop.* There's one *Don Melchor de Guzman*, a Friend and Acquaintance of mine, that is desperately in Love with your eldest Daughter *Donna Theodosia*.

> *Alon. at the same time.* 'Tis the sentence of a Philosopher,
> *Loquere ut te videam*; Speak that I may know thee; (3.ll.342–
> 60)[10]

It is doubtless merely coincidence, because Dryden's direct
source here is Molière, that Alonzo's (mistranslated) philosophical sentence was profoundly important to Jonson, cited in
his *Discoveries* as a fundamental principle of epistemology:
'*language* most shewes a man: speake that I may see thee'. . .[11]
Lopez, unsuccessful in capturing Alonzo's attention with legal
gibberish, runs off to find a bell with which he manages to
interrupt Alonzo's next diatribe against 'perpetual Talkers,
Disputants, Controverters, and Duellers of the Tongue'. Yet,
for all that this frenetic activity has a Jonsonian texture, the
play as an entirety lacks the Jonsonian satiric impulse. Bellamy
and Maskall are not, as are Subtle and Face, calculatedly
manipulating the gullible and the greedy. Cant, trade-talk,
argot—the various languages of duplicity that take on such a
perverse malevolence in Jonson—are a temporary discomfi-
ture for Lopez and a short-lived test for Bellamy's powers of
invention. This point about Dryden's fundamental *difference*
from Jonson might be pursued in respect of another of his
plays, the fabulously successful *The Feign'd Innocence: or Sir
Martin Marall*, premièred in August 1667. The plot is simple
and monolithic. Sir Martin Marall's inept counterplotting foils
all the plans laid by his servant Warner to capture Mrs.
Millisent for him. Despite the argument made by John Loftis,
editor of the California edition, for Jonsonian influence, the
uncomplicated structure of this play, its formula of repeated
situations, its over-reliance on a single actor's performance
(Nokes was apparently a huge success in the title-role)—in
short, its failure to build into any degree of farcical complexity,
makes it a singularly inept imitation of Jonson.[12] This suggests
that Dryden had no real talent for, or understanding of,
Jonsonian stagecraft. Far more central to Dryden are those
scenes in which the witty couples engage in 'repartie'; the
combats of thrust and parry, innuendo and counter-impli-
cation that indicate the young protagonists are suited to each
other through intelligence, rank and sexual appetite. Shadwell
would complain that such couples as Wildblood and Jacinta in

*An Evening's Love*, or Frederick and Lucretia in *The Assignation* or Palamede and Doralice in *Marriage à la Mode* are entirely interchangeable, mouthpieces for the author's wit, prompted by no internal imperatives of character.

Shadwell's response to a kind of comedy in which speech and action are not integrally related is to develop 'humours' characters, where that connection is as tight and predictable as possible. Stanford and Emilia are the 'sullen lovers' of Shadwell's play. Recalling Jonson's Morose (*The Silent Woman*) who cannot abide noise, and his Lovel (*The New Inn*), who can take no pleasure in the present age, this couple are attracted to each other not by the sexual friction of their discourse but by discovery of their symmetrical aberrations. In the characters of the fustian poet Ninny, the squeaking musician Woodcock, and the self-appointed polymath Sir Positive At-All, Shadwell is able to satirize quite identifiably the contemporary figure of the virtuoso, a theme to which he returns in his play *The Virtuoso*. There are moments in *The Sullen Lovers* superficially similar to the passage of action from *An Evening's Love* examined above, but they are more genuinely Jonsonian moments. In 4.1, Woodcock and Ninny have been torturing Emilia with simultaneously-rendered examples of their art, when Sir Positive enters and in short succession proclaims himself to be master of languages, shipbuilding, painting, athletics, mathematics, music, metaphysics, gambling, legerdemain, diplomacy, rope-dancing (perhaps a not altogether innocent juxtaposition, anticipating the rope-dancing in Swift's Lilliput and the connection established between moral philosophy and gymnastics in Stoppard's *Jumpers*) . . . and so on, until Caroline and Lovel, by dint of speaking very quickly one after the other, provoke the following orgy of self-adulation in Sir Positive:

| | |
|---|---|
| *Car.*—Now *Lovel* to your post. | |
| *Lov.* Navigation. | *Lov.* Physick. |
| Sir *Pos.* Navigation d'ye talk of? | *Car.* Divinity. |
| *Car.* Geography | *Car.* Surgery. |
| Sir *Pos.* Geography d'ye talk of? | *Car.* Arithmetick. |
| *Lov.* Astronomy. | *Lov.* Logick. |

Sir *Pos*. Astronomy,        *Car*. Cookery.
    d'ye talk of?
*Car*. Palmestry.                    *Lov*. Magick.
Sir *Pos*. Hold, hold, hold, hold! Navigation, Geography,
Astronomy, Palmistry, Physick, Divinity, Surgery, Arith-
metick, Logick, Cookery and Magick: I'le speak to every
one of these in their order; if I don't understand 'em every
one in perfection, nay, if I don't Fence, Dance, Ride, Sing,
Fight a Duel, speak *French*, Command an Army, play on the
Violin, Bag-pipe, Organ, Harp, Hoboy, Sackbut, and
double Curtal, speak Spanish, Italian, Greek, Hebrew,
Dutch, Welch and Irish, Dance a Jigg, throw the Barr,
Swear, Drink, Swagger, Whore, Quarrel, Cuffe, break
Windowes, manage Affairs of State, Hunt, Hawke, Shoot,
Angle, play at Catte, Stool-ball, Scotch-hope and Trap-
ball, Preach, Dispute, make Speeches.—(Coughs)
Prethee, get me a glass of small beere, *Roger*.
*Stanfo*. Hell and Furies!
*Emil*. Oh, oh—
Sir *Pos*. Nay, hold, I have not told you halfe; if I don't do all
these, and fifty times more, I am the greatest Owle, Pimp,
Monkey, Jack-a-napes, Baboon, Rascal, Oafe, Ignor-
amus, Logger-head, Cur-dog, Block-head, Buffoone, Jack-
pudden, Tony, or what you will; spit upon me, kick me, cuff
me, lugg me by the eares, pull me by the Nose, tread upon
me, and despise me more than the World now values me.[13]

There is a physicality about Shadwell's comedy, evident here
in the turning of Sir Positive into a demented robot, a crazed
pointer revolving madly round a dial, that is absent from Dryden
and that Dryden would finally have condemned as 'low'. Shadwell is always looking for the stage-picture that will transform a
character into the graphic emblem of his humour.[14] It is Shadwell, rather than Dryden, who genuinely enjoys the juxtaposition of bizarre idiolects, the construction of a linguistic tower of
Babel so familiar in Jonson. Dryden will certainly entertain an
individual linguistic humour like the absurdly Frenchified
Amalthea in *Marriage à la Mode*, but as a one-off portrait of vanity
and affectation, not as a sign that irresponsible language has
turned the world upside down. Shadwell's coarse, frequently

grotesque physicality—Snarl being beaten by Mrs Figgup in *The Virtuoso*, Crazy groaning in pain from his pox while being arrested by the bailiffs in *The Humorists*, the cudgelling of La Roch the barber disguised as a count in *Bury Fair*—is quite unlike anything in Dryden's comedy, but very common in Jonson. Violence seeps up through every crack in Shadwell, whereas in Dryden it is controlled by codes of aristocratic honour. It is possible to read *The Virtuoso* as a play written in conscious allusion to *Marriage à la Mode*, since it echoes the basic situations in the subplot of the earlier play, and if that exercise is undertaken, it becomes apparent that Dryden's comedy, at best, was a comedy of ideas which Shadwell's never aspired to be. Of *Marriage à la Mode*, it makes sense to ask what the underlying concerns are, a question that is likely to elicit only disappointing answers in the case of Shadwell, whose comic art is one of surfaces.

Some of the tension to be detected in Dryden's critical writings of this period, then, derives from the fact that he was developing non-Jonsonian forms of comedy while still being obliged not to disown Jonson as a model. Such was the power of Jonson's reputation that Edward Howard, in his play *The Women's Conquest* (1671), went to the length of bringing Jonson's ghost onstage to protest about the Frenchified farces that have displaced the native strain of comedy:

> Did I instruct you (well ne're half an Age)
> To understand the Grandeur of the Stage,
> With the exactest Rules of Comedy,
> Yet now y'are pleased with Wits low frippery,
> Admitting Farce, the trifling mode of France,
> T'infect you with fantastick ignorance,
> Forgetting 'twas your glory to behold,
> Plays wisely form'd such as I made of old;[15]

Yet as Rochester's poem 'An Allusion to Horace' testifies, if Dryden was blamed for failing to follow Jonson's instruction and to respect the eminences of a bygone age:

> But does not Dryden find ev'n Johnson dull?
> Fletcher, and Beaumont, uncorrect and full
> Of Lewd lines as he calls em? Shakespeares Stile
> Stiffe, and Affected?
>
> (ll.81–84)

the opposite charge, that he followed the example of his literary predecessors far too closely, was also being preferred. Picking up from the post-1668 pamphlet war, plagiarism, and its implication that there exists a violable category of literary property, announces itself as an issue at the very outset of 'An Allusion'. Where Horace had begun his poem recalling the terms of his earlier critique of Lucilius in *Satire* 1.4, 'Nempe incomposito dixi pede currere versus / Lucili' ('True, I did say that Lucilius' verses lurched awkwardly along'),[16] Rochester's version registers not just the aesthetic objection to Dryden's 'Rhimes' that they are 'unequal', nor the reception of them as 'dull', but the moral difficulty that they are 'stoln':

> Well Sir, 'tis granted, I said Dryden's Rhimes,
> Were stoln, unequal, nay dull many times:
> (ll.1–2)

The éclat of this opening derives, then, not only from the fact that whereas Lucilius was safely dead, Dryden is very much alive—and this is the first time Rochester has attacked him openly. It also derives from the specific terms in which that attack is constructed. The uneasy suggestion of literary theft continues in ll.5–7:

> But that his Plays, Embroider'd up and downe,
> With Witt, and Learning, justly pleas'd the Town,
> In the same paper, I as freely owne:

The suggestion of 'Embroider'd' is that Dryden embellishes with his wit and learning some base clay that is not his own: and it is right ('justly') that this confection should please those theatrical patrons whose judgement is no better ('the Towne'). Here is a second, more elusive respect in which Jonson's ghost haunts Rochester's poem. In this accusation of lack of original-ity, and in the development of a binary opposition between the merely popular writer and the writer with longer term ambi-tion, Rochester is recapitulating the terms of previous literary controversy—in particular the so-called *poetomachia* involving Jonson, Dekker and Marston at the beginning of the century. In reversing some of the polarities of the earlier struggle, however, Rochester's poem sounds a characteristic note of the

1670's. In *Poetaster*, the bricklayer's son Ben Jonson had figured himself as the English Horace, a court dramatist enjoying the protection of his monarch, ennobled by his talent and chosen for his outstanding ability to advise the ruler. Proving his credentials entailed the exposure of smaller fry like Marston and Dekker (the Crispinus and Demetrius Fannius of the play) the former of whom, through a magnificent literalization of the metaphor of satire as an emetic, is forced to vomit up all the outlandish words in his extraordinary thesaurus. Dekker, in his revenge play *Satiromastix*, ridicules Jonson's pretensions to noble patronage, portraying him as a mere literary hack, who is first discovered hopelessly attempting to find rhymes for a routine epithalamium to celebrate a gentleman's wedding. Interestingly, one charge that is not made against Jonson is that of plagiarism. What appeared to sting Jonson more than any other palpable hit in *Satiromastix* was the repeated claim that he was extremely slow in composition, and could not, or would not, dash off his productions quickly:

> *Tuc.* What wut end? wut hang thy selfe now? has he not writ Finis yet *Iacke?* what will he bee fifteene weekes about this Cockatrices egge too? has he not cackeld yet? not laide yet?
> *Blunt.* Not yet, hee sweares hee will within this houre.
> *Tuc.* His wittes are somewhat hard bound: the Puncke his Muse has sore labour ere the whoore bee deliuered: the poore saffron-cheeke Sun-burnt Gipsie wants Phisicke; give the hungrie-face pudding-pye-eater ten Pilles: ten shillings my faire Angelica, they'l make his Muse as yare as a tumbler.
>
> (1.ii.362–70)[17]

Should Jonson be inclined to consider himself the kind of writer whose work is the product of much study, prolonged revision and careful nurture, Dekker here asserts that his is a prostituted muse just like all the others and will yield its offspring with the help of the customary midwife, money. So acutely did Jonson feel this accusation—that he was pretentiously trying to raise dramatic writing to an undue dignity—that he specifically rebutted it in the Prologue to *Volpone*:

And, when his playes come forth, thinke they can flout
    them,
With saying, he was a yeere about them.
To these there needs no lie, but this his creature,
Which was, two months since, no feature;
And, though he dares give them five lives to mend it,
'Tis knowne, five weekes fully pen'd it:
From his owne hand, without a co-adiutor,
Novice, iourney-man, or tutor.[18]

As Jonson's career developed, he became less defensive about
the degree of creative energy he was prepared to invest in his
plays, as their authorized publication in 1616 would suggest.

In Rochester's poem, this gradual shift in the construction of
poetic value is apparent. It is seen to lie not in a professional
ability to write to order, but in a willingness to ponder carefully
every aspect of one's art—implying a rejection of the professional 'time is money' ethos:

To write what may securely stand the test
Of being well read over Thrice at least
Compare each Phrase, examin ev'ry Line
Weigh ev'ry word, and ev'ry thought refine;
Scorne all Applause the Vile Rout can bestow,
And be content to please those few, who know.
                         (ll.98–103)

Plagiarism takes its place as another corner-cutting, shoddy
technique that the genuinely aspiring author must now out-
grow. Clearly, Rochester's strictures tap a rich vein of guilt
that runs just beneath the surface of the culture. For the
professional writers of the time, who experienced at first hand,
as Rochester did not, the pressures that gave rise to such
expedients, his Horatian advice was difficult to take. Shadwell's preface to *The Sullen Lovers* (1688), for example, acknowledges while minimising the extent of his debt to Molière, and
in nothing-to-lose fashion (since he has as yet no reputation as
a dramatist) confesses that it has been hastily put together:

I freely confess my Theft, and am asham'd on't, though I
have the example of some that never yet wrote a Play
without stealing most of it; And (like Men that lye so long,

till they believe themselves) at length, by continual Thieving, reckon their stolne goods their own too: which is so ignoble a thing, that I cannot but believe that he that makes a common practice of stealing other mens Witt, would, if he could, with the same safety steall any thing else . . . Look upon [this play] as it really was, wrote in haste, by a Young Writer, and you will easily pardon it . . . Nor can you expect a very Correct *Play*, under a Years pains at the least, from the Wittiest Man of the Nation; It is so difficult a thing to write well in this kind. Men of quality, that write for their pleasure, will not trouble themselves with exactness in their *Playes*; and those, that write for profit, would find too little incouragement for so much paines as a correct *Play* would require.[19]

Shadwell was able to manage such 'turd i' your teeth' insouciance in his prefaces, and never more so than in the preface to *Psyche* (1675), where he writes that 'in a thing written in five weeks, as this was, there must needs be many Errors' which must be excused 'since there are so many splendid objects in the Play'.[20] For Dryden, however, the whole business was far more anguished, and it forced out of him, at times, astonishingly frank and painful confessions, as in the following passage from *A Defence of an Essay of Dramatique Poesie* (1668):

For I confess my chief endeavours are to delight the Age in which I live. If the humour of this, be for low Comedy, small Accidents, and Raillery, I will force my Genius to obey it, though with more reputation I could write in Verse. I know I am not so fitted by Nature to write Comedy: I want that gayety of humour which is required to it. My Conversation is slow and dull, my humour Saturnine and reserv'd: In short, I am none of those who endeavour to break Jests in Company, or make reparties.[21]

Equally direct is Dryden's dismissal of his tragedy capitalising on the outbreak of war with the Dutch, *Amboyna*, as 'scarcely [worth] a serious perusal, it being contrived and written in a month, the subject barren, the persons low, and the writing not heightened with many labored scenes'.[22]

One measure of the extent to which the exigencies of professionalism were bearing upon literary production at this period is furnished by the confession, made by both Dryden and Shadwell even if not entirely seriously, that they have abandoned rhyme because it represents poor value for money! It takes too long to write, and brings too little in profit. Shadwell writes, in the prologue to *The Virtuoso* (1676):

> Yet since y'have had Rhime for a relishing Bit,
> To give a better taste to Comick Wit.
> But this requires expence of time and pains,
> Too great, alas, for Poets slender gains.
> For Wit, like *China*, should long buri'd lie,
> Before it ripens to good Comedy;
> A thing we ne'er have seen since *Johnson's* days,
> And but a few of his were perfect Plays.
> Now Drudges of the Stage must oft appear,
> They must be bound to scribble twice a year.
> (ll.5–14)[23]

When, in 1687, Gerard Langbaine published his extraordinary catalogue of all the English plays known to him, he gave his bibliographical project a polemical edge apparent in its title— *Momus Triumphans: or, the Plagiaries of the English Stage*. Langbaine's preface was dedicated to exposing the difference between classical and modern ways of using sources. The ancients borrowed as a mark of respect to their forebears, borrowed only what was beautiful in them, and modestly acknowledged their debts. The moderns are thieves, trying to gain credit for invention not their own, and the worst offender is John Dryden, to whom is preached this homily:

> I cannot but blame him for taxing others with stealing Characters from him . . . when he himself does the same, almost in all the Plays he writes; and for arraigning his Predecessours for stealing from the *Ancients*, as he does *Johnson*; which tis evident that he himself is guilty of the same. I would therefore desire our Laureat, that he would follow that good Advice which the modest History Professor Mr Wheare gives to the young Academick in his *Antelogium, to shun this, Confidence and Self-love, as the worst of*

> *Plagues; and to* consider that *Modesty is it which becomes every Age, and leads all that follow her in the Streight, and right Path to solid Glory* (italics reversed).[24]

Perhaps Langbaine has in mind Dryden's double-edged compliment made to Jonson in *An Essay of Dramatick Poesie*, that 'he invades Authours like a Monarch, and what would be theft in other Poets, is onely victory in him'.[25] From these charges of plagiarism and duplicity, Shadwell is explicitly excepted by Langbaine. He borrows very little and never without acknowledgement. For those whose view of these matters is conditioned by 'Mac Flecknoe', this relative positioning of Dryden and Shadwell comes as something of a surprise.

It should be clear that when, in 'An Allusion to Horace', Rochester counterposes Shadwell to Dryden as 'mighty opposites' and makes this contest the armature of the poem, he is expressing an important insight into the present condition of his culture. 'Mac Flecknoe' will accuse Shadwell of plagiarism wittily and Shadwell's *The Medal of John Bayes* (1682) will make the countercharge bluntly:

> Were from thy Works cull'd out what thou'st purloin'd,
> Even D——fey would excel what's left behind.
> Should all thy borrow'd plumes we from thee tear,
> How truly Poet *Squab* would'st thou appear! . . .
> Thou plunder'st all, t' advance thy mighty Name,
> Look'st big, and triumph'st with thy borrow'd fame.
> But art (while swelling thus thou think'st th'rt Chief)
> *A servile Imitator and a Thief.*

Plagiarism will soon come to be apprehended as a legal matter in increasingly individualistic and professionalized institutions of literature. Already in the 1670's the aesthetic foundation is being laid for this, as writers argue over the question whether 'invention' is to be given higher priority than learning in literary production. As Edward Howard puts it in his preface to *The Women's Conquest*:

> It is very observable, since Translating hath been so much practis'd, and taking from Romances and Foreign Plays, the compositions arising from them appear not less disproportion'd and uneven, then if a painter undertaking

to describe a History, should from the drawings of
Masters, and Figures in Print . . . take a posture from
one, a head from another, a body from a third, and having
put them on such legs as he shall make for them,
confidently averre he hath performed the noble invention
and design that belongs to a Story Painter.

(sig.a2v)

At this historical juncture there is some unresolved contradiction in the demonstrable degree of mounting anxiety
over plagiarism and literary theft, co-existing with the desire to
be most clearly indebted to an eminent predecessor. What
Langbaine upbraids as intellectual dishonesty is not usually
what would now be considered plagiarism: the adaptation of
plots from plays and novels written by authors no longer living,
and/or in languages other than English. In the absence of a law
of copyright, which would define the precise sense in which, to
use Chesterfield's expression, wit could be considered 'a kind of
Property', this cultural tension could not be diffused. If, then,
the reader detects in Rochester's 'An Allusion to Horace' some
degree of inconsistency—Dryden accused of literary theft in
the opening lines but later censured for his upstart refusal to
serve the literary gods of Elizabethan and Jacobean England in
his critical opinions—it may be that s/he has stumbled across a
genuine enough *aporia*. The contradiction here could not admit
of resolution from within the institutional boundaries of
literature, but required the Copyright Act of 1709 and subsequent clarificatory legislation to make sense out of it.

## NOTES

1. William Kupersmith observes that 'although Sprat and Cowley wrote
the earliest Imitations of Horace, John Wilmot, Earl of Rochester, first used
the Imitation as a weapon to attack contemporaries' in *Roman Satirists in
Seventeenth-Century England* (Lincoln, NE and London, 1985), p. 97. Etherege,
it seems, had produced a systematic imitation of Boileau in 1673, which
Dryden had mentioned to Rochester in a letter. See James Winn, *John Dryden
and his World* (New Haven and London, 1987), p. 251.
2. Previous important discussions of the 'Allusion' have not always
observed this point, and have had some tendency to condemn Rochester's

poem as a relatively unsuccessful exploitation of its original. See Howard D. Weinbrot, 'The "Allusion to Horace"': Rochester's Imitative Mode', *Studies in Philology*, 69 (1972), pp. 348–68; David Farley-Hills, *Rochester's Poetry* (London, 1978), p. 203; Pat Rogers, 'An Allusion to Horace', in *Spirit of Wit: Reconsiderations of Rochester*, ed. Jeremy Treglown (Oxford, 1982), pp. 166–76; P. E. Hewison, 'Rochester, the Imitation and An Allusion to Horace', *Seventeenth-Century*, 2.1 (1987), pp. 73–94.

3. See Frank Stack, *Pope and Horace* (Cambridge, 1985), for the most detailed discussion available of Popean technique. On pp. 85–88, Stack provides an excellent example of the way in which Pope employed typography to focus particular attention on Horace's obscenity. In *Sober Advice from Horace*, Pope quotes Horace in block capitals, raising the reader's (somewhat salacious) interest in how he is going to negotiate the translation of 'mirator CUNNI CUPIENNIUS ALBI'.

4. *The Works of John Dryden*, ed. H. T. Swedenberg Jr., *et al.*, 20 vols (Berkeley, Los Angeles and London, 1956–), 11:320–21, 322. (Hereafter, 'California Dryden').

5. All quotations from Rochester are taken from *The Poems of John Wilmot, Earl of Rochester*, ed. Keith Walker (Oxford, 1984) pp. 99–102. Shadwell recorded one of Dryden's allegedly gauche attempts at in-crowd obscenity in *The Medal of John Bayes* (1682):

> Thy Mirth by foolish Bawdry is exprest;
> And so debauch'd, so fulsome, and so odd,
> As . . .
> *Let's Bugger one another now by G— —d*
> (When ask'd how they should spend the Afternoon)
> This was the smart reply of the Heroick Clown.

6. California Dryden, 13:14.
7. Say, that thou pour'st them wheat,
   And they will acornes eat:
   'Twere simple fury, still, thy selfe to waste
   On such as have no taste!..
   If they love lees, and leave the lusty wine,
   Envy them not, their palate's with the swine
   (ll.11–14, 19–20).

*Ben Jonson*, eds. C. H. Herford and Percy and Evelyn Simpson, 8 vols (Oxford, 1938), 6:492.
8. California Dryden, 10:205–06.
9. Thomas Shadwell, Preface to *The Humorists* in *The Complete Works of Thomas Shadwell*, ed. Montague Summers, 5 vols (London, 1927, re-issued New York, 1968), 1:10, 12. (Hereafter, 'Summers').
10. California Dryden, 10:259.
11. Herford and Simpson, 8:625.
12. California Dryden, 9:352–69, *passim*.
13. Summers, 1:74.
14. A few examples might help to elucidate this point. When we are first

introduced to Sir Nicholas Gimcrack, the title-figure of *The Virtuoso* (1676), the *scene opens and discovers* Sir Nicholas *learning to swim upon a table*': or the marvellous stage-direction that opens *Bury Fair* (1689)—'Trim stands jetting out his bum, and bowing all the while'. Throughout his career, Shadwell exploited the possibilities of claustrophobic staging pioneered by Jonson in plays like *The Alchemist* and *The Silent Woman*, enjoying nothing more than to bring together in the same confined space characters who are rivals and antipathetic to one another. Ninny and Woodcock in *The Sullen Lovers* are lured to the same room in an inn, both under the impression that Emilia is to be there. In *The Humorists* (1671), Crazy and Drybob have both been told by the maid Bridget to climb into a window that they understand to be Theodosia's, there to be discovered and beaten by Raymond and Brisk. This device is taken to unprecedented lengths in *The Virtuoso* when Sir Formal Trifle and Sir Samuel Hearty, dressed in drag, find themselves sharing the same pitch-dark vault.

15. The Hon. Edward Howard, *The Women's Conquest* (London, 1671), Second Prologue, ll.11–19.

16. The translation is that of Niall Rudd, *The Satires of Horace and Persius* (Harmondsworth, 1973, rep. 1976), p. 67.

17. Thomas Dekker, *Satiromastix* (1602), ed. Fredson Bowers (Cambridge, 1953), 1: 326. For an excellent account of the quarrel, see David Riggs, *Ben Jonson: a Life* (Cambridge, Mass. and London, 1989), pp. 72–85.

18. Herford and Simpson, 5:23–24.

19. Thomas Shadwell, Preface to *The Sullen Lovers* in Summers, 1: 10,12.

20. Summers, 2:279.

21. *A Defence of an Essay of Dramatique Poesie* (1668), p. 7.

22. *Dramatic Works of John Dryden*, ed. George Saintsbury, 8 vols (Edinburgh, 1882), 5:8.

23. Thomas Shadwell, Prologue to *The Virtuoso* (1676), reproduced in *Dryden and Shadwell: the Literary Controversy*, ed. Richard L. Oden (New York, 1977), n.p.

24. Gerard Langbaine, *Momus Triumphans; or, the Plagiaries of the English Stage* (1687), ed. David Stuart Rodes (Augustan Reprint 150, William Andrews Clark Library, Los Angeles, 1971), Sig. A3v.

25. California Dryden, 17:57.

# Rochester and Oldham: 'High Rants in Profaneness'

RAMAN SELDEN

## I

Rochester died on 26 July 1680. John Oldham's pastoral elegy 'Bion, A Pastoral . . . Bewailing the Death of the Earl of Rochester' suggests that the Earl was his poetic mentor:

> If I am reckon'd not unblest in Song,
> 'Tis what I owe to all-teaching tongue:
> Some of thy Art, some of thy tuneful breath
> Thou didst by Will to worthless me bequeath:
> Others thy Flocks, thy Lands, thy Riches have,
> To me though didst thy Pipe and Skill vouchsafe.[1]

The lines were written about four years after Rochester was first made aware of Oldham, when the latter was working as an assistant master at the Whitgift School in Croydon. More than one account survives of a visit from Rochester and other court wits (including the Earl of Dorset and Sir Charles Sedley, according to the *DNB*, which derived its information from the Memoir attached to the 1722 edition of Oldham's *Works*, l. v–vi), though the venue was more likely to have been Beddington (where Oldham's patron Sir Nicholas Carew lived)[2] than Croydon.

The immediate occasion seems to have been Oldham's so-called 'Satyr Against Vertue', written by July 1676. This title, under which the poem was piratically published in 1679, was repudiated by Oldham who, in the 1682 edition, settled on an epigraph from Juvenal and 'Ode. Suppos'd to be spoken by a Court-Hector at Breaking of the Dial in Privy-Garden'. This drunken exploit of Rochester's had been mentioned in a newsletter report (26 June 1675): 'My Lord Rochester in a frolick after a rant did yesterday beat doune the dyill which stood in the middle of the Privie [Gard]ing, which was

esteemed the rarest in Europ'.[3] The phrase 'after a rant' may
have given Oldham the hint for his poem which, whatever its
intention, seems to have delighted the court wits and roused
their curiosity to meet the poet. Aubrey[4] refers to the exploit
and the presence of Lord Buckhurst and Fleetwood Shepherd.
We know of no other certain contacts between Oldham and
Rochester, but it is quite possible that a Latin letter written by
Oldham on 5 November 1677 was addressed to Rochester. The
letter accompanied a copy of Oldham's poem on the marriage
of William and Mary. The letter shows an appropriate
deference: 'I do not hope that you will admire them [the
verses]: it will be enough for me if you simply pardon them'.
The letter includes a passage in which Oldham suggests that
he lives for the moment and enjoys gay company:

> My first of cares is to put aside all care . . . I enjoy the
> present, . . . and leave the rest to fate, thinking nothing so
> absurd as to allow fear of the future to spoil my present
> happiness. Two or three times a week certain of us good
> companions meet in a tavern; there we drink in moder-
> ation, laugh sufficiently, in stories, wit, jests, songs and
> every cultivated pleasure pass the hours, . . . By heaven,
> you would envy us almost, did I not know you to be a man
> experienced and practised in the same happiness.[5]

The passage combines a tame Horatian hedonism with an
allusion to the epicurism of the Rochester cult, especially in the
probable tribute to Rochester's Hobbesian 'Love and Life: a
Song' (first published in 1677): 'Whatever is to come is not:
The present Moment's all my Lott' (ll.6 and 8).[6]

David Vieth, in his edition of Rochester's poems, discovered
a note on a manuscript copy at Yale (Osborn MS, Chest II, no.
14) of the 'Ode' (Satyr Against Vertue) dated 1677. The
author of the note informs us that Oldham's patron, Sir
Nicholas Carew, showed a Cowleian Pindarique in praise of
virtue and religion to the Duke of Buckingham and 'severall off
the witts at court'. The wits were impressed but did not believe
a man of Oldham's limited social experience could have
written it. They challenged Carew to set his man the task of
writing on the 'Thesis: Aude aliquid, et caet: which was as
much in the dispraise of virtue on the other side'. Oldham (he is

not named, but it must be him) 'to vindicate his reputation, and oblige Sir Nicholas, and that this was only a Tryall of skill . . . made this following poem'.[7] Vieth speculates that, since no surviving poem of Oldham's fits the description 'in praise of virtue and religion', it is likely that the Pindarique was the poem on the marriage of William and Mary. Consequently, Vieth dates the 'Aude aliquid' poem and the wits' visit not before November 1677, since the marriage poem's failure indicates that Oldham had not yet established his connection with the court wits. In fact, the poem was written by July 1676. Presumably Rochester did not exert himself on Oldham's behalf in 1677, having already honoured him with a partial visit in 1676. However, the note does contain some convincing detail. It is characteristic of Oldham, as we shall see, to respond to a 'Tryall of skill' even though it might undermine his 'principles'.

In Paul Hammond's view, 'Bion' should not be taken seriously as evidence of Oldham's discipleship,[8] since the poem itself marks a change of allegiance and a shift towards a more orthodox and classical poetic. It is certainly true that Oldham's poetry of the period 1676–80 is rather more Rochesterian than the ensuing period's. In his Advertisement to *Some New Pieces* he aims to translate Horace's *Ars* in the 'easier and familiar way of writing' associated with Horace's *Epistles*.[9] Hammond also believes that in the earlier phase Oldham had not found his most congenial models in Cowley and Rochester and that his work begins to mature after Rochester's death.[10] I agree that there is a change towards more elegant and classical poetics but I question the value judgement Hammond wishes to place upon it. I would suggest that Oldham's mock-baroque style is not 'immature' but corresponds to a definite phase in English poetry which plays with the instability of baroque rhetoric.

The 'Ode' is a paradoxical encomium,[11] in which the speaker adopts the stance of a committed sinner who inverts the history of ethical exempla, damning the virtuous (Aristotle, Brutus, Socrates) to praise the vicious (Herostratus, Nero, Guy Fawkes, Cain). It is in many ways a rather schoolmasterly performance, full of bookish allusions, mainly inspired by the Pindaric allusive style of Cowley. The poem is explicitly, even

heavy-handedly, ironic in its praise of vice. However, Oldham's exuberant adoption of a mask of vice is sufficiently
pleasurable stylistically to blur the distinction between irony
and sincerity. Rochester was fond of embracing his own vices
as if in pride. His 'To the Postboy' ('Pox on it why do I speak of
these poor things? I have blasphemed my god and libelld
Kings' (ll.13–14), which was written (probably by Rochester)
shortly after 27 June 1676 and therefore contemporaneously
with Oldham's piece, is in the first-person confessional mode
and in that respect differs from Oldham's overt dramatization
of the Rochesterian voice. Rochester evidently enjoyed seeing
his already celebrated persona given such a grandly Marlovian
treatment. Vieth argues that the mythic image of Rochester
was cultivated by the court wits as a 'form of joshing', and that
in 'To the Postboy' Rochester is working 'in the tradition
propagated by the lampoons written against him.[12] There is no
conclusive evidence of Rochester's authorship, so that Vieth's
interpretation remains speculative, especially his interesting
idea that Rochester transcends the myth and 'infuses his self-
portrait with almost satanic energy and grandeur' (Vieth, in
his edition of Rochester's poems, p. 203). If we imagine the
poem to have been written by one of the wits (say, Buckhurst)
we would have to restore the poem to the joshing category,
albeit bordering on denunciation. It is clear that both Rochester's and Oldham's fascination with the myth of the libertine
hero produced an unstable, polysemic form of discourse which
slides between the ironic, the confessional and the heroic
modes.

  Rochester himself wrote poems in which he develops an
ironic persona. 'A Very Heroicall Epistle in Answer to Ephelia', for example, includes passages in which the 'happy Sultan'
is praised by a speaker intended to satirize the boastful lover,
John Sheffield, Earl of Mulgrave:

> Thee, like some God, the trembling Crowd adore;
> Each Man's thy Slave, and Woman-kind, thy Whore . . .
> Secure in Solid Sloth, though there dost Reigne
>                                   (ll.35–36 and 41)

It should be said that Rochester's ironies are usually sparing
and less systematic than Oldham's.

There seems little doubt that Oldham had no desire to embrace the cult of libertinism espoused by the court wits, but his fascination had the effect of giving his writing an errant impetus, a veritable abandonment to the signifier. The pleasure of writing and the heady commitment of identification with the subject-position of the 'other' overcome the qualms of the speaking subject. For example, when Oldham's ranter imagines an even greater career of sin than had been achieved by his predecessors he declares:

> Let your Examples move me with a gen'rous Fire,
> Let them into my daring Thoughts inspire
> Somewhat completely Wicked, some vast giant
> Crime,
> Unknown, unheard, unthought of by all past and present
> Time:
> 'Tis done, 'tis done; me thinks I feel the pow'rfull
> Charms,
> And a new Heat of Sin my Spirits warms;
> I travail with a glorious Mischief, for whose Birth
> My Soul's too narrow, and weak Fate too feeble yet
> to bring it forth[13]

The intertexts seethe and shimmer beneath the surface (Tamburlaine, Virgil's Sibyl, the Alexander and Alcibiades topoi). The pedantry is less apparent than in the passages on the 'Stagyrite' and the Athenian 'sniveling Puritan'. The lines ignite that frisson of abandoned wickedness we associate with Barabas and De Flores. Oldham later employed the same devices for his villainous personae in *Satyrs upon the Jesuits*. No doubt Rochester would have enjoyed the attack on idealism and reason and the celebration of natural instinct. He would have noticed several Rochesterian touches too. When Oldham's ranter declares 'Let fumbling Age be grave and wise' and let virtue 'varnish with her Name a well-dissembled Impotence', we are reminded of Rochester's 'The Disabled Debauchee' who is 'forc'd from the pleasing Billows of debauch, on the dull Shore of lazy temperance' (ll.15–16) and who will, 'shelter'd in impotence, urge you to blows, And being good for nothing else, be wise' (ll.47–48). Rochester's Epilogue to Davenant's *Circe* (1677) contains similar lines:

> 'Twas Impotence did first this Vice begin,
> Fooles censure Wit, as Old men raile of sin,
> Who Envy Pleasure, which they cannot tast,
> And good for nothing, wou'd be wise at last.
>                                        (ll.13–16)

The ranter's concern that vice should be embraced with style and elegance is another Rochesterian theme:

> None, but dull unbred Fools, discredit Vice,
> Who act their Wickedness with an ill Grace;
>     Such their Profession scandalise,
>     And justly forfeit all that Praise,
> All that Esteem, that Credit, and Applause,
> Which we by our wise Menage from a Sin can raise:
>     A true and brave Transgressor ought
> To sin with the same Height of Spirit Caesar fought.[14]

In his 'A letter from Artemiza', which was at some time (possibly before July 1676) transcribed by Oldham along with 'Satyr' the 'fine lady' possesses a 'foppery' which 'without the help of Sense, Could ne're have rose to such an Excellence' (ll.132–33). Artemiza declares that 'An Eminent Foole must be a Foole of parts' (l.161).

It is clearly the ranter's *style* which has such strong affinities with Rochester's persona. Even Rochester's letters contain striking parallel's with Oldham's ironic villain. Writing to Savile (c.1673–74) he begins:

> Do a charity becoming one of your pious principles, in preserving your humble servant Rochester from the imminent peril of sobriety, which, for want of good wine more than company (for I drank like a hermit betwixt God and my own conscience) is very like to befall me. Remember what pains I have formerly taken to wean you from your pernicious resolutions of discretion and wisdom.[15]

The Earl who wrote of 'your pernicious resolutions of discretion and wisdom' would have relished Oldham's 'The Manhood and Discretion of Debauchery'. Of course, Rochester's irony has all the wicked twinkle of aristocratic negligence and playful outrageousness. Oldham's guying of the Earl's transgressive spirit may seem factitious, but he produces a discourse of excess which develops its own momentum.

Anthony à Wood thought the 'Ode' was among 'the mad ranting and debauched specimens of poetry of this author Oldham' which Rochester 'seemed much delighted in'.[16] The pirated edition of 1679 provoked a reply by an anonymous author who evidently saw no irony.[17] Oldham himself was moved to write 'An Apology for the foregoing Ode', in which he clearly underlines the ironical intention of the 'Ode' which was written 'in Masquerade . . . not to Flatter Vice, but to Traduce'. He also implies that his Muse had become rather more involved in the part than he had intended:

> She thought she must be Termagant and mad;
> That made her speak like a lewd Pun O'th' Town,
>     Who, by converse with Bullies wicked grown,
>         Has learnt the Mode to cry all Vertue down;
> But now the Vizard's off, she changes Scene,
> And turns a modest civil Girle agen.[18]

Oldham inverts the libertine mask and becomes the righteous satirist who desires to achieve a 'Poetique Rage' which will make him thought 'Heav'ns just Plague' upon the 'Sins of lewd Mankind'. If the 'Ode' is factitious, the 'Apology' is no less so. In the 'Ode' he assumes a voice whose irony is cast in doubt by rhetoric, while in the 'Apology' he assumes the righteous satirist's stance in a Juvenalian persona. The question arises 'is there a way of discovering the true Oldham?' Is there a coherent identity behind the contradictory surface of his poetry? Modernist poetics looks for a godlike 'mind' behind the personae of a text, but postmodernist theories regard all representations of subjectivity as equally caught up in the order of discourse. A persona is no more than a subject position. Rochester's self-representation in his letters and Oldham's dramatized personae are all constructed voices, always resistant to attempts to stabilize their identity.

## II

Oldham produced a number of other poems under the influence of Rochester and the court wits (but prior to the July

1676 meeting). They are 'Sardanapalus', 'Dithyrambique on Drinking', 'Upon the Author of the Play call'd Sodom' (another obscene poem). Subsequently, Oldham wrote a number of pieces which reveal either the direct influence of or strong similarities with Rochester's poetry. The former include 'The Eighth Satire of Monsieur Boileau, Imitated', 'An Ode of Anacreon Paraphras'd: The Cup', 'The Careless Good Fellow'. However, Oldham also wrote attacks on the wits, both before and after his acquaintance with Rochester.

His first important poem 'To the Memory of My Dear Friend, Mr. Charles Morwent: A Pindarique' (Morwent died of small-pox at the age of twenty in 1675),[19] contrasts Morwent's virtues with the vices of the debauchee. Interestingly, Oldham uses the same rhetorical patterns as he used a year later in the 'Ode' (ll.108ff), but adapted to a virtuous persona. In old age the wicked are forced to abandon vice, and in their virtual impotence have to settle for virtue:

> Let wild Debauche[e]s hug their darling Vice
> And court no other Paradise,
>     Till want of Power
> Bids 'em discard the stale Amour,
> And when disabled strength shall force
>     A short Divorce,
> Miscall that weak forbearance Abstinence,
> Which wise Morality and better Sence
> Stiles but at best a sneaking Impotence.[20]

The passage goes well beyond the needs of its context and reveals Oldham's fascination with the Rochesterian idiom. It is not impossible that Oldham read in manuscript Rochester's 'The Disabled Debauchee', which is dated 1675 by Vieth. In the 'Apology' Oldham makes an explicit attack upon the wits when he laments his own indulgence in their vein:

> He could be Bawdy too, and nick the Times
> In what they dearly love, damn'd Placket-Rhimes,
> Such as our Nobles write,
> Whose nauseous Poetry can reach no higher,
> Then what the Codpiece and its God inspire;
> So lewd, they spend at Quill, you'd justly think,
> They wrote with something nastier than Ink.[21]

Once again, Oldham's text shifts gear from a simple moral denunciation to an unconscious complicity: in old-fashioned terms, his imagination is fired by the rhetoric of obscenity.

Six months after composing the 'Ode', in another elegy (on Harman Atwood, whose niece was married to John Shepheard, Oldham's Whitgift headmaster, and who died 16 February 1676/7), he attacks 'The Men of Sence who in Confederacy join / To damn Religion' and 'try by little Railleries to ruin it, / And jeer't into an unregarded poor defenceless thing.' Had they seen Atwood's piety, we are told, they would acknowledge its power to 'Proselyte as fast as they debauch the Age'. The last phrase reduced, in rhetorical terms, the pious and the lewd to the positions of equivalence in the economy of persuasion. There is no slide into complicity here, but one can say that the binary oppositions which sustain the discourse are freely reversible in Oldham's work of the period; he moves between contrary terms, passing back and forth as if through a mirror.

Rather as Donne wrote both libertine and neoplatonic verses in the same period, so Oldham intersperses his Rochesterian experiments with moments of religious penitence. On 22 June 1677 he wrote to a friend: 'There is not an arranter fool in nature than a rash unguarded unconsidering sinner' and applies this to his own former self[23]. In the undateable 'Sunday Thoughts in Sickness' he laments 'How oft have I triumph'd in my . . . seared insensibility? . . . How have I abus'd and misemployed those parts and Talents . . . which I have made the Patrons of Debauchery, and Pimps and Panders to Vice.'[24] It used to be commonplace to think that Donne repented his youthful poetry in a similar manner. However, in both cases there are less simple and purely diachronic dimensions to their contrary poetic styles (see my conclusion).

### III

In some ways, his most impressive Rochesterian piece is 'Upon the Author of the Play call'd Sodom'. It attacks an author for his obscenity but unexpectedly turns the insults against the insufficiencies of the author's talents:

Disgrace to Libels! Foil to very Shame!
Whom 'tis a scandal to vouchsafe to damn!
What foul Description's foul enough for thee,
Sunk quite beneath the reach of Infamy?
Though covet'st to be lewd, but want'st the Might
And art all over Devil, but in Wit.[25]

This echoes the 'Ode': 'None, but dull unbred Fools, discredit
vice, Who act their Wickedness with an ill Grace.'[26] Sodom's
depravity is a failure of wit, which prevents the author from
achieving the polish which Rochester had in mind when he
praised one of his fellow wits, Sir Charles Sedley, in 'An
Allusion to Horace' (Winter, 1675/6):

For Songs, and Verses, Mannerly Obscene, . . .
Sidley has that prevailing gentle Art,
That can with a resistless Charme impart,
The loosest wishes to the Chastest Heart.
(ll.61 and ll.64–66)

The skills of 'mannerly' obscenity were also cultivated by
Rochester and by Oldham in his Rochesterian poems of
obscenity. In 'Sodom', Oldham separates himself from his
enemy by raising the figurative stakes. The metaphoric
exuberance is shared by Rochester. In his poem 'On Mistress
Willis' he asks the 'Bawdy Powers' to inspire him: 'I'le write
upon a double Clowt, And dipp my Pen in Flowers' [menstrual
discharge] (ll.7–8) Oldham too imagines his author's 'Muse
has got the Flowers'. In the same vein he fancies the bawdy
author's work being used as pornography:

There [Moorfields] Punk, perhaps, may they brave works
                                              rehears,
Frigging the senseless thing with Hand and Verse.

This resembles Rochester's satire on Charles describing Nell
Gwyn trying to raise his member with 'hands, fingers, mouth,
and thighs' (l.30), but Oldham introduces a zeugma ('Frigging
. . . with Hand and Verse') which raises the obscenity to a
higher poetic power. [27]

He anticipates Pope's metaphoric shock-tactics in *The Dunciad*, and makes the 'Author' void 'Corruption':

Like Ulcers, thy Impostum'd addle Brains
Drop out in Matter, which thy Paper stains:
Whence nauseous Rhymes by filthy Births proceed,
As Maggots in some Turd ingendring breed.[28]

Oldham's own rhymes (verses) engender themselves in a
similar way—sliding along the defiles of the discourse of
obscenity. I am not making a moral point, but rather a point
about writing: Oldham turned his poetic talents, at least for a
while, to the task of learning to become one of the 'Debauche[e]s
of the nobler Strain'. H.A. Mason, commenting on Thomas
More's resort to Roman obscenity in his epigrams, makes the
point that 'some Humanists thought that they were doing the
Latin thing in making their epigrams as lewd and indecent as
possible', but also defended their practice by quoting Martial's
own maxim 'Lasciva est nobis pagina, vita proba' (My pages
are lascivious, but my life is clean).[29] One is reminded of
Milton's Latin poems in the Ovidian manner. This might seem
to be hypocrisy or prurience, but, in thinking this, we would be
overlooking the historical nature of cultural codes about writing
and sexuality. Oldham evidently felt the need to repent his
naughty writings but we should not take the apparent alter-
nations of perspective too seriously. It is not so much that his
repentance is 'insincere', but that in flirting with the libertine
wit of his aristocratic model he is engaging in a certain kind of
signifying practice which draws him into a pattern of reversals
and inversions of terms. The fashionably outrageous style of
libertine wit could never be adopted by Oldham *in propria
persona*, but this does not prevent his pious renunciations from
being as fictitious (rhetorical) as his Rochesterian voice. He
produces a variety of dramatis personae (pius or immoral or
ironic), while Rochester interweaves libertine and religious
terms to produce a proto-Lawrentian effect of transcendent
naturalism. He remarks in the 'Advertisement' to the collection
which included the 'Ode' are oddly ambivalent and self-
revelatory. He declares that the poem 'is the most liable to
censure' (either 'frequently censured' or 'vulnerable to censure')
but was never designed to attack virtue:

> Twas meant to abuse those, who valued themselves upon
> their Wit and Parts in praising Vice, and to shew, that

> others of sober Principles, if they would take the same
> liberty in Poetry, could strain as high rants in Profaness
> as they.[30]

The two purposes are hardly consecutive or reinforcing. Moral
principle vies with emulation in a revealing manner. Oldham
does not tell us why he felt the need to 'take the same liberty in
Poetry'. There is clearly something compelling in such fictive
liberty. The same ambivalence appears in Oldham's phrase,
describing Rochester, 'our great witty bawdy Peer' (Rawlinson
MS).

## IV

Of Oldham's three mock-heroic Pindariques (the 'Ode', the
'Dithyrambique' and 'Sardanapalus'), all ironic celebrations of
the Rochester cult, the most impressive is 'Sardanapalus', in
which Oldham glorifies the erotic conquests of the eastern
Prince. The technique anticipates Dryden's and Pope's techniques of bathos, vividly mixing heroic idiom and the obscene.
Since Charles II was commonly associated in satire with
Sardanapalus there are inevitably a number of parallels which
would have amused Rochester who had himself indulged in
mock-heroic ridicule of the monarch, especially in his 'A Satire
on Charles II'. When Oldham ironically praises the monarch's
passivity which left him 'Free from the Trouble, and Imperti-
nence of State; Exempt from all the Anxiety and Fear / Which
other Sceptred Wretches wear', we are reminded of Rochester's
lampoon in which Charles is contrasted with the warlike Louis
XIV:

> Him [Charles] no Ambition mooves, to gett Renowne
> Like the french Foole, . . .
> Peace is his Aime, his Gentlenesse is such
> And Love, he loves, for he loves fucking much.
> (ll.5–6 and ll.8–9)

The following lines make a seemingly direct allusion to the
court wits' satire on Charles. Sardanapalus withstands court
raillery 'with Gen'rous Scorn':

> In vain the Railing Satyrs of the Age
>> Attack thee with Poetic Rage;
> They spread their loose Lampoons in vain,
> And with Leud wit thy sacred Pintle did Profane.[31]

Rochester actually profaned Charles's pintle ('His Sceptter and his Prick are of a Length', (l.11), etc). Even the mixed style ('Pintle', 'Profane') is distinctly Rochesterian ('And may no woman better thrive that dares profane the cunt I swive!', Vieth, p. 46). Oldham seems to be translating Rochester's lampooning style into the formal mock-heroic. For example, Charles's is:

> The proudest peremtoriest Prick alive
> Though Safety, Law, Religion, Life lay on't,
> 'Twould breake through all to make its way to Cunt.
>> (ll.19–21)

Oldham transforms this into full epic dress:

>> Fates, do your worst, said'st though,
>> Our Pr-k shall Reign in spite of you:
> Not all your Heav'n shall bribe me from Delight,
> Nor all your Thunder from my Pleasure fright.
> Sink Nations, Kingdoms perish, Empire fall,
> One thrust in Charming C-t shall over balance all.[32]

This grandiosity of manner did not impress Sir William Soame, who attacked Oldham in 'To the Author of Sardanapalus upon that, and his other writings', in which he twitted the 'School-master' for wrought versification and his ranting style. There is noting impressive, he says, in 'Shew[ing] a Monster for a Man', and in mistaking 'furious Fustian for Sublime' (cited in *Poems*, p. liv). In his advertisement to *Some New Pieces* (1681) Oldham defends himself but also makes concessions, clearly moving towards a more sober and neoclassical aesthetic.

'A Dithyrambique on Drinking', as its subtitle indicates ('Suppos'd to be spoken by Rochester at the Guinny-Club'), resembles the 'Ode' in being both an explicit dramatization of Rochester's persona and a paradoxical encomium. It also resembles 'Sardanapalus' in its use of a sublime mock-heroic style. The poem, based on the drinking song genre described in Cowley's 'Praise of Pindar'[33] is applied to Rochester's self-acknowledged addiction to wine. He confessed to Burnet that his friends engaged him deeper and deeper in 'Intemperance' when they saw how, inflamed by wine, he was lifted to heights of pleasantry and wit. He added that 'five years together he was continually Drunk'.[34] The 'Guinny-Club' presumably refers to a regular gathering of Rochester and the wits where each contributed a guinea to the evening's expenses and where poems like Oldham's would have provided the entertainment. Drinking wine raises the toper above the level of mere mortals, above the level of 'poor tottring Reason'. The drinker's attack on 'base Reason' bears some resemblance to Rochester's 'Satyr', which Oldham transcribed. Oldham's 'Rochester' abuses the 'sober Fool' who called drunkenness 'madness'. He calls the man 'some dull Philosopher, some reas'ning Tool'. In the 'Satyr' Rochester calls that 'vain Animal' man, 'Who is so proud of being rational' (ll.6–7), 'the reasoning Engine' (l.29). However, this similarity should not distract us from recognising the un-Rochesterian features of the poem which is full of Oldham's favourite devices—sublime ranting, heavy irony, and sustained mock-elevation. The following lines are typical and point towards the mock-heroic style of Dryden and Pope rather than the relatively rare pieces of sustained mock-heroic in Rochester:

> Assist Allmighty Wine, for thou alone hast Power,
>     And other I'll invoke nor more,
>     Assist, while with just Praise I thee Adore;
>     Aided by thee I dare thy Worth Rehearse
> In Flights above the common Pitch of groveling Verse:
>     Though art the World's great Soul, that Heav'nly
>                         Fire,
>     Which dost our dull half-kindled Mass Inspire;
> We nothing gallant, and above our selves produce;
>     Till thou dost Finish Man and Reinfuse:
> Thou art the only Source of all the World calls Great,
> Thou didst the Poets first and they the Gods Create.[35]

The lines look backwards towards the rationalized neoplatonism of Cowley and forwards to the satiric sublimities of Pope's

*Dunciad*. The links with Rochester here are mainly biographical. In his letters to Savile Rochester sometimes adopts a mock-serious tone in his references to wine, but his naturalistic zest and libertine philosophy make his idiom more serious. A second bottle of wine, he writes, 'tells us trust of ourselves, and forces us to speak truths of others, banishes flattery from our tongues and distrust from our Hearts, sets us above the meane Pollicy of Court prudence'.[36] In the letter in which he jokes about Savile's 'pernicious resolutions of discretion and wisdom', he concludes with one of his characteristic intensifications in which he appropriates the resonances of religion to the libertine faith:

> Dear Savile, as ever thou dost hope to out-do Machievel or equal me, send me some good wine! So may thy wearied soul at last find rest, no longer hovering 'twixt th' unequal choice of politics and lewdness![37]

Oldham's poem centres on the sublime relief of the insensibility afforded by wine, which helps us 'Sleep out the dull Fatigue, and long Debauch of Life'. He makes no attempt to transmit Rochester's naturalistic convictions, reducing them to irrational and nihilistic gestures.

Closer to Rochester's manner is 'The Careless Good Fellow' (written on 9 March 1680) which uses the stanza form of Rochester's 'Lampoone' which opens:

> To longe the Wise Commons have been in debate
> About Money, and Conscience (those Trifles of State) . . .
> (ll.1–2)

Oldham's poem starts:

> A Pox of this fooling and plotting of late,
> What a pother and stir has it kept in the State![38]

Rochester's lines are directly imitated later in the poem:

> I mind not grave Asses, who idly debate
> About Right and Succession, the trifles of State;
> (ll.19–20)

In the toper's celebration of his fun-loving monarch Oldham takes up in a different fashion Rochester's contrast (in 'A Satire

on Charles II') between the pacific Charles and the warlike
Louis XIV, calling Louis XIV 'The Bully of France' (Rochester calls him 'the Hector of France'). Oldham's poem is
interesting too for its scepticism about the Popish Terror ('Let
the Rabble run mad with Suspicions and Fears') which
Oldham had just helped to ferment in his anti-Popish *Satyrs
upon the Jesuits*. Even though scepticism is in character with the
drinker's persona, the poem confirms one's sense of the
reversibility of the subject positions which Oldham enters in
his poetry of this period. I prefer to read the shifts of position as
symptoms of a labile psyche rather than as rationalized
adjustments of perspective.

Oldham evidently knew Rochester's 'Upon His Drinking a
Bowl' (1673?) which has links with both 'The Careless Good
Fellow' and Oldham's 'An Ode of Anacreon Paraphras'd: the
Cup'. Their common liking for the mock-heroic appears in the
passage in which Oldham's toper waxes hyperbolical:

> Oh what an Ebb of Drink have we?
> Bring, bring a Deluge, fill us up the Sea,
> Let the vast Ocean by our mighty Cup,
> We'll drink't and all its Fishes too like Loaches up.[39]

Rochester's poem, a version of Ronsard's imitation of some
Anacreontic verses, includes a similar grandiose vision:

> Make it [the cup] so large, that fill'd with Sack
> 　　Up to the swelling brim,
> Vast Toasts, on the delicious Lake,
> 　　Like Ships at Sea may swim
> 　　　　　　(ll.5–8)

However, the differences are at least as striking as the
similarities: Oldham's flight of fancy is characteristically more
rhetorically wrought up ('Oh what an', 'Bring, bring', 'the Sea
. . . the Ocean'). Oldham's Anacreontic poem also aims to
inflate his model:

> Make me a Bowl, a mighty Bowl,
> Large, as my capacious Soul,
> Vast, as my thirst is; let it have
> Depth enough to be my Grave.[40]

In one passage in which the drinker asks the potter to decorate the cup, Oldham adds an erotic touch which is taken from Rochester:

> Draw me first a spreading Vine,
> Make its Arms the Bowl entwine,
> With kind embraces, such as I
> Twist about my loving she.[41]

Here are the lines in Rochester's poem which Oldham uses:

> But carve thereon a spreading Vine,
>     Then add Two lovely Boys;
> Their limbs in Amorous folds intwine,
>     The Type of future joys.
>         (ll.17–20)

Rochester's eroticism is more direct, more unorthodox and is complicated by one of his characteristic appropriations of religious discourse ('The Type of future joys'). Oldham translates Rochester's daring, homoerotic vision into a conventional conceit.

Oldham was an important pioneer of the Imitation[42] and his interest in this form was given impetus by the example of Rochester's less systematic kinds of 'allusion' poetry. Oldham's 'The Eighth Satyr of Monsieur Boileau, Imitated' is partly inspired by Rochester's 'Satyr' (1675?) which was transcribed by Oldham in the Rawlinson manuscript.[43] Rochester's famous poem is loosely based on Boileau's satire, but he develops a distinctive argument without following the precise shape of his model. Oldham follows the original's argument and provides a vividly topical sequence of English parallels to Boileau's French. However, there are a number of passages where Oldham has clearly leaned upon Rochester for expressions.[44] Oldham's *adversarius* apostrophizes man as 'Lord of the Universe':

> For him was this fair frame of Nature made . . .
> To him alone of all the living kind,
> Has bounteous Heav'n the reas'ning gift assign'd.[45]

Rochester's *adversarius* declares:

> Blest glorious Man! to whom alone kind Heav'n,
> An everlasting Soul has freely giv'n . . .
> And this fair frame, in shining Reason drest . . .
>                (ll.60–61 and ll.64)

Oldham describes reason leading man astray; he is tossed about by 'wavering doubt' and his 'restless mind still rolls from thought to thought.'[46] Rochester too invokes man as the 'misguided follower' of reason who, 'Stumbling from thought to thought, falls headlong down / into doubts boundless Sea' (ll.16, 18–19). Oldham's 'idle whimsies of his brain' is matched by Rochester's 'Mountains of Whimseys, heap'd in his own Brain' (l.17). Oldham's *adversarius* praises man's intellect in phrases not based on Boileau: man's 'boundless wit, with souring wings durst fly, / Beyond the flaming borders of the sky'. Rochester's speaker sees reason enabling man to take 'flight' and 'then souring pierce, / The flaming limits of the Universe' (ll.68–69).

Oldham wrote a number of other poems in the period before Rochester's death which might well have entertained the wits at the 'Guinny Club', but which owe almost everything to the neoclassical wit of Cowley and Waller rather than the more down-to-earth eroticism of Rochester. In these poems (for example, the 'Cosmelia' poems and 'Upon a Lady . . . Out of *Voiture*') there is once again a typical alternation between rhetorical elevation and mock-heroic vulgarity. In like manner Oldham's attempts to mimic or to assimilate the fashionable wit and obscenity of Rochester's circle seem always to produce a radical ambivalence of stance—a swinging between classical sublimity and mock-seriousness, between heroic libertinism and puritan self-recrimination. Oldham clearly aspired at some moments to become a member of the school of elegant outrage. Rochester, in the Beddington visit, briefly acknowledges Oldham's right to notice. Rochester succeeded in capturing a devotee in an unlikely quarter—the lodgings of an assistant schoolmaster. However, Oldham's poetic career, which began under the tutelage of the neoclassical tradition (especially Cowley), took a partially contradictory turn in the years 1676–79 when, in search of patronage and in troubled times, he allowed subconscious drives to shape the surface of his writings. The poetry of this period releases the forbidden voices of anger and desire: the forms of rant, denunciation, curse, mock-encomium, drinking song and impersonation all facilitate the unblocking of strong feelings. However, neoclassical decorum and the authority of the allusive mode exercise a shaping and restraining effect,[47] elevating lewdness to the level of the 'mannerly obscene' and abuse to the level of heroic satire.

Rochester's 'all-teaching tongue' cannot be given all the credit for Oldham's stylistic exuberance. Oldham's own brand of heroic satire is not Rochester's. The latter held to a much more personal aesthetic of satire, and believed that he could not 'write with life, unless he were heated by Revenge.' Satire is founded upon 'Resentments' (Burnet, p. 26). Also, Hammond is right to see a new poetic emerging in Oldham's 'Bion', his elegy on Rochester. Oldham seems to attribute to Rochester's influence the qualities of smoothness ('thy tuneful breath') to which Oldham aspired rather than those he had cultivated under the influence of that 'witty bawdy Peer'.

## NOTES

1. All quotations are from *The Poems of John Oldham*, ed. Harold F. Brooks with the collaboration of Raman Selden (Oxford, 1987). David Farley-Hills's review, *RES*, 39 (1988), pp. 445–46, contains a supplementary list of possible echoes of Rochester in Oldham's poetry. Subsequently, *RES* published a letter from Brooks and Selden correcting some misapprehensions of Farley-Hills.

2. David Vieth quotes an anonymous note on the poem, which indicates that the author of the note was aware that Carew was Oldham's patron. See 'John Oldham, the Wits, and *A Satyr against Vertue*', *PQ*, 32 (1953), pp. 91–93. Harold Brooks deduced the Carew connection independently (see *Poems*, xxviii and n.16).

3. *The Poems and Letters of Andrew Marvell*, ed. H. M. Margoliouth, 3rd edition (Oxford, 1971), 1.409.

4. *Brief Lives*, ed. Andrew Clark, 2 vols (1898), ll.34.

5. Translated from Bodl. MS Rawlinson, Poet. 123, p. 106.

6. All quotations from Rochester's poems are from Keith Walker's edition, *The Poems of John Wilmot, Earl of Rochester* (Oxford, 1984).

7. Vieth, 'John Oldham, the Wits, and *A Satyr Against Vertue*', *op. cit.*, p. 91.

8. Dustin H. Griffin, *Satires Against Man: The Poems of Rochester* (Berkeley, 1973), p. 257n: 'Rochester had surprisingly little influence on . . . Oldham'.

9. *Poems*, p. 88.

10. Paul Hammond, *John Oldham and the Renewal of Classical Culture* (Cambridge, 1983), pp. 36–41.

11. H. K. Miller, 'The Paradoxical Encomium with Special Reference to Its Vogue in England, 1600–1800', *Modern Philology*, 53 (1956), pp. 45–78.

12. David M. Vieth, *Attribution in Restoration Poetry: A Study of Rochester's Poems of 1680* (New Haven and London, 1963), pp. 198, 203.

13. *Poems*, p. 66.

14. *Poems*, p. 63.

15. *The Letters*, ed. Jeremy Treglown (Oxford, 1980), pp. 91–92.

16. *Athenae Oxonienses*, ed. P. Bliss, 4 vols (1813–20), IV. 121.

17. *Poems*, p. 400.

18. *Poems*, p. 68.

19. For a discussion of Morwent see *Poems*, p. 513.

20. *Poems*, pp. 305–06.

21. *Poems*, p. 69.

22. *Poems*, pp. 318–19.

23. *Poems*, p. xliii.

24. *Poems*, p. xliii.

25. *Poems*, p. 342

26. *Poems*, p. 63

27. A surviving prologue to *Sodom* confirms a pornographic intention by the author. See Roger Thompson, *Unfit for Modest Ears*, London and Basingstoke, 1979, p. 127.

28. *Poems*, p. 342.

29. H. A. Mason, *Humanism and Poetry in the Early Tudor Period* (London, 1959), p. 42.

30. *Poems*, p. 4.

31. *Poems*, p. 347.

32. *Poems*, p. 348.

33. *Poems*, p. 500.

34. Gilbert Burnet, *Some Passages of the Life and Death of the Right Honourable John Earl of Rochester* (London, 1680), p. 12.

35. *Poems*, p. 261.

36. *The Letters*, ed. Jeremy Treglown (Oxford, 1980), p. 67.

37. *Ibid.*, p. 92.

38. *Poems*, p. 237.

39. *Poems*, p. 263.

40. *Poems*, p. 216.

41. *Poems*, p. 217.

42. See Harold F. Brooks, ' "The Imitation" in English Poetry, Especially in Formal Satire, Before the Age of Pope', *RES*, 25 (1949), pp. 124–40.

43. *Poems*, p. 436.

44. For a full listing of parallels, see *Poems*, pp. 436–45.

45. *Poems*, p. 162.

46. *Poems*, p. 163.

47. Cf. Felicity A. Nussbaum, *The Brink of All We Hate: English Satires on Women, 1660–1750* (Lexington, 1984), p. 24.

# 'The Present Moment' and 'Times Whiter Series': Rochester and Dryden

## BERNARD BEATTY

Dryden and Rochester are the most considerable poets of their day and knowingly represent their times. Both poets are fascinated, too, by their occupancy of time but they understand and represent this in entirely different ways. This divergence is most easily marked in their reading of Charles II and his court but it controls, too, their attitude to sexuality and, finally, distinguishes the specific nature of their religious conversions.

The opposition is not difficult to see for it cuts to the centre of their interests and literary procedures. Rochester insists upon the impossibly 'present moment' and, as corollary and consequence, reveals himself in impersonation. Dryden is concerned with a 'now' in which 'Times whiter Series is begun' and, as corollary and consequence, is enfolded in visions of history. These are poles apart but, as such, are complementary. Rochester's 'present moment' is 'all my Lott' and disappears 'as fast as it is got' ('Love and Life', ll.8–10).[1] He does not possess as 'mine' any past or future. The 'present moment', however, at the very point of its appropriation is liable to be hapless. It is always an amalgam of the 'lucky' or 'happy minute' and 'The Imperfect Enjoyment'. The character of such moments is most obviously revealed in sexual interchange but that, in turn, discloses an inescapably general state of affairs. We find ourselves with the wrong companions, in the wrong house, wearing the wrong shape, thinking with the wrong consciousness. Enjoyment does not wait on our desire nor does our will control our members. As this is the case even the 'livelong minute' eludes consciousness but tests and reveals our discomfort. Lovers may 'Long to be often tried' in this way but have to convince themselves and others that their hearts 'do justly swell, with no vain-glorious pride' ('Against Constancy', ll.13–16). Even if, for the precarious moment, such pride is deserved, it exists as assertion and willed performance encircled by doubt and it will be cancelled by the inevitable change to old age and then to worms. Indeed, confidence in the swelling life of legitimate pride is always undermined at its moment of exultation by the invisible worm of detumescence, impotence and death. All debauchees know themselves to be disabled. When Rochester is not identifying himself in this alias, he tries to distance himself from himself by publicly naming the king as the original of all maimed and disabled debauchees.

In Rochester's view, surprisingly close to Dryden's, the health of the Court and England, like that of some elemental tribe, is bound up with the interchangeability of Charles II's 'Sceptter and his Prick' ('A Satire on Charles II', l.11). *His* desires, we are told, are not 'above his Strength'. This condition, instead of ensconcing him in the primal 'blest . . . Created State' ('The Fall', l.1), renders him contemptible insofar as he is governed as man and king by any 'she' who can activate that all too reliable potency. Characteristically, Rochester cannot sustain this focus but has to undermine the vindicated present moment which escapes the accusation brought to it. Instead, he goes on to displace it by the more familiar Wilmotian picture of Charles's exhausted virility and Nell Gwyn's laborious stimulation of the fallen sceptre back to life. This later image is logically inconsistent with the earlier attack. It is connected, however, quite plausibly by consistency of tone and by Rochester's ingrained assumption that virility and impotence, though decisively opposed again and again in his verse, are almost interchangeable. If we wanted to find a parallel for this there is a famous one close at hand in Marvell's 'To his Coy Mistress' which, too, seems to merge erotic vaunting with deep, though witty, despair. Marvell, praised in 'Tunbridge Wells' (l.64), had little respect for Charles. He could not relate the monarch to his own respect for Nature's fecundity and for impossible purity. It is here that Dryden established a connection from the beginning, though it is to flower best in poems written after Rochester's death.

Dryden begins the last paragraph of *Astraea Redux* in this way:

And now times whiter Series is begun
Which in soft Centuries shall smoothly run.
(ll.292–93)

The thought is characteristic of the poet. Dryden reads current
history as he reads the Scriptures. Time as such wastes away in
repeated cycles of folly but Time is renewed 'now' in a 'whiter
Series' as it were *ab initio* in a fresh creation. Here, the
usurpation of Royal government under Cromwell is interpreted as sin converted into penitence. So Charles returning to
England sees its white cliffs in a witty double focus:

The Land returns, and in the white it wears
The marks of penitence and sorrow bears.
(ll.254–55)

The whiteness of penitence and of England's originating purity
is the foundation for the new 'whiter Series' of Time that is
inaugurated by the Restoration and renewed, according to
*Annus Mirabilis*, after the Great Fire. Twenty years later, not
without some desperation, Dryden claims that yet again
Charles's England, despite severe interim training, is to be
renewed directly from its sacred sources. At the end of *Absalom
and Achitophel* he repeats, as prophesy, the claim of *Astraea
Redux*:

Henceforth a Series of new time began
The mighty Years in long Procession ran:
(ll.1028–29)

It would be hard to imagine a vocabulary and point of view
further from Rochester's than this. We see this most clearly
when we notice what Dryden does with the interchangeability
of Charles's phallus and sceptre. This is an insight that Dryden
shares with Rochester but, characteristically, the derisive
metaphor is enlarged into vision. Charles has three important
attributes for the author of *Absalom and Achitophel*. He is,
magnificently, what Rochester would call a 'swiver'. His
natural temperament is one of 'ease'. He is, nevertheless, a
sceptred monarch representing the intersection of sacred and
secular history. Dryden reads these facts and their inter-
relation in a completely different way from Rochester. They

are not at odds with one another. Charles's 'vigorous warmth' is not haunted by impotence because it participates in and is an emblem of a fecundity both natural and divine. Charles's authority (his sceptre) is unashamedly bound up with the uncontrollable energies of germination. Thus the opening lines of *Absalom and Achitophel* accept and reverse the standard sneers at Charles's promiscuous use of concubine and bride made by Rochester and others. Charles's sexuality, as presented by Dryden, is not dependent on, or a sign of, his will. Rochester's fraught distinctions between enjoyment, desire and will are swept away. Charles does not seek to control, hold on to, or interiorly possess the livelong minute. On the contrary, he is an emblem of what is given to him who, in turn, scatters 'his Maker's Image through the Land'.[2] By the same token, Dryden sees him as at ease in nature and by nature. Rochester, in 'A Satire on Charles II', presents him as never at ease:

> Restlesse he roalles about from Whore to Whore,
> A merry Monarch, scandalous and poor.
>
> (ll.14–15)

Once again, Rochester in these later lines cancels the encomium, however ironic, of his earlier opening address:

> There reigns and oh long may hee reigne and thrive
> The easiest King and bestbred man alive.
>
> (ll.3–4)

Dryden is perfectly well aware of Rochester's perspective. Achitophel urges Absalom to 'Commit a pleasing Rape upon the Crown' (1.473). The implication is that Charles, 'like womens leachery' (1.471) would wish to be constrained in this fashion much as he would welcome the determined ingenuity of Nell Gwyn in Rochester's satire. Similarly, Absalom repeats Rochester's analysis of Charles's ease, impotence, and dependence on French cash:

> My Father, whom with reverence yet I name,
> Charm'd into Ease, is careless of his Fame:
> And, brib'd with petty sums of Foreign Gold,
> Is grown in *Bathsheba's* Embraces old.
>
> (ll.707–10)

Dryden puts these lines in so as to present a perspective that he can wean us away from. This is his normal method of argument and one that Rochester never employs. Using this method, Dryden writes plays, sets Achitophel against David, Hind against Panther, Sigismunda against her father. We have to admit, to be sure, that David, Hind, and Sigismunda are clearly commended and that Dryden cannot maintain complete neutrality even in *An Essay of Dramatick Poesie*. Dryden seems to be more committed and doctrinaire than Rochester but this is an illusion. It is not here a matter of insisting that Rochester has a stateable and stable position of his own. This is a minor bugbear of Rochester criticism.

It is certainly valuable to isolate and collect articulated suppositions from Rochester's reported conversations with Burnet, letters to Savile and so forth. It would be odd if these did not surface in his poems but Rochester does not find all the resources for his poetry in some all too easily discernible compound of Hobbes, La Rochefoucauld, deism and libertinism. Where, for example, would we find Rochester's sustained preoccupation with impotence and testing in this milieu? If we shift focus back to Spenser or sideways to Bunyan, we will better place Rochester's mixed concern with cowardice, failure, bravado, restlessness and exalted but humble self-consciousness. Rochester's famous line 'For all Men wou'd be Cowards if they durst' is an inversion of Crashaw's 'Tis cowardise that keeps this field / And want of courage not to yield.'[3] Rochester's fascination with 'Melting Joys' whether decorous (in song: 'My dear Mistriss has a heart', l.1), or disgusted ('A Ramble in St. James's Park', ll.113–22) is a long way from but still closer to Crashaw's liquefying intensities than to French libertinism or Carew's 'A Rapture'. Mutability is literally and horrifyingly fluid for him. Above all, he is interested in the untranscribable presentness of the moment insofar as the will lays claim to it, whereas Crashaw is interested in the transcendence disclosed in the moment as it is yielded. Hence, Rochester's blankness ('nothing') and fear. Fear is relished by the religious consciousness,[4] sought out by heroes, such as Rochester at Bergen, and by aesthetic sensibility too. *Pilgrim's Progress* unifies all three. In Rochester's impromptus and the studied nonchalance of Dryden's prose prefaces, for instance, we catch a comparable sense of style, exhilarating because precarious.

Nevertheless, if we are going to demonstrate that Rochester is more dogmatic than Dryden, the route will involve some daunting paradoxes of Rochester's own making. The most important of these is contained in the formula already instanced: 'For all Men wou'd be Cowards if they durst'. This is a sapiential aphorism but also a brag. The brag consists of an aggressive modesty since the speaker plainly dares to be a coward. Such aggressive reduction is Rochester's peculiar forte. Because it is so ostentatiously based on human nature and common sense, it is manifestly élitist, for it is the tone which is the tenor here. The apparent content is simply a vehicle for the tone. Hence style is crucial.

Jeremy Treglown first brought Rochester's disparagement of effort to our attention.[5] I don't wish to quarrel with this helpful insight but it does leave some problems. If Rochester disapproved of effort, why does he repeat Horace's injunction with approval in 'An Allusion to Horace'?

> Compare each Phrase, examin ev'ry line,
> Weigh ev'ry word, and ev'ry thought refine.
> (ll.100–01)

The next lines, with their reference to 'the unthinking Laughter' which makes 'a Play-house ring' probably refer to Dryden. We can answer this question by repeating Rochester's criticism of Dryden in 'Satyr' (Timon):

> Mine *Host*, who had said nothing in an hour,
> Rose up, and prais'd the *Indian Emperor.*
> *As if our Old World, modestly withdrew,*
> *And here in private had brought forth a New.*
> There are Two *Lines*! Who but he durst presume
> To make the old *World*, a new withdrawing Room,
> Whereof another *World* she's brought to *Bed*!
> What a brave *Midwife* is a *Laureats* head!
> (ll.143–50)

We notice the importance of 'durst' here. The host admires it; Rochester does not. Rochester only dares to be a coward. Both Rochester and Dryden, in fact, contributed to that tempering of excess in diction and image which Pope was going to establish as mainstream practice. Both poets, in different ways and from different social positions, valued habits of excess current in the insecurely established, aristocratic world of the Court. Excess, therefore, could be seen as evidence of a vulgarly *passé* idiom or of true aristocratic manner. Similarly but oppositely, 'ease' could be construed as evidence of good breeding or of ignominious sloth. From Rochester's viewpoint, Dryden's excess is evidence of vulgarity. It is the obviousness of Dryden's effort, not effort as such, which is here ridiculed. Indeed, one part of the charge is that Dryden tries but does not try hard enough. This accusation will focus indiscriminately on the writer and the man. The daring which makes 'the old World, a new withdrawing room' is an unconvincing, flaunted reversal of scale which only shows that the 'Laureats head' does not 'ev'ry thought refine'. In the same way, according to 'An Allusion',

> Dryden, in vaine, try'd this nice way of Witt,
> For he, to be a tearing Blade thought fit.
> 
> (ll.71–72)

If we take all the implications here, it is clear that the speaker himself would not fail if he 'try'd this nice way of witt' and that he is, as much as anyone of taste would wish to be, an authentic 'tearing Blade'. His adjustments of effort are right. Both these implications are quite justified. How deep they go may be seen by picking up the word 'tried' in this couplet and referring it back to familiar lines in another context:

> But we, whose hearts do justly swell,
>     With no vain-glorious pride,
> Who know how we in love, excell,
>     Long to be often try'd.[6]

There is no fear of failure here or, rather, there is a sense of absolute failure but the speaker has the energies both for interim success and to look death in the face. This kind of pride is not 'vain-glorious' and can be sharply distinguished from Dryden's or from that of his detested patron, Mulgrave who is 'My Lord All-Pride'. Here we can repeat the same trick and note what happens to the important word, 'swell' in a different context.

> Bursting with Pride, the Loath'd Impostume swells,
> Prick him, he sheds his Venom strait, and smells;
> But tis soe Lewd a Scribler, that he writes,
> With as much force to Nature, as he fights.
>                        ('My Lord All-Pride' (ll.1–4))

Mulgrave, like Dryden, swells and dares to scribble but the next lines tell us that he is so little of a 'tearing Blade' 'That ev'ry Schoole-Boy, whips him like a Topp'.

Against these wrongly judged efforts at bravery and wit, Rochester boasts of the reliability of his cowardice, final failure ('And fate change me for worms' (l.20)), modesty in speculation, and non-figurative idiom. This stance is that of proto-dandy for it is an aggressively minimal style that holds these things together. It is the style which, if it is to work at all, has to be supremely successful. The form of this success is worth noting.

Rochester's most successful verses rarely depend upon overt or striking images. His best lines, to my taste, are founded upon adroit syntax, diction and cadence. A couplet such as this well-known one from 'Satyr' (Timon) will stand as a representative example of this:

> Though nothing else, she (in despight of time)
> Preserv'd the affectation of her prime.
>                        (ll.53–54)[7]

Of course, Rochester's lyrics utilize a number of recognized love-conceits and rhetorical figures but it is often the case that these are most charged when drastically reduced to the univocal. For instance, the early 'A Dialogue between Strephon and Daphne' has Strephon justifying inconstancy by developing a familiar analogy between sexual passion and thunderstorms. The whole section needs to be quoted in order to establish the deft simplification of Daphne's reply. Strephon is speaking:

> See the Heav'ns in Lightnings break,
> Next in Storms of Thunder Speak;

Till a kind Rain from above
Makes a Calm—so 'tis in love.
Flames begin our first Address,
Like meeting Thunder we embrace:
Then you know the show'rs that fall
Quench the fire, and quiet all.

### DAPHNE

How shou'd I these show'rs forget,
'Twas so pleasant to be wet;
(ll.33–42)

Daphne's reply, of course, deliciously maintains Strephon's
*double-entendre* even in her best line, "'Twas so pleasant to be
wet', but that line is literally true. Its force does not lie in a
conjunction of the metaphorical and the literal, nor in the
ironic disjunction of the two. It is the simplicity of the
vocabulary and sufficiency of the literal meaning which are
decisive. It may be helpful to contrast this passage with what
must be the best use of this metaphor in English:

Maidens and youths filling their wild arms in air
    As their feet twinkle: now recede and now
Bending within each other's atmosphere

    Kindle invisibly; and as they glow
Like moths by light attracted and repelled,
    Oft to new bright destruction come and go,

Till like two clouds into one vale impelled
    That shake the mountains when their lightnings
                                                mingle
And die in Rain.
(*The Triumph of Life*, ll.149–57)[8]

We would not expect Rochester to write and think like Shelley
but this method of letting one image generate another, confus-
ing scale, risking incoherence but triumphantly avoiding it, is
one that Dryden would understand and admire. His poetry,
too, often depends upon 'the rapid abstraction of parallels'.[9]
*Annus Mirabilis*, for instance, depends wholly upon this. It is
such daring that 'Mine host' commends: 'Who but *he* durst

presume To make the old *World* a new withdrawing Room',
('Satyr' (Timon), ll.147–48). Dryden generates images in order
to astonish us but he relies, not without strain, on the old trust
in the underlying analogies between all forms of temporal and
spatial existence with one another and with consciousness.[10]
Thus Dryden's enlarging imagination, despite its proud
manner, is a means of showing that he and we are constituted
by the history and nature in which we participate. However
arbitrary these appear, and Dryden is acutely and sceptically
conscious of their experienced randomness, they manifest
'Times whiter Series'. Dryden's metaphor, ridiculed in 'Satyr'
(Timon), does recognize and is genuinely excited by the
transformation of European consciousness, still in process,
which is needed to accommodate the New World. In this sense,
the 'Laureats head' is indeed 'a brave Midwife'. Rochester is
impervious to these acknowledgements. The entire thrust of
his imagination is towards reduction and against enlargement.
The bath and bed to which he heroically binds himself in
'Against Constancy' are as narrow as the coffin of an anchor-
ite's perpetual recollection. Under no circumstances is that bed
the focus of enlarging metaphors. His mistress will never be
encountered as Rochester's America or Newfoundland.

Hence we can understand why it is that Rochester excels in
both satire and lyric. As he understands it, both depend upon
reduction, unostentatious management of tone, compression,
and refined but casual diction. Dryden's lyrics, as his other
verse, depends upon energy, manifest bravura, and uncon-
cealed intelligence. The *brio* of this verse invariably announces
its author but in all other ways he is concealed. His dramatic
inventions are never impersonations. Dryden observes them,
as we do, from outside. The natural summation of Dryden's
lyric manner is in the ode. Rochester writes no odes. The
closest he comes to one—'Upon Nothing'—is an anti-metap-
hysic of reduction which denies its character as an ode.

The real opposition here is of form rather than ideology.
Dryden's 1687 St. Cecilia ode wings its way through song and
metaphor to a 'Grand CHORUS' and a resounding last line
'And Musick shall untune the Sky'. Rochester's 'ode' releases
its energies in choice sardonic understatements ('spoil', 'line',
'assists') and dwindles into satiric formulas for familiar targets

('statesmens braines', 'Kings promises', 'Whors vowes') which displace Nothing as an object of attention. It is hard to know whether this effect of diminution and terminating boredom is exactly calculated or not. Certainly Rochester could not risk sustaining the feat of imagining that the opening stanzas delight in. Would he not then be merely 'a brave Midwife' like Dryden? Quite the opposite, his intention is to reverse all generative imagery including that of his poem. Rochester's poetry, like Nothing itself, has to be mock modestly anterior to the circumstances which it discloses. It cannot take life from them since it would then lose the disengagement which is its constitutive attribute.

We can detect a similar reticence in 'Satyr'. There are here, we must grant, some memorably fashioned images. In particular, lines 11–30 seem to depend upon 'the rapid abstraction of parallels'. Editors oblige with analogous passages in *Paradise Lost* and Quarles's *Divine Fancies*. It is not the imagery as such, then, which is crucial but the deftness of its handling in Rochester's context and the absolute mastery of cadence in its articulation. The images do not multiply and slip their leash as they would in Donne and might in Dryden. We are implicitly referred back to the author but not thereby, as in Donne and Dryden, to a self-manifesting creativity. The comparison with a dandy is again appropriate. Nothing precisely is asserted either. We should avoid reading lines like the following as though they are Rochester's version of the *Essay on Man*.

> Our *sphere* of Action, is lifes happiness,
> And he who thinks Beyond, thinks like an *Ass*.
> (ll.96–97)

Asses, after all, 'are in their degree, As wise at least, and better far than he' (ll.115–16). Rochester is not, in any useful sense, giving us a reliable insight into the proper relationship of thought and action. He is, on the contrary, cancelling any 'beyond' so that we, as readers, are forced to accept the reduced space given to us. Rochester himself remains outside this contracted territory. His initiating ruefulness ('who to my cost already am', l.1) is evidence of his superiority, not of his predicament. The 'Sphere of Action' offered to us as 'lifes happiness', and therefore sufficient, can only turn out to be

that same 'present moment' which defeats those brave enough
to lay claim to it. Nevertheless, the poem itself is evidence of a
sphere of understanding disclosed only in its form and manner.
It is always the implied claim to insight and vitality in the very
abandonment of such claims that makes Rochester (the poet)
impregnable. He could not, to press the point, be so unassail-
ably a 'tearing Blade' if he was not at such pains to be a coward
and insist on telling us. The best of all his images in this poem
makes the larger point for us:

> Those Reverend Bedlams, Colledges and Schools;
> Borne on whose wings, each heavy Sot can pierce,
> The limits of the boundless Universe.
> So charming Oyntments, make an Old Witch Flie,
> And bear a Crippled Carcass through the Skie.
>
> (ll.83–87)

The words 'bear' and 'through', in the last line, play as much
part in its cutting edge as 'crippled Carcass'. The latter is a *tour
de force* but it does not break away from its context. On the
contrary, the verb pairs back with the earlier 'pierce' and the
unexceptionable 'heavy Sot'. We are not caught up in the brave
midwifery of the poet's imagination here. The poet is other
than this act of imagining because he must be framing the sky
filled with contemptible objects and pierced by fools. The
latter are ridiculous to take such pains to pierce apparent limits
which only take them into boundless skies, just as earlier their
equivalent struggled in 'doubts boundless Sea' (l.15). But the
poet's consciousness must be anteriorly one with the boun-
dlessness which he sees as thus invaded. In the same way, his
earlier complaint about the 'Myte' who 'Think he's the Image
of the Infinite' (l.77) expects us to recognize ourselves in the
metaphor but, in so doing, accepts the poet's right to defend
the infinite on its own behalf. None of this can be explicit or the
effect would be lost. Dryden's imagination takes us up into its
own exaltation. His horror at Achitophel or MacFlecknoe is
because they cheapen a possible sublimity. By attacking them,
he explicitly invites us to share the grounding of his imagination in that sublimity. Rochester shares his exasperation with
us but remains apart.

    If we look, for instance, at 'The Second Prologue at Court to

*The Empress of Morocco*', we can see how Rochester wriggles out of Dryden's shoes whilst caught wearing them. His task was to write, as Dryden had so often done, a prologue to a play and a complimentary address to the king. Mulgrave provided another prologue for the same play. These functions are separated symmetrically into a general address (22 lines) followed by a direct speech to Charles (23 lines). The two parts are held together by the same conceit that the play is virtually played by women for a male audience of which Charles is the supreme representative. Therefore, we are told, men should not laugh at those women who now seek to 'divert' them because, implicitly, successful sexual interaction is destroyed by ridicule. Further, women as young and beautiful as the prologue speaker (Lady Elizabeth Howard[11]) are sure to conquer them so Charles should, as a wise diplomat, extend his patronage to the play which is an embodiment of women's power to charm.

This argument, on inspection, is based on Rochester's customary paradox. The power of the ladies' case resides in its weakness. The male audience is not to exercise its wit or judgement 'though you see reason for it' (1.3) because such judgement, even if correct, will invite a reciprocal laughter by women when men do 'their best' (1.8). There is thus an implicit paralleling of the performance of the play with sexual performance. In both of these, as with Rochester's poetry, the tone, not the apparent content, is central. For instance:

> Few so ill bred will venture to a Play
> To spy out Faults in what we Women say.
> For us no matter what we speak, but how:
> How kindly can we say—I hate you now.
> (ll.15–18)

Male judgement cannot be exercised on the script ('what we speak') when its constituents ('I hate you now') can reverse meaning in the 'how' of performance. A 'now' is always a 'how' for Rochester. It has no existence apart from the style displayed in it. The word 'now' occurs constantly in Dryden's prologues and major poems [12] with quite different force. The opening lines of Rochester's Prologue seem to establish something comparable:

> Wit has of late took up a Trick t'appear,
> Unmannerly, or at the best severe,
>                     (ll.1–2)

It is easy to find parallels to this in Dryden.[13] The 'now' beyond this 'of late' is fashioned by the flow of history. The play thus announced is an event within a wider sequence. Taste itself is part of history. There is a similarly Drydenesque touch in Rochester's later suggestion that Lady Elizabeth's 'force of charms' may check even Charles's 'prosperous arms'. This refers, evidently, to Charles's current successes against the Dutch.[14] Nevertheless, Rochester is uninterested in Time in this sense. We are forced to distinguish a 'present moment' from a 'now' with more precision.

Dryden's 'now' is history's medium. It comes from the past but is only intelligible through the subsequent history which it brings about. This is true of Biblical history but it operates even in the lowest and grossest examples. For example, in the 'Epilogue to the King and Queen at the Opening of their Theatre', Dryden imagines some 'Vizard Masque' attracting male attention in the 'mid Gallery' of the theatre as the epilogue is being spoken and comments:

> Fine love no doubt, but e'er two days are o'er ye,
> The Surgeon will be told a wofull story.
>                     (ll.17–18)

Dryden cannot imagine, even in the most trivial instances, any 'now', which is without antecedents and outcome and is therefore unavailable for judgement. Rochester's Lady Elizabeth, and even his Charles II, are not part of historical time in this way; they occupy a present moment of interplay in which the all-reversing powers of will and the irreversible decline of the flesh are the only operatives. Hence 'I hate you now' is an instance of tone's customary triumph over content. It is a theatrical moment in theatrical time but transcribes publicly what takes place elsewhere when:

> To love's Theatre, the Bed,
>      Youth and beauty fly together,
> And act soe well it may be said

> The Lawrell there was due to either.
> ('Leave this gawdy gilded stage', ll.5–8)

Acting seeks out, manipulates, but never inhabits the 'now' whose possession it anticipates and recalls. Sexual theatre is always being tested and tried in the present moment and seeks recognition ('the laurel') there but is uninterested in the judgements of history or the stable written word on its performance. Dryden respects the history and writing which he unites as historiographer and laureate. He subordinates his strong theatrical imagination to them.

When Rochester, in the second half of his prologue, addresses Charles ('great sir') in the person of Lady Elizabeth Howard impersonating herself, what is at stake is simply the present moment of their implied interchange. This is a theatrical, courteous and sexual moment, not an historical one. And if this moment is itself knowingly referred to the known character of Charles's life and court, then this too is from one style to another, not from a 'now' to an historical epoch which encompasses it. Charles, we are told, cannot escape:

> Our soft Captivitie,
> From which old Age alone must set you free.
> Then tremble at the fatal Consequence—
> Since 'tis well known for your own part (Great Prince)
> 'Gainst us you still have made a weak defence.
> (ll.33–37)

No editor, I think, glosses 'part' here in the same way as the 'nobler part' of the young lady's 'Ancient Lover' or the 'frailer part' of 'The Fall'. It would be heavy-handed to do so, as we see if we follow the implication through in the next couplet:

> Be generous, and wise, and take our part;
> Remember we have Eyes, and you a Heart.
> (ll.38–39)

Nevertheless, the banter of this exchange must depend upon 'part' meaning, not without some delicacy, the member raised by 'poor laborious Nelly', and theatrical part, and military side. Charles is invited into this theatrical and sexual moment because, as the prologue makes clear, his court acknowledges no other sense of Time. Therefore the triumph of the ladies over him ('Our victory') will, the last line assures us, be Charles's own 'triumph'. This triumph will be a conquest of Time in the present moment through the victorious pleasures of sexual yielding. Only 'old Age' will set the king 'free' from this 'soft Captivitie'. The diagnosis of Charles's life-style made so courteously here turns out to be identical with the contemptuous indictment made in 'A Satire on Charles II' and, as that, would equally furnish the conclusion:

> I hate all Monarchs, and the Thrones they sit on
> From the Hector of France to the Culley of Britaine.
>
> (ll.32–33)

The reverse proposition must also be true. Rochester's disgust is real but its present object, Charles, is the epitome of a style in which Rochester is implicated much as he sups with Timon and takes the waters with the other fools in Tunbridge Wells. There is nowhere else to be but in, not of, such moments impersonating yourself or others. That is why I cannot agree with Keith Walker's apparently unexceptionable and representative comment: 'His conversion, whether real or fantasy, figured largely in his reputation but has little to do with the quality of his poetry'.[15] The argument here seems designed to defeat some latter day Burnetites. Even Graham Greene would hardly fit this description and it is difficult to think of other candidates.

Conversion is not a minor matter. The conversions, markedly different though they were of Donne, Crashaw, Vaughan, Bunyan, Dryden, Rochester and other major seventeenth century figures constitute a fact of some literary consequence. On Rochester's own assumptions, his conversion and deathbed must throw light on the interconnections of style, will, and moment, at that point of evacuation which obsessed his imagination. On Dryden's very different assumptions, such conversion, as outcome and change, clarifies what precedes it. In both cases, we must be not unprepared to find faith consonant with apparently opposed declarations. How else could we keep track of the phenomenon of conversion?

In Dryden's case, we know virtually nothing of his conversion to Catholicism. We have no equivalents to Burnet,

Rochester's Remonstrance, and the letters of Rochester's friends, mother, and wife. We do have, however, *The Hind and the Panther* which, on even the most ahistorical theory, must bear some relation to Dryden's conversion. As we would expect, Dryden's new religious conviction returns the transcendence implicit in 'Times whiter Series' back to its source. He can thus allow himself a much bleaker look at the likely prospects for England's secular history than in his earlier poems. He has largely surrendered that vision of England as a vehicle for poetic imagination and providential care which nourished *Astraea Redux, Annus Mirabilis, Absalom and Achitophel* and (negatively) *The Medal*. Those hopes are now transferred via the Hind to the sacred but largely hidden history of the Catholic Church. Dryden still sees himself, and writes out of, a 'now' fashioned by historical contingency and sustained by vertical renewal but the King and Court no longer lie at the centre.[16] The Hind has replaced Charles II. Her power, like his, is rooted in apparent yielding to the time that same 'ease' which Dryden so much admired in Charles and looked for in vain in James II. Unlike Charles, however, the Hind will never die and is always available in a 'now' never entirely occluded. Dryden renders this vulnerable, untainted availability with a real tenderness. This Hind, too, suffering in Time is still the unassailable summation of all temporal process. This, we may reasonably presume, is how Dryden understands his own conversion. It is fully consonant with the revised cultural programme that Dryden set himself in *The Fables*.

It is clear that Rochester, who was responsible for the reconversion of his wife from Catholicism to Protestantism, did not jump from his awkward 'present moment' into Dryden's transcendently reinforced 'now'. It might seem impertinent and inappropriate to guess at the final volitional movements of Rochester's exhausted psyche and frame but it is not. Rochester himself invites us to do so much as Donne's poetry makes us imagine the real death which, if Walton [17] is even no more than half accurate, is so helpful a commentary on the control *in extremis* exercised in his verse. But Rochester is not really like Donne either. We have no good reason to doubt the sequence proposed in Burnet's account in which, according to Rochester's own account, it was not Burnet's rational arguments but direct reading of the suffering servant passage from Isaiah 53 by his mother's chaplain that precipitated a specific 'present moment' of conversion. The Biblical text uses a past tense for the servant: 'But he was wounded for our transgression, he was bruised for our iniquities: the chastisement of our peace was upon him; and with his stripes we are healed' (Is.53, 5). But the application is in the present ('we are healed'). Rochester receives the text in that present moment and in so doing, identifies the text, Christ (an application of this text made only by Christians in faith) and himself. The transference of the text from Old to New Testament and to 1680 in the light of such an immediate recognition is closely analogous to the impersonations by which Rochester has hitherto performed himself. Christianity has always offered a way of being yourself by being another. The only difference, and this constitutes the conversion, is that the will is now yielded to and through the moment rather than displacing it and governing the resultant space by acting a part. Hence, this moment of conversion has an afterwards which will acknowledge it. This, so far as we can tell, is exactly what occurred. It is not a matter of new convictions or a new interpretation of Life. Religious conversion, in its own terms (that is to say, the terms of Rochester's acceptance), is a death and rebirth into Life. It is Dryden's 'now' and Rochester's 'present moment' which are suddenly accepted by a will that gains them by ceasing to claim them.

Rochester's friend, Fanshawe, explained this, by insisting that Rochester had gone mad.[18] Dryden's contemporaries insisted that Dryden's conversion (like Keith Walker[19] they would say 'conversion') was no more than a political act. In both cases, their poetry is a better guide to the possibilities that their conversions actualize than their biographies as such or recorded convictions. Conversion is a surprising thing but, once in place, can then be understood as of a piece with the personality. We have argued that the 'present moment' of awkward alienation from the Court, Tunbridge Wells society, or sexual interchange is displaced by a mode of assertion in reduction which is authenticated only by Rochester's style. Rochester lines up Dryden with Mulgrave as an embodiment of assertion in enlargement rooted in a confessedly inhabited

# Rochester and Dryden

'now'. This difference is carried through in their conversions. Rochester's salvific recognition of a more extreme reduction than his own (the Suffering Servant) may be compared to Dryden's dissociation of the Panther of power from the gentle Hind 'Immortal and unchang'd'. In both cases, powerlessness in the perceived archetype is suddenly accepted as life-giving and transforming in present time. Their conversions may not necessitate the 'quality' of their writings but they are illuminating confirmations of their character, depth and concerns. There is no good reason to think them improper matters of literary attention.

## NOTES

1. All quotations of Rochester's poems taken from *The Poems of John Wilmot, Earl of Rochester*, ed. Keith Walker (Oxford, 1984).

2. *Absalom and Achitophel*, l.10 in J. Kinsley, ed., *The Poems and Fables of John Dryden* (Oxford, 1958; pb. edit. 1970), p. 190. All quotations from Dryden's poems are taken from this edition.

3. 'A letter to the Countess of Denbigh', ll.61–62 in G. W. Williams, ed., *The Complete Poetry of Richard Crashaw* (New York, 1974), pp. 150–52. 'Satyr', l.158, pp. 91–97.

4. The fear of the Lord is the beginning of religious wisdom and, as such, derided in the passage from Act II of Seneca's *Troades*, p. 51 translated by Rochester. Such an appeal to fear is increasingly less prominent in mainstream religious apology in the seventeenth century and is not pressed, for example, by the smug interlocutor of 'Satyr' nor by Burnet in his interchanges with Rochester. Fear, however, appears to be a discernible though not decisive element in Rochester's conversion.

5. 'He knew my style, he swore', Jeremy Treglown, ed., *Spirit of Wit* (Oxford, 1982), p. 80.

6. 'Against Constancy', ll.13–16, pp. 42–43.

7. Lines of formally similar character and quality can be found, for instance, in 'The Imperfect Enjoyment', ll.29–30, pp. 30–32; 'Tunbridge Wells', ll.8–10; 'Satyr', ll.39–40, pp. 91–97; 'A letter from Artemiza in the Towne to Chloe in the Countrey', ll.30–31, pp. 83–90.

8. D. H. Reiman and S. B. Powers, eds., *Shelley's Poetry and Prose* (New York, 1977), p. 459.

9. The phrase is Rosamund Tuve's in *Elizabethan and Metaphysical Imagery* (1947; Phoenix pb. edit., 1961), p. 318. It is there applied to 'Upon the Death of the Lord Hastings' but would be equally apt for late poems such as 'Eleonora' or the Anne Killigrew and St Cecilia Odes.

10. This is Harold Love's argument in 'Dryden's Unideal Vacancy' in *Eighteenth-Century Studies*, xii, no.1 (Fall, 1978), pp. 74–89.

11. Lady Elizabeth Howard turns up again as 'Lady Betty' in 'Signor Dildo', ll.23–24.

12. The word 'now' or an equivalent like 'this day' occurs in the majority of Dryden's Prologues. It is in the first line of 'Heroique Stanzas' and in the last line of 'To my Honour'd Friend, Dr. Charleton'. It occurs about every twelfth quatrain including the last one in *Annus Mirabilis*. It is used less, but crucially in David's final speech, in *Absalom and Achitophel*. In 'Threnodia Augustalis' it is used with equal confidence of Charles II as corpse ('An image, now, of Death', l.66) and as transcendent ('Our patron once, our Guardian Angel now', l.397). Dryden uses it in an erotic, non-historical way in his songs, e.g. 'Till at length she cry'd, Now, my dear, now let us go' ('Whilst Alexis lay prest', l.15). Rochester uses it in a similar way in his songs, e.g. 'A Dialogue between Strephon and Daphne', ll.1,7, pp. 12–14.

13. e.g.   Wit's now arriv'd to a more high degree
Our native language more refined and free.
Our ladies and our men now speak more wit
In conversation than those Poets writ.
('Epilogue to the second part of GRANADA', ll.22–25)

14. There is a straight historical 'now' too in Rochester's 'Lampoone', ll.5–6, pp. 68–69:

Unlesse (as agaynst Irish cattle before)
You now make an Act to forbid Irish whore.

15. Walker, *Rochester*, p. xi.

16. 'Good life be now my task: my doubts are done', *The Hind and the Panther*, I, 78.

17. See Izaak Walton, *The Lives of John Donne, Sir Henry Wotton, Richard Hooker, George Herbert & Robert Sanderson*, ed. S. G. Saintsbury (Oxford, 1927), especially pp. 74–82.

18. See the two letters of Rochester's mother quoted in Graham Greene's *Lord Rochester's Monkey* (London, 1974), p. 217.

19. Walker, *Rochester*, p. xi, 'his deathbed "conversion" '. This, of course, is a very small bone to pick with a wonderfully helpful edition of Rochester's poems.

# Index of Proper Names
# and Works